The Writer's Art

James J. Kilpatrick

THE WRITER'S ART

Andrews, McMeel & Parker

A Universal Press Syndicate Company

Kansas City • New York

Library of Congress Cataloging in Publication Data

Kilpatrick, James Jackson, 1920-
    The writer's art.

    1. English language—Errors of usage.   2. English
language—Style.   I. Title.
PE1460.K54   1984   808'.042   84-2892
ISBN 0-8362-7925-5

For

Heather, Douglas, Alina,

Charlotte Alyce, Maria,

Jamie, and Marc

Contents

Foreword

Most people have heard the wisecrack about laws and sausages, how they resemble one another in what went into making them. Or something like that. James Jackson Kilpatrick warns against the cliché, and it is never too soon to heed James Jackson Kilpatrick when he is laying down the law on English usage. In fact, sausages have it in common with much else. There isn't anything especially eye-catching about the rocky stones that in due course yielded the marble that in due course yielded the Parthenon. Those of us disinclined to biological curiosity experience no temptation to look at pictures of livers, upper intestines, or tonsils, let alone the real thing. And we all know about those many who having experienced grammar at school, and been made to parse sentences, and distinguish between dependent and independent clauses, subjunctive and indicative moods, have no more curiosity about the morphology of English than most of us have about the innards of a diesel engine. But now listen.

Spring is coming to Scrabble, Virginia. There is the profusion of flowers. Among them "the trillium, loveliest of them all, which kneels as modestly as a spring bride, all in white, beside the altar of an old oak stump. If you're not familiar with the trillium, imagine the flower that would come from a flute if a flute could make a flower. That is the trillium, a work of God from a theme by Mozart."

I shouldn't really need, in order to make my point that prejudices about anatomical structures are not always warranted, to do much more than to say that the man who brought off those lovely sentences—casual commentary on a natural cycle in an earlier book—has up and written

1

an engrossing and majestic treatise on the English language. He calls it *The Writer's Art*. It is not only the best book of its kind I have ever experienced (the incomparable Fowler wrote a different kind of a book), it is the most compelling reading about writing I have ever seen. If such a book were written about human biology, I would be tempted to become a doctor. But never mind if you have a vocation: James Jackson Kilpatrick's book will be read for the sheer pleasure of the experience; read by people who intend to make no special effort to improve their writing, let alone harbor any ambition to write belletristically. But I warn that Mr. Kilpatrick's book is so seductive that the temptation to improve is not easily resisted. It requires a chastity belt on the spirit to read, and not to experience temptation in the voluptuous delights of language.

It requires only a reading of a few paragraphs of the book to know that you are embarked on an important trip, under the direction of a guide who (most important) has labored intensively to understand what it is that works in English, what it is that does not work in English; moreover, a writer whose aptitude (indispensable) for words, and for the composition of sentences, is so marked that the distinctions he makes convince us in part because they hit with revelatory force, in part because we have come to trust him deeply. Kilpatrick engages at first attention; then respect; finally devotion. This last is done, I think, because he insinuates his own veneration for the proper sentence and, sensing now what it is that we may have been missing, we are grateful to the man (person?—see Chapter 4) who helped open our eyes.

Notice that JJK has named his book *The Writer's Art*. It is art he speaks of in two senses. The first is that fine writing—he speaks of Rebecca West, for instance; Lawrence Durrell, Hemingway, and Twain—is not something we can master in the sense that, say, we can master a word processor. But it is also true, where art is the object of our scrutiny, that differing judgments can be made. It required many centuries before the aesthetic consensus crystallized that Notre Dame de Chartres was possibly the most beautiful thirteenth-century cathedral in Europe and that Westminster Abbey was possibly the ugliest thirteenth-century cathedral in Europe. Some questions about English are unresolved ("It's I" or "It's me"?) And then, too, there is the matter of usage. Although the overwhelming majority of technicians may agree that a particular usage is offensive and should be quarantined, manacled, exported—maybe even executed, if only the Supreme Court will go along—that use will at some point overwhelm us, like old age. JJK is sensitive to the autonomous inertia of words and for that reason accepts the likes of "access" as a transitive verb. But his ear is so good, his good sense so gratifyingly reliable, that we find ourselves volunteers in the good usage army, disposed to spend blood, sweat, and tears.

Over the years I have been much interested, and frequently amused, by the author's Hundred Years' War against Unusual Words. Interested because he makes his case so well; amused because he is not particularly constrained by it. He tells several amusing stories in this volume, one of them about stumbling into the word *limicolous*, which is to say, "living in mud." He found himself using the word, and woke the next day with a most dreadful hangover. "No advice is more elementary, and no advice is more difficult to accept: When we feel an impulse to use a marvelously exotic word, let us lie down until the impulse goes away. . . . My brother pundit, Bill Buckley, falls into sin even more easily than I. He has had affairs with *decoctable, anfractuosity,* and *endogamous.* He has taken to bed with *chiliastic, phlogistonic, sciolism, incondite,* and *osmotically.* He has fallen for *hubristic, otiose, repristinate, adumbrated,* and *synecdoche.*" Two sentences later, the author uses in a dense little cluster, *arcane, syntactically,* and *bibulousness.* And this notwithstanding that there are those who believe that *arcane* is an arcane word, that *syntactically* can be made to sound like the malapropism of someone far gone in bibulousness.

I have a private theory about unusual words so simple it is embarrassing, in such august auspices, to disclose. It is as simple as that, say, we tend to conclude that people who use words with which we happen not to be familiar are using unfamiliar words. If John knows 8,000 words and Susan knows 8,000 words, inevitably John will know 250 words that Susan does not, and Susan will know 250 words that John does not, and John will think Susan exhibitionistic, and Susan will think John affected. I like to cite the waiter of a restaurant in Garden City who approached me twenty-five years ago to complain that he had subscribed to National Review and was absolutely certain that its circulation would greatly increase if only it stopped tolerating such unfamiliar words. Exactly two years later I was at the same restaurant, same table, same waiter, who greeted me joyfully, congratulating me on having taken his advice.

There are reasons for using words even when they are unfamiliar, a term which has to mean unfamiliar to those unfamiliar with them, a description whose geographical coordinates I would hate to have to specify. It can be a matter of rhythm, it can be a matter of the exact fit— and it can be something by way of obeisance to the people whose honed verbal appetites created the need for such a word, which therefore came into being. Call it supply-side linguistics; but whatever you call it, pray be thankful that someone invented the word *velleity* and that a few refuse to permit it to die, even as others would die to preserve the lousewort. Kilpo tells us that "as writers, we ought to take advantage of all the glorious riches of the English tongue, and to use them as best we can, but always taking into account one thing: the audience we are writing for." I would not dispute the relevance of this injunction directed at those terrible people who write those inscrutable instruction manuals (the computer-folk now call this "documentation"), but I think that writers also have an obligation to keep the frontiers of language open, else the weeds grow, the tall trees out there atrophy, and our patrimony is eroded.

I would not have thought it possible for someone other than a professional bibliographer to gather so many pointed examples of the kind of thing that is awfully wrong, that is less than quite right, that is okay, that is quite beautiful. In one section, JJK gives us Version One of a paragraph he wrote, lets us see its weaknesses even as he slowly descries them; lets us trace his corrections, on into drafts four and five. This is truly exciting stuff, like seeing a documentary on Picasso painting a canvas. And listen to the names of the subchapters in Chapter 4, which are: "The Things We Ought Not to Do." They are: 1. "We ought not to use clichés." 2. "We ought never to fall into gobbledegook." 3. "We ought not to mangle our sentences." 4. "As a general rule, we ought not to use euphemisms." 5. "We ought not to pile up our nouns as adjectives." 6. "We ought not to coin words wantonly." 7. "We must not break the rules of grammar." 8. "We ought not to write dialect or slang unless we are certain of both our ear and our audience." 9. "We ought not to be redundant." 10. "We ought not to use words that have double meanings." 11. "We ought not to write portmanteau sentences." 12. "We ought not unintentionally to give offense by sexist words or phrases, but we ought not to be intimidated either." 13. "We ought not to make mistakes in spelling."

Right there we have the plainspokenness that characterizes Kilpatrick together with evidence of the ear that exactly catches what it is he wants to say, and, I guess I should add, a whiff of the imperial manner. If you feel strongly about words, it is downright offensive when someone says "hopefully," unless he is referring to a whaler's wife, looking hopefully out over the horizon of her widow's walk. Kilpatrick, while understanding and flexible to the point of acknowledging the dynamic imperative, is a firm custodian. I would trust the family treasure with him, you bet. There will be no attrition of the language at the gravesite of the collected works of James Jackson Kilpatrick.

He confesses that this is in some ways a personal book. I would guess that most proficient word-users would agree with somewhere between 90 and 95 percent of what he pronounces upon. But some things aggrieve him more than others, and that is both to be expected and, in a sense, welcomed, because once again it reminds us of the factor of art. He provides a huge chapter devoted to at least a hundred personal crotchets, of which the initial dozen are "A" AND "AN"; A.M. IN THE MORNING; ABSOLUTE WORDS; ABSTRACT/ABSTRACTION; ACCESS (V); AD HOC; AD NAUSEAM; ADAGES, OLD; ADAPT/ADOPT; ADVERSE/AVERSE; AFFECT/EFFECT; and AFFIDAVIT. Under ABSOLUTE WORDS we read, "My own modest list of words that cannot be qualified by 'very' or 'rather' or 'a little bit' includes *unique, imperative, universal, final, fatal, complete, virgin, dead, equal, eternal, total, unanimous, essential,* and *indispensable.*"

I dunno. Wouldn't the idiomatic ring of "altogether unique" strike you as okay? Or how about, "It was, so to speak, rather a final gesture when Dominguin dedicated the bull to his loyal public and proceeded to get killed." But . . . we are taking advice from a man whose ear is a Stradivarius, and there is reason to give him the benefit of the doubt, always allowing for the supremacy of one's own conscience. And again, everyone has his own crotchets. While I was reading Kilpo's manuscript aboard an airliner, the captain's voice rang in, "We will land at La Guardia in approximately fifty-nine minutes." *Approximately?* What's approximately for, if not imperatively conjoined to one hour, or forty-five minutes; or, at most, fifty-five minutes?

But this kind of thing can go on and on. For instance, we can agree that the "h" is not pronounced, requiring therefore "an" as the indefinite article. But then doesn't a difference come in precisely in the emphasis the individual elocutionist gives to the "h" sound? *I* would say, "a historical novel" because it happens that when I pronounce the adjective, the aitch is definitely present and accounted for. Again, mightn't a historian, even one so sure of tone that he would never think heedlessly of an "old cliché," find himself so situated as desiring to distinguish between a new and an old cliché? ("The arsenal of democracy, that very old cliché, has given way to a new cliché, namely the military-industrial complex.")

If you wish to pursue the game, the list of demurrals grows (I said I agreed with 95 percent, and 5 percent is, really, a whole lot). Consider the author's dislike for such locutions as "with deference to the learned opinion of my able and distinguished friend." But, don't you see, there is a rhetorical point to be served in occasional tushery. You are reminding the reader—and your distinctly unlearned and undistinguished colleague—that you are aware of the boundaries of diplomatic exchange, and willing to observe them, even as Winston Churchill would have addressed a communication to his German counterpart, "Dear Mr. Hitler."

While I am at it, Mr. Kilpatrick uses the exclamation *aargh!* to communicate disgust: wrongly, I think, influenced as I was when thirty years ago, reading the letters of Swinburne, I came upon him using it to express orgasmic delight in one of his vapulatory fantasies. (Mr. Kilpatrick is reaching for ugh!) Again, do we proper word-users need to stay away from the "long day" on the martinet's grounds that a day cannot have more than a fixed number of hours, and didn't Galileo or somebody go to jail to prove Kilpo's point?

On the matter of *expertise* I get deadly serious. It happens that I learned the word from a scholar bilingual in French, and that I was present when he and a renowned philosopher discussed ruefully the deterioration in the use of the word, whose corruption has been depriving us of a marvelously useful resource. Invited formally to define the word, they came up with: "*Expertise* is the body of operative knowledge" (that attaches to the subject under discussion). So that, for instance, you can say, "There is expertise in politics up to a point, after which it becomes an art." There is no way of saying this if you attach to *expertise* the vulgar meaning Mr. Kilpatrick correctly advises us would justify throwing the word away altogether. Throw out the bad word, struggle to reclaim the good one.

And then, as lagniappe, I am amused by the author's insistence that *remains to be seen* is tolerable only when you are talking about a corpse awaiting inspection in a funeral parlor. I see (and use) the phrase intending to inject doubt. Man-from-Missouri-wise-kind-of-thing. "It remains to be seen whether Harry Truman's bid for the farm vote is going to pay off." Remember that by authorizing one usage you are not committed to preferring it. "I am not so sure that Harry Truman's bid for the farm vote is going to work" would satisfy whatever doubt I desire to invest in the observation.

But what a barrel of fun. The author wrote to me that this would be his "last book." But then we find, under Number 10 above ("Avoid Words That Have Double Meanings"), "Another word that occasionally gives trouble is *last*. Its first meaning, unmistakably understood, is *final, terminal, ultimate*. But *last* also can mean 'most recent.' If we fall into a sentence involving *the last few months* or *his last book*, we may cause a flicker. By contrast, *past* admits of no confusion in a context of time: the *past few* months. Instead of *his last book*, I would suggest *his latest book*."

Just so. It may be that James Jackson Kilpatrick will never write another book at once so charming, instructive, resourceful, and useful. But something will gestate in his mind, you watch. You know what? Something like the coming of spring we began with. This is a spring that

tiptoes in. It pauses, overcome by shyness, like a grandchild at the door, peeping in, ducking out of sight, giggling in the hallway. "Heather!" I want to cry, "I know you're out there. Come in!" And April slips into our arms. The maples do not come forth in green; they are flowering red, soft as slippers, in tassels like a jester's scepter. The flowering almond is pink, absurdly pink, little-girl pink, as pink as peppermint and cream. The apples display their milliner's scraps of ivory silk, rose-tinged. All the sleeping things wake up—primrose, baby iris, candytuft, blue phlox, the Scotch heather that had seemed dead beyond resurrection. The earth warms—you can smell it, feel it, crumble April in your hands.

Kilpatrick was writing about the coming of spring, but as much could be written about the materialization of another book in the mind of a man who cannot stop making poetry, whether he is writing about the spring, the Supreme Court, or the English language.

WILLIAM F. BUCKLEY, JR.

Introduction

My purpose in this book is primarily to venture a few suggestions, based upon a lifetime as a writer, on how good writers can get to be better writers. I want to speculate on some of the reasons why so much bad writing abounds. Over the years I have acquired a hundred pretty little crotchets, and I propose to trot them out for critical inspection.

You will accurately infer that I approach these happy tasks in a *prescriptive* frame of mind. No apologies. Two groups of mariners sail on the semantic ocean. There are *descriptive* linguists, whose primary concern is with what is. And there are *prescriptive* linguists, whose primary concern is with what should be.

Laurence Urdang, the engaging and scholarly editor of Verbatim, has described his function in this way:

"I am a descriptive linguist. That means I regard language as the substance that it is my function, as a scientist, to describe. I cannot express distaste or dissatisfaction with the corpus of data I examine any more than a doctor can refuse to deal with cholera or leprosy. It is my job to describe what I observe. It is that that makes me a 'descriptive linguist.' As a professional lexicographer, I cannot execrate words I dislike for their denotative meaning *(cancer)*, their connotative meaning *(bribery, fraud)*, their pronunciation *(cacophony)*, or on any other grounds, any more than I can extol them for their beauty *(chocolate, Catherine Deneuve, murmur).*"

For my own part, I most assuredly cannot qualify as a "linguist," whether descriptive or prescriptive. I am a writer. I began writing professionally in 1941 and I have been writing ever since. The years have given me some sturdy convictions—or pure prejudices, as you will—on what ought to be. I am wholly prescriptive, and I am thus free from the bonds that restrain my brother Urdang. I can condemn; I can express both distaste and dissatisfaction; and when I conclude that a particular usage is execrable, I can execrate at the top of my lungs.

The word *replica* provides an example of what I am getting at. The descriptive linguist accurately observes that the word has come to mean *copy, model, reproduction,* and *facsimile.* This is what is. The descriptive scholars make no judgment calls. I have no quarrel with the important function they perform. We need descriptive linguists just as we need mapmakers, pathologists, tape recorders, and copying machines. But over in my camp, I am free to plead for the restoration of *replica* to its original meaning: a work of art, or other object, re-created by its original creator.

The descriptive scholars observe that in the looking-glass world of language, Humpty Dumpty reigns supreme. "When I use a word," said His Majesty, "it means just what I choose it to mean—neither more nor less." Large numbers of English-speaking people now speak of *parameters* to mean *boundaries, limits, agendas, specifications, contents, inventories, variables,* and *possibilities*—among other things. The word is understood in all these senses—and to be understood is the primary purpose of communication. We want to convey ideas, images, commands, directions, or whatever, from the mind of the speaker or writer to the mind of his audience or his readers. Communication fails if it is not effective communication.

But effectiveness, I submit, is only the beginning of the communicative art. My thought is that, just as there is more to eating than merely stuffing one's belly, so there is more to writing than merely being "effective." If the purpose of housing were solely to provide shelter from the rain, the Sun King could have erected an A-frame. Instead, he built the Palace of Versailles.

My argument is that the well-established rules of grammar and syntax do indeed matter. Punctuation matters; if punctuation did not matter, as Wilson Follett has observed, we would be hard put to distinguish between a *pretty tall woman* and a *pretty, tall woman.*

My argument, further, is that values matter in speech or in writing just as they matter in every other aspect of our lives. Some of the descriptive linguists insist that "grammar is manners," and in so doing they yield the point at issue. No one doubts that when a guest at dinner spits on the floor, it may properly be said of him that he has "bad manners." Why, then, should the prescriptive linguist be reproached when he pronounces *Him and I done been there* "bad grammar"? We put values on behavior; we put values on food, clothes, housing, automobiles; we put them on morals. Without differing values, we have nothing; we are reduced to saying that "whatever is, is right." And this is nonsense. True enough, *whatever is, is* (though that elementary thought is assisted by the comma in the middle), but the mere fact of the whatever's existence does not make the whatever right.

There is more to communication than the merely effective conveyance of an idea or image. Let me convey an image: *After a rainy and windy night, the sun came up.* The sentence is effective; it is good enough for any ordinary purpose. But this is Wordsworth:

> There was a roaring in the wind all night;
> The rain came heavily and fell in floods;
> But now the sun is rising, calm and bright.

We value "good writing" for the author's skillful use of simile and metaphor, for his sense of cadence, for the orderly arrangement of his thesis. We put a lower value, or no value at all, on writing that is loose and flabby. We may laugh at the mangled sentence, *Rosemary started cooking herself when she was eighteen,* but we are not laughing with the writer, we are laughing at him.

In sum, my first proposition is that writing comes in grades of quality in the fashion of beer and baseball games: good, better, and best. Some usages, in my opinion, are better—not merely more effective, but better—than other usages. In this book, I want to make a few judgment calls.

Second, I advance the proposition that these better ways can be mastered by writers who are serious about their writing. There is nothing arcane or mysterious about the crafting of a respectable sentence. Writing is carpentry; it is the craft of joining words together. The construction of a good, solid sentence is no more a matter of instinct than the putting together of a dovetailed drawer. Writing is a skill; at higher levels of writing, it becomes an art. The country fiddler brings skill to his instrument, and often a remarkable level of skill; Menuhin on a Stradivarius is something else. My hope in this book is not to make greater Menuhins, but to make better fiddlers.

*   *   *

Let me acknowledge with thanks the kindness of so many persons who have helped to bring about this book. Roger Rosenblatt's beautiful essay on "The Man in the Water" is reprinted by special permission from Time magazine. Professor Anders Henriksson's melancholy collection of student boners is reprinted by special permission from The Wilson Quarterly. The translations by Brown University students to and from gobbledegook are reprinted by special permission from the Brown Alumni Monthly. The correspondence between William F. Buckley, Jr., and Hugh Kenner is reprinted by special permission from National Review.

There is no way individually to thank all the readers of my "Writer's Art" column who contributed so generously to this book, but collectively I express my debt to them. Neither is there any way adequately to thank Jinnie Beattie, who helped with the manuscript at every step along the way and fed the whole thing into the maw of an IBM Personal Computer. Having a book is like having a baby, and Jinnie midwifed this one all the way.

James J. Kilpatrick
White Walnut Hill
Scrabble, Virginia 22749

1 How Fares the English Language?

The assertion is heard from time to time that the common language of the United States is not really "English." On the contrary, goes the chauvinist argument, we speak "American," and the title of H.L. Mencken's most enduring labor is cited as proof that there is an "American Language." Up to a point—up to a very narrow point—the assertion is valid. Our British cousins spell it *labour,* we spell it *labor;* their cars run on *petrol,* ours on *gas.* To *knock up* means one thing in London, something else in New York. But when these differences have been taken fully into account, our mother tongue remains—English. Our distinctively American contributions amount to no more than a few late afternoon freckles on a venerable visage. This book has to do with the use of the English language in the late twentieth century.

Ours is a beautiful language, beautiful to speak and to hear, beautiful to read and to write. It is a changing language, as constantly changing as some eternal train that now picks up a few passengers and now lets some off. English is strong; it is soft and supple; it lends itself to majestic speech and to comedy as well. In this century it has largely replaced French as the international language of diplomacy and trade.

English is also a puzzling and often infuriating language. Doubtless there is some reason, buried in the mounds of Middle English, why we run through such rhymes as *dint, flint, hint, mint,* and *tint,* and then fall upon *pint.* As verbs go, our verbs are reasonably regular, but these days our subjunctive is a sometime thing; now you see it, now you don't. Our parts of speech are maverick horses; they will not stay put in the corrals in which we would fence them, for sometimes nouns are nouns and sometimes they trot away to serve as adjectives instead. It is not as if we had no rules; we have an abundance of rules: Do not split infinitives! Do not end a sentence with a preposition! But few of our rules of composition are rigid rules; like willows in a wind, they bend to the shape of a sentence.

One of the century's great grammarians, Professor George Curme, was in most matters a purist's purist, but he long ago provided some sound observations on the "resistless forces of life" that create change in language.

"To the conservative grammarian," Curme wrote, "all change is decay. Although he knows well that an old house often has to be torn down in part or as a whole in order that it may be rebuilt to suit modern conditions, he never sees the constructive forces at work in the destruction of old grammatical forms. He is fond of mourning over the loss of the subjunctive and the present slovenly use of the indicative. . . . The English-speaking people will chase after fads and eagerly employ the latest slang as long as it lives, for play is as necessary as work, but as long as it remains a great people it will strive unceasingly to find more convenient and more perfect forms of expression. It will do that as naturally as it breathes. . . ."

We should realize, said Curme, "that English grammar is not a body of set, unchangeable rules, but a description of English expression, bequeathed to us by our forefathers, not to be piously preserved, but to be constantly used and adapted to our needs as they adapted it to their needs."

I mention Curme's wise admonitions for a reason: It is mistaken—it is not merely mistaken, it is silly and futile—to lay down absolute rules for English and to insist that they be obeyed absolutely. I happen to look upon many -*ize* endings as preposterous formations, as in, "Southern Louisiana last night was disasterized by widespread floods," but we would be hard put, in the exigency, to get along without *memorize, plagiarize, hypnotize* and their kin. I long ago yielded on the matter of *to contact;* it is a nice, taut verb that conveys a well-understood meaning, and it is significantly shorter than, "When you reach Chicago, get in touch with . . ."

Yet when the inevitability of change has been willingly acknowledged, much more remains to be said. A large body of tradition and popular acceptance provides a foundation on which reasonable rules and respectable opinions may be erected. It is immaterial that Shakespeare once lapsed into *between you and I.* Such a confusion of nominative and objective pronouns today is quite simply wrong. Except for comic effect, no serious writer would tolerate the construction.

My thesis is that English composition does indeed have standards of excellence and levels of quality. As a general rule, it is better to use words precisely than to use words sloppily; the meaning we convey by the exact word ordinarily is bound to be clearer than the meaning we convey by an inexact word. The purpose of the written word, of course, is to communicate thought, and a writer's vocabulary has to be adapted to his audience. For one audience, we may write of carcinogens; for a different audience, of substances likely to cause cancer. This is elementary, but the point needs to be made.

Opinions on what is "correct" in grammar and syntax always will vary widely. Professional writers fuss incessantly among themselves on questions of usage, but at the bottom of their disputes is a conviction that there is a right way and a wrong way of putting words to work. It is rare to encounter an apostle of "anything goes," but one such apostle, Jim Quinn, has made a lively career of debunking the idea of good, better, and best in English usage.

Quinn identifies himself as "a poet, a satirist, and the food columnist for Philadelphia Magazine." In 1980 he published a polemical little work, *American Tongue in Cheek.* Some anonymous scoundrel, hoping to throw me into apoplexy, sent me a copy of the paperback Penguin edition. In the same compulsive way that a clean-plate eater will eat most of the brussels sprouts that are served him, I read most of Quinn's regurgitated heresy. Never having seen the fellow's poetry or his satire, I venture no opinion thereon, though I am filled with a dreadful surmise. But if this professional tail-twister is as cavalier in his approach to the spice rack as he is contemptuous in his attitude toward the written word, may a merciful providence protect the people of Philadelphia from his sauce Béarnaise.

Quinn's pronouncements are directed at "lovers of the language." His purpose is to make them "angry," and he accomplishes that aim superbly. He happily embraces *him and I;* he suffers not the slightest pain at *giftable;* he adopts as his motto, *Let anybody do what they want.* If a participial phrase dangles, he advises us, let it dangle; let it all hang out. He perceives no useful difference between *less* and *fewer.* He terms it a simple fact that *ain't* is in current cultivated usage. Barking yap-yap-yap, he bites at the ankles of such "pop grammarians" and "language purifiers" as John Simon, Edwin Newman, and Thomas Middleton. He is a real shoot-'em-up Saturday night hell-raiser, this one.

But such flashy exhibitionism, accompanied by the pseudo-scholarship of a bright sophomore, has about as much appeal as graffiti on the outer walls of Notre Dame. Quinn is an intellectual streaker, mooning his way through the English language, but he writes with a matador's skill at teasing a bull, and his polemics serve a useful purpose. He compels us to think about values.

Are there values? If *He do his chores this morning* is just as "good" a sentence as *He did his chores this morning,* then the game is up. In this event, it makes no difference how we write, on account of the whole idea, y'know, is just that somebody dig what we say, get it? Right! But if there are qualitative differences—if there are enduring values—then these differences merit our careful consideration.

Let me offer an analogy: In 1969 my wife and I built our home in the Blue Ridge Mountains. Good fortune led us to a wonderful old man, Arthur Griffith by name. He called himself a carpenter; he was in fact a cabinetmaker. Mr. Griffith discarded lumber he regarded as inferior. He would cut a board, and test it, and trim a little, and test it, and take off a little more with his plane, and finally he would fit the board precisely. He cut every mortise as if he were a jeweler cutting the facets of diamonds. He sandpapered; he polished; he filled every nail hole. He made square corners. He cared.

Ten years later, when a tool shed needed building and Mr. Griffith was unavailable, we hired a jackleg. He was the Quinn of carpentry. He sawed a mortise by kind of squinting at the board. His joints gapped like the teeth of a six-year-old. When he finished, the shed was a functional shed. Nothing more could be said for it.

Yes, there are qualitative standards in writing. The good craftsman will go at every sentence as Arthur Griffith went at the kitchen cupboards, with love and discipline and skill, and with a reverence for the keen-edged tools of our trade. John Updike set the standard for writers to aspire to: It is "to work steadily, even shyly, in the spirit of those medieval carvers who so fondly sculpted the undersides of choir seats." To be sure, that standard is not necessarily the standard we employ in writing a letter to the gas company, but it is important to understand that such a standard exists.

One of the melancholy truths of our time is that many young people are largely unaware of what writing is all about. Doubtless this has been true throughout all ages; until this century, only a privileged few had much of an education beyond elementary school. But it is poignantly, ironically true that among high school graduates, levels of achievement in reading and writing have declined steadily in recent years. The opportunities for enlargement of the mind never have been greater; a technological revolution has swept over the old sedentary libraries, endowing them with computers, cassettes, data retrieval systems, and all the rest. Appropriations for public education have grown to a point that many states spend more than $3,000 a year on each pupil in average daily attendance. Yet the more resources we make available, and the more money we spend, the less we seem to accomplish. The 1983 report from the National Commission on Excellence in Education brought in a sad indictment of the public schools: They are drowning in rising tides of mediocrity.

Professor Hugh Kenner of Johns Hopkins, one of the most literate men in the land, has remarked that "most people today do less writing than people did fifty years ago." Obviously this is so. Once hostesses wrote invitations to come to lunch, and prospective guests wrote notes in reply. Once our political leaders wrote long and thoughtful letters – individual letters—to their constituents. Form letters and robot typewriters have assumed this role. Business affairs that once were conducted through correspondence now are conducted by telephone. The day rapidly approaches when all the records of our civilization, or what passes for civilization, will wind up on a single floppy disk.

The National Commission estimated that 23 million American adults must be judged "functionally illiterate by the simplest tests of everyday reading, writing, and comprehension." W.H. Auden back in 1967 guessed that "nine-tenths of the population do not know what 30 percent of the words they use actually mean." Standard tests of literacy among high school students reflect a discouraging trend.

We are bound to ask ourselves why these things have happened. Answers and explanations come from every quarter. It is first said that the statistics are deceptive and the test scores are misleading. Part of the blame, said the National Commission, lies with state legislatures and local school boards. "Secondary school curricula have been homogenized, diluted, and diffused to the point that they no longer have a central purpose. In effect, we have a cafeteria-style curriculum in which the appetizers and desserts can easily be mistaken for the main course."

The Supreme Court, it is said, has made the bad matter of discipline even worse, by requiring full-blown due process hearings before a student may be suspended or expelled. Our easygoing society has concluded that 175 or 180 days of schooling every year are enough; our legislatures have concluded that the people won't pay for anything more. Various pressure groups have imposed upon the public schools a burden of responsibilities that schools were not required to manage in the past—sex education, nutrition education, brotherhood education, driver education, a greatly expanded program of physical education.

Television, a convenient ogre, also is blamed for the pathetic state of reading and writing. The child who spends three thousand hours a year watching the boob tube is learning *something* in the process, but much of that *something* may not be worth learning.

Changing times have wrought changing methods of teaching. In my own nonage, back in the twenties and thirties, we learned English in the same way that golfers practice putting, pianists run their scales, and skaters do their school figures. We worked at it. We had spelling bees. We had homework every night, and I suppose. we regarded this as intolerable oppression, but we did it. We wrote themes and plays and book reviews and verse. We memorized great chunks of poetry and drama. We *recited,* if you please, with gestures, and the more affluent families provided their sons and daughters with private lessons in elocution.

One tool was especially valuable for the youngster who wanted to write: We diagramed sentences. I am told this old discipline has gone the way of *hic, haec, hoc,* and more's the pity. Diagraming is to prose composition as the study of skeletons is to the mastery of human anatomy. If we learn the bones first, we know where the ligaments attach. "Find the subject!" I can still hear a seventh-grade teacher crying. "Find the subject!"

Diagraming was an exercise, and to the extent that this teaching device still is used, it remains one of the best exercises. Looking back at homework in Taft Junior High School, I suppose I found no more pleasure in diagraming a dozen sentences than I found in running the twelve arpeggios. Of what use, I wondered, are subjects, predicates, prepositional phrases, and subordinate clauses? In time I would discover that they are the raw material of a writer's life.

Another discipline has been almost eliminated by the chefs in charge of the smorgasbord. Two years of Latin used to be required for graduation from high school; now two years of Latin rarely are taught at all. My recollection is that I took four years of Latin, and late in life I found that the experience gave me a little something in common with Evelyn Waugh. He too took great quantities of Latin (and Greek as well), and recalled in his autobiography that he forgot all of it as he grew older. He doubted that he could compose "even a simple epitaph" in impeccable Latin.

"But I do not regret my superficial classical studies," Waugh said. "I believe that the conventional defense of them is valid, and that only by them can a boy fully understand that a sentence is a logical construction, and that words have meanings, departure from which is either a conscious metaphor or inexcusable vulgarity. Those who have not been so taught . . . betray their deprivation."

Were our teachers better teachers back in the old days? As a general proposition, I surmise that they were. Prior to World War II, the brightest young women went into teaching. The pay was as low as respect was high, but the situation gave the schools some highly competent people in the classroom. Today the brightest young women find many other opportunities opening for them. These opportunities pay better salaries than the public schools are willing or able to pay; the intellectual challenges often are more appealing; evenings are free for more amusing pastimes than correcting the abysmal spelling on a ninth-grader's paper.

While these circumstances were changing, the educational establishment was changing also. The old professional associations of teachers, by a notably unfortunate alchemy, turned into trade unions. In this regard, teachers today cannot be distinguished from teamsters, hod carriers, or plumbers. At the top of the establishment, an industrious lobby worked for changes in the requirements for the licensing of teachers. Emphasis shifted from the *what* to teach to the *how* to teach; methodology replaced course content; master's theses appeared on such cosmic topics as *The Designing of Storage Space in a High School Gymnasium;* and the teachers' colleges prospered as never before.

Richard Mitchell, a professor of English at Glassboro State College in New Jersey, attacked these wretched developments in a polemical book in 1982, *The Graves of Academe.* He dipped his pen in sulfuric acid, and he etched a bitter picture. Within the teachers' colleges, he said, the teachers of English who are charged with teaching potential teachers of English are themselves an illiterate bunch. No wonder Johnny can't write! His teacher doesn't know how to write either.

Mitchell provided an example of the prose that oozes from the educationist establishment:

> Recent research has shown that a number of student variables—authoritarianism, dogmatism, intelligence, conceptual level, convergent-divergent ability, locus of control, anxiety, compulsivity, need for achievement, achievement orientation, independence-dependence, and extraversion-introversion—may moderate the relationship between teacher directiveness and grades and satisfaction . . . The purpose of the present research is to develop multivariate mathematical models of the interactive relationships using stepwise regression strategies.

How do you like that tapioca? Have another serving:

> An Academic Planning Model must involve a futures planning component. Goals should be set for some time in the future. These goals should be translated into shorter term objectives for which the degree of detail and concreteness varies inversely with the lead time. There should also be reasonable suspense dates for implementation of plans and a definitive methodology for evaluation and feedback. The interfacing of long-term . . . and short-term planning should result.

And yet one more example, this one from a superintendent of schools in Michigan. He arranged to have this message circulated to parents, teachers, and pupils:

> STUDENT RIGHTS/RESPONSIBILITIES
> One constant and over-riding concern of all district personnel is the rights of our students. Aside from this, it shall no longer be implied because along with rights for the students, efforts shall be obviated in their inculcation as to responsibilities and obligations they have also. A board document of due process shall be prepared and which shall contain as well, Rights, Responsibilities.

At Mitchell's own institution in New Jersey, the communications department proposed to establish an "ideal classroom" for the teaching of the basic writing course. Traditional classrooms, it was said, have a way of perpetuating traditional approaches. Away with them! "By bringing together in one room a large variety of audio-visual implements, creating a relaxed atmosphere by having the room carpeted with pictures on the walls and easy chairs and tables and by having duplicating equipment and a variety of newspapers and magazines readily available, we can encourage attempts to change both students' perceptions and teachers' approaches to the task of learning how to write.''

There's a vision for you—a room carpeted with pictures on the walls and easy chairs. But desks? Typewriters? Tablets? Dictionaries? How does one learn to write with an audio-visual implement going?

Mitchell also cited a recommendation from the Educational Testing Service that teachers grade student writing "holistically." That is, writing should be judged "for a total impression of its quality rather than for such separate aspects of writing skill as organization, punctuation, diction, or spelling." The idea is to take a positive approach to the rating of compositions by concentrating on "what the student has accomplished rather than on what the student has failed to do or has done badly."

This is a neat idea. Applied to a student of the piano, the approach would ignore wrong notes. Applied to a budding surgeon, the approach would overlook what the potential doctor had failed to do or had done badly. If the student, having been assigned to remove an appendix, mistakenly took out the tonsils instead, we should be forgiving; we should think holistically. It is the total impression that counts.

Given such instruction, let us pity the poor children who would like to be writers. Their teachers' teachers are infected; their teachers are Typhoid Marys, and the epidemic of poor writing spreads.

Our high school graduates—not all of them, but vast numbers of them—are deficient not only in writing but in other humane studies also. Anders Henriksson, a teacher of history at McMaster University and the University of Alberta, made a nice malicious hobby of collecting fragments from his students' papers. He put them together in a sorrowfully revealing essay for The Wilson Quarterly.

History, as we know, is always bias, because human beings have to be studied by other human beings, not by independent observers of another species.

During the Middle Ages, everybody was middle aged. Church and state were co-operatic. Middle Evil society was made up of monks, lords, and surfs. It is unfortuante that we do not have a medivel European laid out on a table before us, ready for dissection. After a revival of infantile commerce slowly creeped into Europe, merchants appeared. Some were sitters and some were drifters. They roamed from town to town exposing themselves and organized big fairies in the countryside. Mideval people were violent. Murder during this period was nothing. Everybody killed someone. England fought numerously for land in France and ended up wining and losing. The Crusades were a series of military expaditions made by Christians seeking to free the holy land (the "Home Town" of Christ) from the Islams.

In the 1400 hundreds most Englishmen were perpendicular. A class of yeowls arose. Finally Europe caught the Black Death. The bubonic plague is a social disease in the sense that it can be transmitted by intercourse and other etceteras. It was spread from port to port by inflected rats. Victims of the Black Death grew boobs on their necks. The plague also helped the emergance of the English language as the national language of England, France and Italy.

The Middle Ages slimpared to a halt. The renasence bolted in from the blue. Life reeked with joy. Italy became robust, and more individuals felt the value of their human being. Italy, of course, was much closer to the rest of the world, thanks to northern Europe.

Man was determined to civilise himself and his brothers, even if heads had to roll! It became sheik to be educated. Art was on a more associated level. Europe was full of incredable churches with great art bulging out their doors. Renaissance merchants were beautiful and almost lifelike.

The Reformnation happened when German nobles resented the idea that tithes were going to Papal France or the Pope thus enriching Catholic coiffures. Traditions had become oppressive so they too were crushed in the wake of man's quest for ressurection above the not-just-social beast he had become. An angry Martin Luther nailed 95 theocrats to a church door. Theologically, Luthar was into reorientation mutation. Calvinism was the most convenient religion since the days of the ancients. Anabaptist services tended to be migratory. The Popes, of course, were usually Catholic. Monks went right on seeing themselves as worms. The Last Jesuit priest died in the 19th century.

After the refirmation were wars both foreign and infernal. If the Spanish could gain the Netherlands they would have a stronghold throughout northern Europe which would include their posetions in Italy, Burgangy, central Europe and India thus serrounding France.

The German Emperor's lower passage was blocked by the French for years and years.

Louise XIV became King of the Sun. He gave the people food and artillery. If he didn't like someone, he sent them to the gallows to row for the rest of their lives. Vauban was the royal minister of flirtation. In Russia the 17th century was known as the time of the bounding of the serfs. Russian nobles wore clothes only to humour Peter the Great. Peter filled his government with accidental people and built a new capital near the European boarder. Orthodox priests became government antennae.

The enlightenment was a reasonable time. Voltare wrote a book called "Candy" that got him into trouble with Frederick the Great. Philosophers were unknown yet, and the fundamental stake was one of religious toleration slightly confused with defeatism. France was in a very serious state. Taxation was a great drain on the state budget. The French revolution was accomplished before it happened. The revolution evolved through monarchial, republican and tolarian phases until it catapulted into Napolean. Napoleon was ill with bladder problems and was very tense and unrestrained.

History, a record of things left behind by past generations, started in 1815. Throughout the comparatively radical years 1815-1870 the western European continent was undergoing a Rampant period of economic modification. Industrialization was precipitating in England. Problems were so complexicated that in Paris, out of a city population of 1 million people, 2 million able bodies were on the loose.

Great Brittain, the USA and other European countrys had demicratic leanings. The middle class was tired and needed a rest. The old order could see the lid holding down new ideas beginning to shake. Among the goals of the chartists were universal suferage and an anal parliment. Voting was to be done by ballad.

A new time zone of national unification roared over the horizon. Founder of the new Italy was Cavour, an intelligent Sardine from the north. Nationalism aided Itally because nationalism is the growth of an army. We can see that nationalism succeeded for Itally because of France's big army. Napoleam III-IV mounted the French thrown. One thinks of Napoleon III as a live extension of the late, but great, Napoleon. Here too was the new Germany: loud, bold, vulgar and full of reality.

Culture fomented from Europe's tip to its top. Richard Strauss, who was violent but methodical like his wife made him, plunged into vicious and perverse plays. Dramatized were adventures in seduction and abortion. Music reeked with reality. Wagner was master of music, and people did not forget his contribution. When he died they labeled his seat "historical." Other countries had their own artists. France had Chekhov.

World War I broke out around 1912-1914. Germany was on one side of France and Russia was on the other. At war people get killed, and then they aren't people any more, but friends. Peace was proclaimed at Versigh, which was attended by George Loid, Primal Minister of England. President Wilson arrived with 14 pointers. In 1937 Lenin revolted Russia. Communism raged among the peasants, and the civil war "team colours" were red and white.

Germany was displaced after WWI. This gave rise to Hitler. Germany was morbidly overexcited and unbalanced. Berlin became the decadent capital, where all forms of sexual deprivations were practised. A huge anti-semantic movement arose. Attractive slogans like "death to all Jews" were used by governmental groups. Hitler remilitarized the Rineland over a squirmish between Germany and France. The appeasers were blinded by the great red of the Soviets. Moosealini rested his foundations on 8 million bayonets and invaded Hi Lee Salasy. Germany invaded Poland, France invaded Belgium, and Russia invaded everybody. War screeched to an end when a nukuleer explosion was dropped on Heroshima. A whole generation had been wipe out in two world wars, and their forlorne families were left to pick up the peaces.

According to Fromm, individuation began historically in medieval times. This was a period of small childhood. There is increasing experience as adolescence experiences its life development. The last stage is us.

Professor Henriksson's students were not exceptions. Other teachers of history could compile essays that would be similar, if not so delightful. The wonder is that we have as many lovers of the humanities as we do, but I advance this proposition out of a gratifying personal experience: People do care about the language. They care passionately about the language. The columnist who writes about writing, such as William Safire of The New York Times, swiftly discovers that in some quarters he is regarded as a hero. Mail arrives by the bagful. Readers overwhelm him with applause for his efforts—and readers also pounce mercilessly upon the columnist's own blunders.

Toward the end of 1981 I wrote a column asking for help in the matter of the subjunctive mood. Earlier I had written that a campaign to oust Interior Secretary James Watt was an exercise in futility *if there ever was one.* I also had written of an air traffic controller who suffered severe stress at a major tower, but *if he were assigned to a lower level,* he would suffer no more stress than men suffer in other jobs. A reader in Chicago wrote to reprimand me for using the indicative; I should have written *if there ever were one.* A reader in Alabama admonished me for using the subjunctive; I should have written *if he was assigned.*

Well, I inquired despairingly of my readers, Who's right? I thought I might get two or three letters of advice. After all, who cares about the subjunctive? Within a week forty-six letters arrived in response. Believe me, that is a phenomenal response, and it was evident from the tone and content of the mail that my correspondents had strong convictions on the matter.

I'll return to the subjunctive after a while. My point here is that we ought never to despair. For all the illiteracy detected by the National Commission, and for all the dimwittedness exemplified in the papers of Professor Henriksson's students, great numbers of the American people care deeply about the use and abuse of language. In a typical day's mail in my office, a sixty-seven-year-old mechanical engineer in Kokomo is upset about *have got.* A housewife in Chicago hopes I will never use the phrase, *to throw a party.* A gentleman in Texas protests the use of *Anglo* to mean a white person not of Hispanic descent. A reader in Greenwood, S.C., prays that I will wage war against *time frame.*

From Lake Worth, Fla., comes a letter from a mathematically minded reader who is irritated by *times,* as in *The new film is 100 times the thinness of.* A gentleman in Indianapolis echoes the complaint: *Two times as much,* he asserts, is 100 percent more, whereas *two times more* is 200 percent more.

Lovers of the language are filled with peeves and irks. They are annoyed by redundancies: *Gobi desert, rice paddy, the hoi polloi, true facts, free gift, rain shower.* I hear regularly from a crotchety fellow who resents the use of *both* when *each* would be better, as in "both teams have two time-outs remaining." It is marvelous—I use the word respectfully, as something to marvel at—that in the midst of our permissive times, so many persons should care for discipline so much.

Let us take heart. Now and then I get a letter reproaching me for picking grammatical nits, or for being "a purist," or for losing sight of what *writing* is all about. A reader in Olympia, Wash., wondered if "the rule-makers" of language "have ever convened to try to determine what helps and what hinders communication through written language." His thought was that writing should get closer to speech. What purpose is served, he asked, by fine distinctions in language that are appreciated "only by the very few who have equal knowledge"? He proposed that writers who write for a general audience should settle upon a core of words commonly understood, "and then pretty much stick to it." A sound idea?

My own answer, of course, would be, no. It seems to me that, as writers, we ought to take advantage of all the glories of the English tongue, and to use them as best we can, but always taking into account one thing: the audience we are writing for. The danger in trying to communicate with everybody, all the time, is the danger of "writing down" to some perceived common denominator of comprehension. This way lies the cornmeal mush of Dick and Jane and Spot the dog, who incessantly ran-ran-ran through a second-grade reader.

We write for two reasons. Sometimes we write solely for the sake of self-expression; we want to write something out of our system. This is why non-professionals keep diaries and write sonnets. Most of the time we write to communicate; we write personal letters or business letters; we write manuals of instruction and office memoranda; we write novels, plays, biographies, recipes, diet books, newspaper pieces, and magazine articles. But always, inescapably, we are writing for a perceived audience.

It follows that we cannot stick to some agreed-upon core of words. Beyond a basic vocabulary, we find hundreds of special vocabularies. My friend in Washington implicitly recognized this. He enclosed some verses written by a black co-worker in "black English." I could guess at most of the unfamiliar words, but the author did not set out to communicate with me. He had another audience in mind. So it goes. If we are writing for the Religious Herald, we have one core of words; if we write for Penthouse, the core (a pretty hard core, at that) is different because the audience is different.

Our shifting vocabularies ought to be as accurate as we can make them. I was reminded of this by a piece in National Review by mathematician John Saxon, the author of a textbook on algebra that could revolutionize the teaching of that discipline. "Algebra," he wrote, "is the basic language of all mathematics beyond arithmetic." I looked in total mystification at the illustrative problems that accompanied his piece. They were written in his basic language—and I do not read or speak that language. I am as ignorant of Algebra as I am of Arabic, Hebrew, or Greek.

That depressing realization reminded me anew of the astounding number of languages that are spoken and written in our polyglot world. All of us know someone who speaks French or German or Spanish. That is not what I have in mind. My grandchildren will grow up speaking Computer; they will be lost in the next century if they don't. I have friends who speak Architecture, who speak Music, who speak Medicine. Each of these tongues has a vocabulary all its own. Those of us who write for a living should be careful when trying to speak in languages we do not comprehend.

My wife, by way of example, was for many years a professional sculptor. She speaks Art. Whenever she reads of a "light shade" or a "dark tint," she climbs a wall. When she is told that someone has painted an "abstract," she throws things. I have a son in the Navy. When someone calls his destroyer a "boat," he goes up the mast. In his presence I do not speak of "by and large" or "windward edge" unless I want to hear more about sailing than I truly want to know.

For my own part, I speak a little Printing, fluent Government, and pretty fair Law. These are my languages. When I see that some alien has confused a bill and a resolution, I react with the pain of a Parisian listening to a Mississippian speaking French.

Let me add a story with a moral to it: One October, a few years back, I wrote a pretty column about autumn in the Blue Ridge Mountains. I said our hills were Persian carpets—an old metaphor, but an apt one. Then I threw in a sentence to this effect, that "the old women of Karastan, weaving their rugs by hand, could not contrive," and so forth. The sentence had a nice lilt and ring. I liked that sentence.

By good fortune, I am blessed at my syndicate with the greatest copy editor who ever sat in a slot. He takes nothing for granted. My phone rang. It was my mentor, complaining that he had checked two atlases, and nowhere in what used to be Persia could he find a city or town of "Karastan." Much humbled, I made a couple of calls. In the end we inserted "Tabriz" instead.

My problem, obviously, was that I do not speak Carpets. Karastan, I now can inform you, is located not in Iran but in North Carolina. Behind every reckless writer should lie a careful copy editor. The moral to the story is, if you plunge into such foreign tongues as Algebra, Art, or Architecture, and you do not truly know a parameter from a pediment, you are likely to make a public fool of yourself. I almost did.

The late David W. Maurer was a professor emeritus of linguistics at the University of Louisville. He specialized in the languages of crime. If you speak Pickpocket, you will know that a *John Bates* is a middle-aged victim, a *blute* is a newspaper carried by a *tool* to obscure his active hand as he *gets his duke down* or *reefs a kick.* In 1981 the University Press of Kentucky published a 390-page volume of Maurer's researches, *Language of the Underworld.* It is not a dictionary I would use every day, but if I were a novelist writing about common thieves and flimflam artists, Maurer's work would lead me to the accurate word.

That always should be our goal, as Mark Twain has reminded us, "to use the right word, and not its second cousin." When we read that a "house has been robbed," we are meeting a second cousin, for houses are burglarized; people are robbed. When we read that a "partially nude" body has been found, we experience an imperceptible hesitation—for *nude* is just that; it is synonymous with *naked,* and we would not write of a "partially naked" body. The right word in this instance would be partially *clad.*

There was a time when sly fellows nipped tiny bits of gold or silver from coins in circulation, until at last the coins lost much of their value. Then a diemaker invented the milled edge, and the practice ceased. All I am saying is that words have milled edges too, and we ought to keep them that way.

2 Faith, Hope, and Clarity

Off and on for more than thirty years I have tried to preach this gospel to students of journalism and to cub reporters: Before anything else, we must be *writers*. We may be known as reporters, or critics, or columnists, or reviewers, or editorialists. We may specialize in news of business or labor or politics or sports. No matter. First of all, we are *writers*. This is how we make our living: We write. We put words together. In the end, the test of how well we do our job is not in how well we cover the news, or review the movies, or chide a president, or criticize an actor, but in how well we write.

I have a theory about writing. The theory goes to this effect: The chief difference between good writing and better writing may be measured by the number of imperceptible hesitations the reader experiences as he goes along.

An author functions as a kind of forest guide. His duty is to escort the tenderfoot along an unfamiliar trail. The pleasure of the hike depends to a large extent upon how often the reader stumbles. Does our reader trip over unfamiliar words? Does he bump his head on an overhanging clause, or stub his toe on an ambiguous antecedent? If so, the reader tends to give up. It's too much, he says, and he turns to something else.

These are among the hazards that cause the reader to suffer those imperceptible hesitations that characterize poor writing. It is the little uncertainty that matters—the small confusion, the modifier that isn't badly lost but only slightly misplaced. At such pauses along the trail, the reader's eye flickers and wanders—back up to the subject, down again to the verb. The process may consume no more than a fraction of a second, but these fractions are like Everett Dirksen's "a billion dollars here and a billion dollars there." Pretty soon, said the Illinois statesman, those billions add up to real money. Imperceptible hesitations add up the same way. A cardinal principle of good writing, says Wilson Follett, "is that no one should ever have to read a sentence twice because of the way it is put together."

Notice Follett's qualification: We may often want to read a sentence twice because the sentence has beauty or punch or wit, or because it contains provocative thought, but we ought never to have to read a sentence twice "because of the way it is put together."

This is what we are talking about, or so it seems to me, when we talk of the writer's *art*. By definition, art is "skill acquired by experience, study, or observation." Art is also "an occupation requiring knowledge or skill." Yet again, art is "the conscious use of skill and creative imagination, especially in the production of aesthetic objects."

The common theme is *skill*. Skills can be taught. It may be that "creative imagination," like perfect pitch in a musician, is an inherited characteristic. I wouldn't know about that. My guess is that imagination also may be cultivated, but when it comes to prose composition, imagination is primarily a property of fiction. I leave that to others. My concern is with—I was about to say plain old ordinary prose, but it is more than that. My concern is with the writing art that begins with the writing craft but aspires to be something better.

How does one get to be a writer? The first two requirements are these—to read insatiably, and to write incessantly.

We ought of course to read selectively. It is all very well to read trash, for the writer can learn something useful, I suppose, from even the gluppiest novel of romance. But there never is time to read all that we would like to read, and the writer's time is best spent on works that endure. It is by such reading that we fill our storehouse with the devices of allusion and comparison; we store the patience of Job, the labors of Hercules. We read for style, for the rolling surf of Gibbon's majestic paragraphs, for the elegance of Macaulay's magisterial reviews, for the exaggerations of Mark Twain and Henry Mencken. We read for information; we read newspapers, magazines, encyclopedias. We read for the fun of it; we read Art Buchwald and Calvin Trillin. We read in the bathroom, we read in bed, we read on the airplane, we never stop reading.

And we never stop writing. We write letters, we write book reviews, we write doggerel verse and marshmallow sonnets. We try our hand at writing fiction, writing plays, writing speeches. We write for anyone who will read our stuff. We write to get something out of our system.

The more we read, and the more we write, the more likely we are to perfect the craft that aspires to the art. Granted, the writer who wants to be a serious writer cannot spend *all* his time by the lamp. Roscoe Ellard, one of the great teachers of journalism, used to urge his students to learn all they could learn of life. "People who lead dull lives," he would say, "write dull copy." Let us be whole persons. But if we ourselves would be read, we must first read what others have written. If we would be writers, we must write. We must try constantly to write as well as we can.

The quality of one's writing should be a concern not only of those whose profession is to write. Businessmen, lawyers, ministers, accountants, and fund-raisers ought also to be concerned. A man is known, so the proverb goes, by the company he keeps. At certain levels of correspondence, a man may be judged by the letters he writes.

Early in 1983 I received a letter from a lawyer in a Midwestern city. He was lobbying hard for a bill he wanted passed, and he enclosed copies of letters he had sent to local newspapers and to his state legislators. I started into the file with sympathy for his cause. I wound up with other emotions entirely.

It was embarrassing. Here was a graduate of a school of law, a member of the bar, a gentleman who evidently had been in practice for a considerable number of years. If he had read his letters after they were typed but before he signed them, no evidence of such scrutiny could be found. Thus one stumbled over *rules* when the author intended *roles*. The fellow confused *it's* and *its* and *who's* and *whose*. He spoke of a constitutional *prohibitation* when presumably he meant *prohibition*.

The gentleman, it appeared, never had met a gerund. He appreciated *you taking the time to read my letter.* The appearance of certain witnesses, he said, *is tantamount to them ostensibly speaking for their organizations.* He had problems with plural subjects and singular verbs: *Everyone who has appeared . . . speak only on a personal basis.* He spoke of a party who could seek redress *in the courts which has the final say.* His failures in punctuation made it almost impossible to make heads or tails of his convoluted sentences.

What impression did he leave, I wondered, on the newspaper editors and the legislators he hoped to influence? Would they take the time and go to the trouble to track through his incoherent paragraphs, and then to backtrack in search of a spoor of meaning? I gravely doubt it.

To be sure, niceties in syntax may not matter in wholly personal correspondence, though history and court records suggest that even love letters may get to be public. It was said of the much-married Tommy Manville that after many a lawsuit he began his letters with a fatalistic salutation: Dear Gladys and Members of the Jury. If we are engaged in what may become public correspondence, we ought to take pains. If we do, we won't cause so many of them.

In brief, we ought to cultivate skills. Toward that end, I venture a few suggestions.

Have Something to Say

This is the first and greatest commandment for a writer, and on many of the nation's editorial pages it is the commandment most often disobeyed. *Have something to say.* This is the whole purpose of writing. We must start with an idea or an image. If there is no substantive idea or image worth conveying, the venture fails at the outset. The idea may be that man is descended from the apes, or that Millard Fillmore has been unjustly maligned, or that a mastery of geometry is essential to the development of an orderly mind. The image may be an image of a forest fire, or a field of wheat, or a stein of beer. No matter. We ought not to blather along, pointlessly and disjointedly, toward no foreseeable conclusion. The idea comes first.

Remember What Saint Paul Might Have Said

If Saint Paul had been talking to a classroom of prospective writers, he might have changed a consonant. Faith and hope must abide, for the writer must have faith in his own ideas and he must hope that his words will be read, but after faith and hope comes clarity. Without clarity we are not even sounding brass or tinkling cymbals. Be clear, be clear, be clear! Your idea or image may be murky, but do not write murkily about it. Be murky clearly!

The techniques of clear writing are neither formidable nor obscure. They echo the same elementary requirements of carpentry. One of these is:

Take Your Time

I know, I know. It isn't always possible, especially with a deadline pressing, to take the time required for polishing our prose. But if somehow we make the time, we will do a better job of putting our words together.

Thus we may trim away the dangling clause. One of the many fine restaurants in Washington is Jacqueline's, at 20th and M streets, but an advertisement for Jacqueline's left a vaguely sepulchral impression: "Although tucked away below ground, you are pleasantly surprised by the charming decor." The writer of an ad for a Virginia hotel had the same problem: "Elegantly appointed, its strategic locale in the heart of Richmond puts you only minutes away," and so forth. The orphan clauses had no subject mother.

We cause hesitations when we employ a poor relation of the right word instead of the right word itself. Thus the respected Wall Street Journal once reported the case of a woman who quit work because cigar smoke gave her headaches and made her "nauseous." The right word would have been "nauseated."

Sometimes we startle the reader with thoughts that are unintentionally profound. From an obituary in the old Washington Star: "She leaves no living survivors." From the term paper of a Virginia high school student: "To execute Gary Gilmore would infringe seriously upon his human rights."

We snag our readers on the briers of "all" and "not all." From The Washingtonian magazine: "Because all new cars aren't bought by little old ladies, finding well-preserved secondhand cars can be a tricky affair." From anthologies of proverbs: "All that glitters is not gold."

Our compasses fail, and we leave our readers lost amid misplaced elements. Abigail Van Buren once wrote that she found it inconceivable "that a registered nurse would be 'ashamed' to take her child to a doctor with recurring pinworms."

In our haste, we slip into lapses of grammar. A staff writer for The Miami Herald, reporting the mugging of a British couple who had just arrived in Florida, said the hoodlums "beat both he and his wife." We lurch into backward formations. A diplomat goes to the Middle East "at no small risk to his own skin." A stranded sailor displays "not a little grit." An investor makes a gain "of no small consequence." United Press International describes Washington's National Airport as "surrounded on three sides by water.'' It is an interesting trick, to surround something on three sides. The New York Times, great newspaper that it is, often errs. The Times has reported upon ''falsely padded expense accounts,'' upon a playwright who was a ''lifelong native of New York,'' upon a man ''shot fatally three times.''

Most of these goofs, gaffes, and blunders are the result of a single cause: haste. If there is one sin against clear writing more serious than all others, it is the sin of careless copyreading. Every city editor has known the bumptious and overconfident reporter who spins his piece from the typewriter (in the days when reporters wrote on typewriters) and supposes the copy iş ready for immediate publication. To borrow from Truman Capote, who was voicing his incredulity at Jack Kerouac's boast that he never changed a line, ''That isn't writing, that's typing.'' Careful editing would have saved Abby from the doctor with pinworms. Careful editing would have eliminated the ''falsely'' in ''falsely padded expense accounts.'' Even a moment's scrutiny would have caught the beating of ''he and his wife.'' The more we read our copy after we believe we are finished with it, the more we will catch obscurities in expression, roughnesses in style, mistakes in spelling, and inexactness in our choice of words. Yes, most of us write on sand, but let us write clearly on sand. Let us be understood before tomorrow's waves come rolling in.

Know Where You're Going Before You Start

Our metaphorical forest ranger would find himself in trouble if he embarked upon a hike with no plan of getting from Point A to Point B. Before we begin a letter, an editorial, a brief, or a note of instructions to the babysitter, we ought to have a clear idea of the points we intend to make and the order in which we mean to make them.

It has been a long time since I made a formal outline for this purpose, neatly done up in Roman numerals, topics, and subtopics, but I find that less formal reminders can be a big help in keeping me from wandering off into the underbrush of a passing thought. There remains much merit in the old advice to the public speaker: Tell them what you're going to say; say it; and tell them what you've said. It may help you to resort to numbering your points: *The Supreme Court erred in three ways. First, it distorted the statute; second, it trampled upon the Constitution; third, it trespassed upon the power of Congress.* You would then go on to expand upon these offenses, taking them in the same order. The court would not pay the slightest attention to your remonstrances, but at least you would have given the justices an orderly hiding.

Keep It Simple

If your aim is chiefly to be clear, keep this in mind: Short words ordinarily are better than long words. Short sentences generally are better than long sentences. At the moment we are not trying for "style." We are trying to communicate clearly. Style will come later.

As a general proposition, the active voice is better suited to clarity than the passive voice. *Dan Rather reported* beats *It was reported by Dan Rather.* Still speaking generally, I suggest that the indicative mood is better than the subjunctive mood. The subjunctive can get you into all kinds of trouble.

"The first law of writing," said Macaulay, "that law to which all other laws are subordinate, is this: that the words employed shall be such as to convey to the reader the meaning of the writer." Toward that end, use familiar words—words that your readers will understand, and not words they will have to look up. No advice is more elementary, and no advice is more difficult to accept. When we feel an impulse to use a marvelously exotic word, let us lie down until the impulse goes away.

A good many years ago, the battleship *Missouri* sailed into the port of Hampton Roads and got stuck on silt in the channel. A few weeks earlier, browsing through the *L* section of the dictionary in search of what is meant by *limbo,* I stumbled over the word *limicolous.* It means "living in mud." Gazing upon *limicolous,* I knew love at first sight. Then the battleship got stuck and I wrote an editorial about "The Limicolous Mo." Not one reader in a thousand knew what on earth I was talking about.

Another time, I was writing a column about the remarkable increase in the number of political action committees. In 1972 these committees numbered 113; ten years later they numbered 3,149. I wanted a word to describe the proliferation. Now, *proliferation* in itself is about a two-dollar word, but that was not enough. The devil was in me.

At precisely that moment, a word wandered by. These things are like knowing sin. Sitting at their typewriters, all writers know the experience. The word is seductive. It slithers along, wet-lipped, scented with exotic perfume; it gazes at the writer with a come-hither glance. "Take me," says this gorgeous creature. "I dare you." Thus are we led into temptation.

The word was *mitotically*. I could not resist it. "Political action committees," I wrote, "tend to multiply mitotically." I hated myself in the morning, but it was too late. A few days later the mail brought a grumpy letter of rebuke and reproach from Jim Lund at The Biloxi (Miss.) Daily Herald. I had it coming.

It is no defense, but I mention it anyhow, to say that my mentor and brother pundit, Bill Buckley, falls into sin even more easily than I. He has had affairs with *decoctable, anfractuosity,* and *endogamous.* He has taken to bed with *chiliastic, phlogistonic, sciolism, incondite,* and *osmotically.* He has fallen for *hubristic, otiose, repristinate, adumbrated,* and *synecdoche.* Once he ventured a kindly comment on Nelson Rockefeller. He said Mr. Rockefeller's opsimathy should be welcomed. It was perhaps the nicest thing Bill Buckley ever said about Nelson Rockefeller, and doubtless it is better to be praised for one's opsimathy than not to be praised at all. But what did it mean? It meant the ability to learn late in life.

These are what Westbrook Pegler used to call "out-of-town words." Edwin M. Yoder Jr., former editor of the editorial page of The Washington Star, once said that among writers, an addiction to big words is worse than an addiction to alcohol. No cure is known to exist. Once the young writer succumbs to arcane polysyllables, he remains syntactically stewed. His rhetorical bibulousness can no longer be restrained. He cannot get enough. He begins to invent words. The editors of the Columbia Journalism Review in 1975 invented *celebrification.* It will make it to Webster's yet.

My younger brother in the pundit business, George F. Will, had been a columnist for only a year when he wrote a splendid piece on Patty Hearst. Her arrest, he informed us, "provided a coda to a decade of political infantilism, the exegesis of which could be comprehended as a manifestation of bourgeois Weltanschauung." With that out of his system, George went on to win a Pulitzer Prize for commentary and to become a polished and literate essayist for Newsweek.

Two writers for Time magazine went butterfly chasing in the same issue back in April of 1981. In the cinema section we learned that "When a film attempts to soar into the oneiric, it is likely to be grounded by the critics." In the books section, the reviewer said of a romantic novel that Masters and Johnson could have explained some things to the heroine, "but even the more oestrous Richard Gallen Books line purrs only a little louder." Well, *oneiric* has to do with dreams, and *oestrous* (which Webster's Collegiate spells *estrous*) has to do with an animal in heat, and now we all know.

In June of 1983, Time took many of its readers over some difficult jumps. In an obituary on Kenneth Clark, we learned that he was a *pre-Freudian* with *mandarin decorum;* that some critics felt Clark had little regard for *Realpolitik;* that his television programs constituted a *didactic* series; that for nearly a decade the American middle class had been battered by the *Oedipal* vengeance of their offspring and accused of being the *otiose* relics of an oppressive culture, but then came Clark and the TV screen to deliver its *thaumaturge.* A review of a production of *School for Scandal* found the characters in *umbrous* quarters; the director, who was abandoning the theater to practice medicine, was a *quixotic* fellow who emulated nineteenth-century *polymaths.* In a review of Sam Shepard's *Fool for Love,* the characters meet in a *mingy* motel. (Newsweek, reviewing the same play, described the motel as *crummy.* Question for Friday's quiz: Which was the better choice of words?) Elsewhere in this same issue of Time, readers could grapple with *pristine, laconic, misogyny,* and *nascent.*

The use of such words depends upon the nature of one's readership and the judgment of the writers and editors. In the Blue Ridge Mountain country where I live, the local weekly aims at the vocabulary and the acquired learning of the ninth-grade level. Small-city dailies aim at high school seniors of average or above average achievement. Reader's Digest targets college freshmen. The New York Times and The Wall Street Journal appear to shoot for the college graduate. It is a mistake, and a grievous mistake at that, to "write down" to our readers, but if a basic purpose of communication is merely to be understood, we ought also to beware of writing over their heads. When a business columnist tells us that the administration's economic forecasts are run through a *Panglossian filter,* we must hope that his readers have met Candide somewhere along the way.

The admonition to avoid unfamiliar words applies with special force to the avoidance of foreign words and phrases. Again, we are talking here of aiming at clarity, of keeping things simple. If we are serving sophisticated prose to sophisticated readers, a soupçon of French or Latin may add brandy to our sauce, but be forewarned: Few semantic offenses are more ludicrous than the foreign phrase used wrongly.

Several years ago in Pennsylvania a man went on trial for murder, even though the body of his supposed victim had not been found. A reporter said the *corpus delicti* was missing; he had not learned that *corpus delicti* has to do with the body of the crime, that is, with the basic legal elements of the offense. A writer in the old Washington Star, weary of the pervasive sexiness of American advertising, said the theme ran on *ad nauseum*. It's *ad nauseam*. In Newsweek magazine, early in 1979, a critic of ballet went into rhapsodies over a performance in which Baryshnikov executed a series of turns that are exciting, "even when served up plain." This time the dancer added something special: "In the middle of this smooth stunt, Baryshnikov delivered the *coup de grace,* elevating his anchored foot, rising in the air like a helicopter, the blade of his whipping leg still whirling him around. . . ." Whatever the gentleman delivered, God knows it wasn't a *coup de grace.* And then there was the sportswriter for Newsday who in 1983 reported a three-way swap among seven baseball clubs and twelve players. "The *ménage à trois* trade," he said, "appeared to set the stage for another three-club deal."

So much for out-of-town words. In the name of clarity, the rule is this: Strike 'em out!

Beware the Elongated Yellow Fruit

I'm not sure that this next piece of advice falls properly under the heading of "aids to clarity," but I insert it here as a precautionary note: Have no unreasonable fear of repetition. True, the repetition of a particular word several times in the same paragraph can strike a jarring note, but ordinarily the problem arises differently. The story is told of a feature writer who was doing a piece on the United Fruit Company. He spoke of bananas once; he spoke of bananas twice; he spoke of bananas yet a third time, and now he was desperate. "The world's leading shippers of the elongated yellow fruit," he wrote. A fourth bananas would have been better.

A writer for The New York Times toppled into this pitfall in a piece about the Alaskan oil pipeline. He wrote oil once, oil twice, and then he fled: From Valdez, "fleets of tankers will carry the lucrative liquid to the United States."

This foolishness used to afflict sportswriters especially, though I believe the disease is not so prevalent among them now. At one time it appeared impossible for baseball writers to speak of "the ball." It was the *horsehide*, the *pill*, the *spheroid*, or even the *white pellet*. A bat was a *wand*, a *hickory*, or the *ash*. Bases were *sacks* or *bags*. Footballs were *pigskins*. Political writers provide evidence of the syndrome when they speak of members of the House and Senate as *solons*. Maybe it is permissible to refer to women as the *distaff side*, or to a wife as a *helpmate* or *better half,* but only for comic effect.

Much more could be said, of course, about the basic techniques of writing clearly. It might even be useful to put in a few reminders about the physical preparation of copy submitted for publication—clean typewriter keys, good black ribbons, return envelopes, and so forth—but we have to get away from the kindergarten stuff. On with it.

3   Beyond the Toothpaste Tube

Consider, if you please, an altogether admirable sentence: FOR BEST RESULTS, SQUEEZE TUBE FROM THE BOTTOM AND FLATTEN IT AS YOU GO UP. That comes off the side of a tube of Crest toothpaste. It is an eminently sound, serviceable, workaday sentence. It could not be improved by shifting "for best results" to some other point. I find it a sentence without a flaw.

But that sentence is far removed from such a sentence as, "In the beginning God created the heaven and the earth." The different authors had different purposes in mind. The translators who put together the King James Bible were concerned with uplifting our hearts; the package designers at Procter & Gamble were concerned with brushing our teeth.

Most of us, if we truly want to be writers, want to get beyond the toothpaste tube. We want to amuse, to persuade, to arouse, to delight, to describe, and we want to do an effective job of amusing, persuading, arousing, delighting, and describing. We aspire to more than merely writing clearly; we aspire now to write gracefully, or literately, or wittily, or perceptively. We have built a sufficiency of chicken coops and would try our hand at the art of the cabinetmaker instead.

How do we go about it? A short answer, I suppose, is that God alone knows how we go about it. At higher levels of skill, where craft becomes an art, there is some truth in the melancholy thought that fiddlers are made, but Menuhins are born. If the Lord has not blessed us with the writer's eye, the writer's ear, and the writer's insatiable appetite for the high-calorie richness of words, no instruction may suffice to get us beyond FOR BEST RESULTS, SQUEEZE TUBE FROM THE BOTTOM. The phrase that ignites a sentence and leaves an incandescent glow behind is fused from within. Even so, I hold to the conviction that much can be done to make the spark more effective.

To avoid misunderstanding, let me emphasize that the fundamentals have to come first. A few years ago I happened to be in Barcelona and took an hour or so before plane time to stroll through the Picasso Museum. We think of Picasso, and ordinarily we think of the distortions that characterized his most famous works—the one-eyed, one-breasted, two-nosed women; the flippered hands and feet, the grotesque distillation of animal forms, the whole dazzling exhibition of abstract expressionism. The museum has plenty of these from the last fifty years of Picasso's life. But in the first two or three rooms, where his student work and early work are displayed, we learn a lesson worth remembering. Here the paintings and drawings are wholly representational. Picasso learned all the rules of draftsmanship—all the disciplines of anatomy and portraiture and the handling of his tools—before he launched into the experiments that would ensure him a place among the immortals. For fifteen years he painted the human figure realistically. It wasn't until he had mastered the rules that about 1907 he began to break them.

I thought about that Barcelona museum when I received an exasperated letter from a young woman at a college in Kansas. She was annoyed with me. I had written a column about restrictive and non-restrictive clauses in which I cited a rule of thumb: If the qualifying phrase is set off by commas, use *which;* if not, use *that.* "It reminded me," she wrote, "of those grade school days when I was drilled on the rules of capitalization and such. I don't believe that art lies in technique. . . . Sometimes when you preach structure and format in your articles, I feel like you would enjoy seeing everyone speak in the Newspeak out of *1984.*"

Miss Kansas, I suggested gently, might benefit from a trip to Barcelona. We must first learn to draw two eyes and one nose, and when that technique has been mastered it will be time enough to draw one eye and two noses. Stravinsky labored for years on conventional harmonies; then he got to "The Rite of Spring." Henry Moore's early work is representational; it was not until he learned how the female torso is put together that he began to take it apart. Once my young friend in Kansas has endured these same disciplines in writing, she may not be so inclined to use *like* as a conjunction. Spelling, grammar, syntax, punctuation—these provide a threshold to composition, but the threshold has to be passed before we move on beyond the tube that is flattened as we roll it up. End of lecture.

Back in 1968, novelist Lee Smith spun an autobiographical story of a nine-year-old girl. The book was *The Last Day the Dogbushes Bloomed.*

In the summer of her story, young Susan liked to go to a nearby pond and think about things: "Sometimes I would sit and look at everything very hard, so it would stay in my head for always." In *Pilgrim at Tinker Creek,* Annie Dillard said much the same thing. She used to sit for hours beside a stream, "sensitive and mute as a photographic plate," while impressions were deposited on her mind.

This is the first secret of good writing: We must look *intently,* and hear *intently,* and taste *intently.* Like nine-year-old Susan, we must look at everything *very hard.* Is it the task at hand to describe a snowfall? Very well. We begin by observing that the snow is white. Is it as white as bond paper? White as whipped cream? Is the snow daisy white, or eggwhite white, or whitewash white? Let us look very hard. We will see that snow comes in different textures. The light snow that looks like powdered sugar is not the heavy snow that clings like wet cotton. When we write matter-of-factly that *Last night it snowed and this morning the fields were white,* we haven't said much. We have not looked *intently.*

A long time ago, when I was maybe twelve years old and had more romantic notions about newspapering than I have today, I used to try an exercise intended to improve a reporter's powers of observation. While I was out of the room, my sister would put five or ten randomly selected objects on the kitchen table. Then I had three seconds or five seconds—I forget which—to look at the objects before she covered them with a cloth.

The point of the game was to recall as many of the objects as possible—a pocketknife, a deck of cards, the jack of spades, a yellow napkin, two spoons, a spool of thread, and so on. Then came the inquisition: What color was the thread? Was the pocketknife open? Was there anything odd about the deck of cards? Were the spoons teaspoons or tablespoons?

My sister used to make things tough. She would include three pennies, but one would be an Indian head. Or she would toss in an obvious pencil, but the pencil's point would be broken. Two milk bottles would have their paper caps; one would not. Which one? Sometimes we played under a rule that permitted the five-second peek at breakfast but required recall in the afternoon after school. This was really tough. It has been many years since I thought about "What Did You See?" but Lee Smith's sentence kindles a flame of memory. As writers, let us look at everything very hard, so it will stay in our heads for always.

Out of this intensity of observation—out of this sensuousness—we derive two important gains. We learn to write precisely; and we fill our storehouse with the images that one day we will fashion into similes and metaphors.

As we look and hear and taste and feel, we are searching for what Somerset Maugham sought all his life—"not the right word, but the *inevitable* word." Edwin Arlington Robinson went through the same experience. Late in life, in a letter to a friend, he wrote of his boyhood struggles to capture a line of poetry. In those days, he said,

> time had no special significance for a certain juvenile and incorrigible fisher of words who thought nothing of fishing for two weeks to catch a stanza, or even a line, that he would not throw back into a squirming sea of language where there was every word but the one he wanted. There were strange and iridescent and impossible words that would seize the bait and swallow the hook and all but drag the excited angler in after them, but like that famous catch of Hiawatha's, they were generally not the fish he wanted. He wanted fish that were smooth and shining and subtle, and very much alive, and not too strange, and presently, after long patience and many rejections, they began to bite.

Robinson's experience is common to every one of us who revel in the jewelry of our language. We see words that blow like leaves in the winds of autumn—golden words, bronze words, words that catch the light like opals. We learn that words have an independent life of their own, grown out of echoes and connotations and associations. We see that words are tactile; we find rough words, smooth words, words with splintered edges; words to shout or to whisper with; words that caress; words that strike. After a long while, as Robinson said, we begin at last to catch the words we want.

If we would write well—if we would get beyond the toothpaste tube, flattening it as we go—we must collect words, store them, hoard them, fasten them into albums. They will be there when we need them. We will collect useless specimens, as I suggested in Chapter 2, but that is not our purpose. We want to collect words that are both inevitable and understandable. H.L. Mencken once wrote of the "inmates" of Washington, D.C. It was the exact word he wanted. Poet Ezra Pound came out of St. Elizabeth's Hospital after his long imprisonment as a lunatic. I interviewed him, and I inquired about the offense that had caused his long confinement. "I committed truth," he snapped. It was the perfect verb.

The intensity I am urging not only will enrich our vocabularies and induce more accurate writing, it also will do something else: It will give us images. We look intently at a caterpillar, and perhaps we see a covered wagon. We look closely at a hill of close-cropped stubble, and perhaps we see the head of a fresh-caught recruit in the U.S. Marines. We look at daffodils and see the trumpets of a marching band. We look at grape hyacinths and see toy soldiers. Graham Greene looked intently at a row of crows, and he saw old black broken umbrellas.

One of the finest writers in the business today is Shana Alexander, my old sparring partner on *60 Minutes*. She uses her pen as Picasso used a brush, catching a perfect image in a single stroke. Looking around a deserted pressroom at a political convention, she saw the rows of silent telephones. They had "the forlorn look of wallflowers at a dance." Once she interviewed a lawyer from the Department of Justice. He was "a man of Teflon, cold and perfectly smooth." She interviewed Marlon Brando. "He is as comfortable in ambiguity as a sailor in a hammock."

For my money, Shana Alexander is the finest court reporter to practice that demanding art since Dame Rebecca West went to Nuremberg. In 1976 Shana went to California to cover the trial of Patty Hearst for armed robbery of a bank; out of that experience came a book, *Anyone's Daughter.* In 1980 she went to Westchester County to cover the trial of Jean Harris for the murder of Herman Tarnower; out of that assignment came another book, *Very Much a Lady.* The two books never sold as well as they should have sold, but every writer could read them with profit. This is what descriptive writing is all about.

At the Hearst trial, Shana looked intently at the defendant on her first day in court: Patty signaled to her parents with a quick, secret wave. "Below the table, emerging from a tailored sleeve, five pink and perfectly enameled fingers flutter like the frilly fin of a Siamese fighting fish."

She continued with marine images. The bailiff raps his gavel twice. "We rise as if he were tapping on the glass. Feeding time." Nearby was Patty's lawyer, F. Lee Bailey. He is "the big fish, grouper or a sheepshead bass, all massive head and strong shoulders." Presiding over the courtroom, "dead center and motionless, sitting so still he might be barnacled to the back wall of the tank, hangs the black-robed judge."

Shana looked intently at the court stenotypists, "human ear trumpets who funnel every word through trained fingers into the little, terrier-sized tripod that sits between their legs." She felt the tension in the chamber: "It hangs across the court like a trapeze net." After several days of the trial, reporters and spectators came to recognize one another, but they kept their thoughts to themselves. "We behave as if we were meeting at a bus stop, not in a courtroom."

Early in the Hearst trial, everyone stands as the day's proceedings are about to begin. Shana's view is blocked by a phalanx of marshals.

> Then a crack appeared in the row of beefy shoulders, and a small pale girl was suddenly *there,* as if materialized by The Great Zombo. She was tiny and jailhouse sallow, with a copper coin's profile, Roman nose, red-gold hair gone dark at the roots, no makeup, dressed in a matronly brown pants suit . . . Directly behind her, in a straight line, sat her team, their faces rigid, formal, and familiar as faces painted on a billboard.

As the trial nears its end, Patty Hearst

> is a Madonna dolorosa, a classic image of female suffering. She sits motionlessly, and tears fall from her eyes as from a Sicilian painting. Fine-featured, smooth-skinned, narrow, and pale, she is almost as white as the "Pieta" of Michelangelo.

The trial of Jean Harris presented a different defendant. Here too there were tears:

> Jean Harris starts to cry. Her crying is unpleasant to watch. Her face reddens and contorts in total silence. Perhaps that is why some observers will write that she failed to cry. She cries almost daily, but recovers quickly. She takes notes briskly, studies transcripts, looks cool, impatient, and bossy.

At forty-three, when her love affair with Dr. Tarnower had obsessed her, the defendant still was a provincial schoolteacher, "about as worldly as Winnie the Pooh." Painfully vulnerable, bruised by her lover's psychological blows, Jean Harris "imagined a rock in every snowball." As Tarnower's disdain increased, "She died from the inside out, the way a tree dies, the heartwood drying out while the bark still stands."

Let me pause to make a point or two about writing. How does Shana Alexander bring it off? As a reporter she long ago learned to look intently and to tuck away images—familiar images—for someday use. Before she went to the Hearst trial, she had looked at the fins of Siamese fighting fish, at groupers and sheepshead bass, at barnacles on a ship's bottom, at terriers, at trapeze nets, at people at bus stops, at copper coins, at hair gone dark at the roots, at billboards, at Sicilian paintings. These were her billets of mahogany and walnut, left to season, from which she would one day carve the finial of a bedpost or the arm of a chair. This is the carpentry of words. This is how a writer writes.

A moment ago I mentioned Rebecca West. One of these years, when I am comfortably in my dotage and have come down with the retirement fidgets, I may yet accept a post at some small and civilized college where the writer's art still is held in high esteem. My first assignment will direct my students to read the books—especially the books of reportage and criticism—of Rebecca West. That could well be the last assignment also, for there is not much to learn about the writing art that cannot be learned from the legacy she left with her death in 1983. She was one of the truly beautiful writers of this century.

In the autumn of 1946 Rebecca West went to Nuremberg to cover the final days of the trial of the Nazi war criminals. Out of that experience came the three dispatches she titled, "Greenhouse with Cyclamens." She pulled them together in a book, *A Train of Powder,* that Viking published in 1955. My prospective students would begin by reading the first of the pieces, and after that, unless they were as insensitive as cinder blocks, they would be better writers.

Dame Rebecca's skill—her art, if you please—was at bottom the skill of observation: intense, unwavering, encompassing observation. Hers was not the camera's eye, which photographs all details of a given scene in the same light; hers was the artist's eye, which emphasizes the significant details and discards the rest. To this power of observation she added the gifts of a rich and disciplined vocabulary and a sense of the cadence of words.

One of the Nazi defendants was Streicher: "He was a dirty old man of the sort that gives trouble in parks." Another was Goering: "He was so very soft . . . He had thick brown young hair, the coarse bright skin of an actor who has used grease paint for decades. . . ." Yet another defendant was Schacht, who at one point "became stiffer than ever, stiff as an iron stag in the garden of an old house."

Rebecca West studied the judges. Among them was a French judge, de Vabres. He was "small and stocky, with a white moustache, and a brow kept wrinkled by the constant offenses against logic perpetrated by this chaotic universe." She watched the interpreters, "twittering unhappily in their glass box like caged birds kept awake by a bright light.'' She watched the courtroom guards, who stood ''as still and hard as metal save their childish faces, which were puffy with boredom.''

Because she had learned to look intently, and to store impressions and comparisons, she was able to construct perfect similes. She saw a group of German laborers joking with their foreman. They stood ''grinning in the sunlight, their grey hairs falling stiff as bootlaces round their leathery faces.'' She gazed at ''a monstrous statue of Bismarck, with a number of women round the base, with breasts like artillery pieces.''

The following winter—this would have been February of 1947—Rebecca West covered a very different trial. She went to Greenville, S.C., for the trial of thirty-one defendants charged with the lynching of a Negro. One of the defendants was a man of forty-five ''with hair that stood up like a badger's coat, eyes set close together, and staring out under glum brows through strong glasses, and a mouth that was unremitting in its compression. He looked like an itinerant preacher devoted to the worship of a tetchy and uncooperative God.'' The defendants had their families in the courtroom.

> Several of the wives sat in close embrace with their husbands, shaken from time to time by the inimitable convulsions of distress. One pregnant girl in a green dress sat throughout the trial with an arm thrown about her young husband's shoulder, rubbing her pudgy and honest and tear-stained face against his arm.

Rebecca West's eye picked up a detail:

> The Bible belonging to Greenville County Court House is in terrible shape. Like many Bibles, it has a flounce, or valance, of leather protecting its edges, and this is torn and crumbling, while its boards are cracked, and no small wonder. Its quietest hours are when it is being sworn upon; at any other time it is likely to be snatched up from the small stand on which it rests, which is like that used for potted plants in some homes, and waved in the air, held to an attorney's breast, thrust out over the jury box, and hurled back to its resting place in a convulsion of religious ecstasy.

Let me pause again. Rebecca West had looked intently at dirty old men who give trouble in parks, at aging actors whose skin had suffered from grease paint, at iron stags, at caged birds, at bootlaces, at artillery pieces, at the hair of badgers, at cracked and crumbling Bibles. To describe the action of the Bible-thumping lawyers, she used active verbs: *snatched, thrust, hurled.* She used adverbs and adjectives sparingly, letting the principal parts of speech carry her narrative. But her greatest gift, to make the point one more time, is that she never stopped looking; she never stopped looking intently.

In *Clea,* the last volume of that dazzling series of novels, *The Alexandria Quartet,* Lawrence Durrell brings us into the harbor of Alexandria on the night of a bombardment in 1944. Out of a sea that had become "a vast empty anteroom, a hollow bubble of blackness," we watch the city's defenses spring to life:

> Then suddenly there passed a sudden breath, a whiff like a wind passing across a bed of embers, and the nearer distance glowed pink as a seashell, deepening gradually into the rose-richness of a flower. A faint and terrible moaning came out across the water towards us, pulsing like the wingbeats of some fearful prehistoric bird—sirens which howled as the damned must howl in limbo. One's nerves were shaken like the branches of a tree. And as if in response to this sound lights began to prick out everywhere, sporadically at first,
> then in ribbons, bands, squares of crystal. The harbour suddenly outlined itself with complete clarity upon the dark panels of heaven, while long white fingers of powder-white light began to stalk about the sky in ungainly fashion, as if they were the legs of some awkward insect struggling to gain a purchase on the slippery black. A dense stream of coloured rockets now began to mount from the haze among the battleships, emptying on the sky their brilliant clusters of stars and diamonds and smashed pearl snuff-boxes with a marvelous prodigality. The air shook in strokes. Clouds of pink and yellow dust arose with the maroons to shine upon the greasy buttocks of the barrage balloons which were flying everywhere. The very sea seemed to tremble . . .
> It was as beautiful as it was stupefying. In the top left hand corner of the tableau the searchlights had begun to congregate, quivering and sliding in their ungainly fashion, like daddy long-legs. They intersected and collided feverishly, and it was clear that some signal had reached them which told of the struggles of some trapped insect on the outer cobweb of darkness. Again and again they crossed, probed, merged, divided. Then at last we saw what they were

bracketing: six tiny silver moths moving down the skylanes with what seemed unbearable slowness.

That was Lawrence Durrell, novelist. The anatomists of style, if they bent to a dissection of that brief passage, might call attention to variations in sentence length: Most of the fourteen sentences are long, but one sentence consists of only five words, one of six, a third of only ten. The anatomists, busy counting syllables like bones of the foot, would find relatively few multisyllabic words—*prehistoric, sporadically, prodigality, stupefying.* By applying word count A to syllable count B to formula C, they might undertake to explain why the passage is a small jewel of writing.

I would go at such an analysis quite differently, and insist that the beauty of Durrell's writing lies simply in the intentness of his vision. He *saw* the searchlights, the rockets, the barrage balloons, the incoming bombers; he saw them with a writer's eye, and his eye translated them into images from everyday experience. Thus we see them too.

We have been talking mostly about the discipline of *looking* intently, but the same principles apply to the other senses also. If we are to write about the sounds of the city, we must listen very hard to the honking of horns, the surf-sound of traffic, and the dentist's drills of sirens. I once tried to listen very hard to the sound of a crowd at Shea Stadium. In between the sudden crescendos of a triple or a triumphant strikeout, it was the sound of an orchestra steadily tuning up—a subdued sound, cellos and bass viols, with an occasional French horn cadenza from the hot dog man. In the country I have listened to a rooster's crow, and I can tell you that roosters rarely say cock-a-doodle-do. They have more the sound of the horns on Model A Fords; it is the croak of a contralto with a bad cold in the head. I have listened to the brass choir of night-hunting hounds, to the bawl of a cow who has mislaid her calf, to the snap of twigs and the papery rustle of autumn leaves. We must look, and hear, and smell, and taste so that the evidence of our senses will stay in our heads for always.

Let me get back to an earlier piece of advice, to read insatiably. For the past few pages I have been talking about reading the best of such contemporary writers as Shana Alexander, Rebecca West, and Lawrence Durrell. But we ought to read everything. Read matchbox covers; read labels on cans of cleaner; read the graffiti on lavatory walls. Read for information, read for style, read for instruction, read for the sheer love of reading.

Read, if you must, simply for pragmatic reasons, because incessant reading will help your everyday composition. Writers ought not to look with awe upon libraries, as if libraries were Greek temples or holy shrines. Libraries must always be lumberyards to us, houses of building supplies. There we go for the facts, dates, documentation that are the cinderblocks and cellar beams of our work. But we also go there for the columns and pediments and finials that add grace and adornment. We read in order to look through the great windows of Shakespeare, opening wide upon mankind; we borrow good worn coins from the Bible; and if we put these resources to prudent use, we fashion new contracts of understanding and allusion with our readers. We borrow wealth and pay no interest on it.

There is this gain also: A process of cross-fertilization occurs whenever we wander through the work of good writers. Their similes, their metaphors, their insights have a way of stimulating fresh images all our own. In the passage from *Clea* I quoted awhile ago, Durrell evoked the image of the daddy longlegs, and we saw those frail beams of light scrambling up the Egyptian sky; we saw them more clearly because all of us have seen the daddy longlegs. If you have the instincts of a writer, which are very like the instincts of a good cook, you may put the novel aside as if you were putting down your fork after a remarkably good dish. Hmmm, you think to yourself, how did the chef bring it off? What did he have in that sentence? (Bugs, you think, if you are thinking of Lawrence Durrell.) Or a pinch of oregano, if you are planning to improve upon your host's spaghetti sauce.

So you promise yourself to look intently at bugs: How does a spider build its web? I once stood entranced in the moonlight for two hours, scarcely moving, watching a spider at work. How sits the praying mantis? What *exactly* is the sound of an angry wasp? Free of charge, I pass along this entomological truth to you: If you want to swat a fly, aim an inch behind him. This is because a fly takes off backwards. That wisdom came to me courtesy of my father-in-law. He was a naturalist; he looked intently. So should we all, for if we observe the fly, the wasp, the mantis, the Japanese beetle on a grape leaf, one day we will take the observation out of our storeroom and put it to use: We will see a thin man who looks like a praying mantis; we will see an Oriental bowl and recall the beetle's rich enamel; we will see squad cars converging on the scene of a crime, and we will remember wasps attacking a windfall apple.

I suggested that we ought to read insatiably for this reason also, to cultivate a sense of style. This is dangerous advice, and ought to be taken strictly as directed. I happen to have an enormous admiration for the style of Henry Mencken. He went at his targets with shillelaghs, fungo bats, and bung starters; he had a way of honing his carving knife with a couple of extra licks, just for dramatic effect, before he began slicing some suckling pig. But I have learned to read Mencken in small helpings, one spoonful at a time, so as not to fall into the clutches of narcotic addiction. We ought not to try to write like Mencken; it is futile, if not absolutely plagiaristic; we look absurd when we try. But we ought to understand how Mencken wrote, how he seasoned his sauces.

Mencken had some things to say on this matter of style that are worth keeping in mind. The Sage of Baltimore had a style too distinctive to be missed and too individualistic ever to be emulated successfully. Back in 1926 he unloaded some thoughts on style.

"The essence of a sound style," said Mencken, "is that it cannot be reduced to rules—that it is a living and breathing thing, with something of the demoniacal in it—that it fits its proprietor tightly and yet ever so loosely, as his skin fits him. It is, in fact, quite as securely an integral part of him as that skin is. It hardens as his arteries harden. It is gaudy when he is young and gathers decorum when he grows old. On the day after he makes a mash on a new girl it glows and glitters. If he has fed well, it is mellow. If he has gastritis it is bitter. In brief, a style is always the outward and visible symbol of a man, and it cannot be anything else. To attempt to teach it is as silly as to set up courses in making love."

Before there can be style, Mencken went on to say, there has to be thought; there has to be an idea. Lacking something to say, a writer tends to write mush; he cannot conceal his dismal efforts with a sauce of applied technique. None of the conjurer's tricks that I might teach in my someday course in Writing 101 will help him—the little dog tricks of long and short sentences, of active and passive verbs, of alliteration and cadence.

"What is in the head," said Mencken, "infallibly oozes out of the nub of the pen. . . . But style cannot go beyond the ideas which lie at the heart of it. If they are clear, it too will be clear. If they are held passionately, it will be eloquent."

All this is true enough, for "style" is hard to pin down. The difficulty recalls Justice Stewart's remark about obscenity; he couldn't define it, but he knew it when he saw it. Whatever it is, style provides the individual hallmark that writers stamp upon their work—but that metaphor is inapt, for it suggests that style is something you put onto a piece after you have finished it, as if it were ketchup on chili or lemon on fish. Style doesn't work that way. It's more of a marinade, permeating the whole composition.

Think, if you will, of some of our own stylists of the past century. Mark Twain comes to mind, maybe F. Scott Fitzgerald, certainly Ernest Hemingway and William Faulkner. Copy five hundred words from each of them, conceal the bylines, and any literate high school senior could identify the authors. On the lower slopes of Olympus, the same test would disclose the individual styles of such popular writers as Norman Mailer, Kurt Vonnegut, Tom Wolfe, Westbrook Pegler, Damon Runyon, Ring Lardner, and William F. Buckley, Jr.

Look back to a couple of great English stylists, Edward Gibbon and Thomas Babington Lord Macaulay. Analyze this sentence: "The various modes of worship which prevailed in the Roman world were all considered by the people as equally true; by the philosophers as equally false; and by the magistrate as equally useful." Or this sentence: "Augustus was accustomed to boast that he had found his capital of brick, and that he had left it of marble." Or this: "Before an assembly thus modeled and prepared, Augustus pronounced a studied oration, which displayed his patriotism and disguised his ambition."

Gibbon fashioned his sentences just as Bach and Mozart fashioned counterpoint. In the first example, the deliberate repetition of *equally* makes the sentence ring. In the second example, Gibbon employed the device of antithesis, setting *found* against *left* and *brick* against *marble*. These devices are the literary equivalent of ribbons and bows; they are the packaging of style in which the idea is wrapped.

So, too, with Macaulay. Here he is criticizing the works of Samuel Johnson. "All his books are written in a learned language, in a language which nobody hears from his mother or his nurse, in a language in which nobody ever quarrels, or drives bargains, or makes love, in a language in which nobody ever thinks." From the same essay: "The habits of his early life had accustomed him to bear privation with fortitude, but not to taste pleasure with moderation." And speaking of Edmund Burke: "He generally chose his side like a fanatic, and defended it like a philosopher."

Do we hear the beat of Macaulay's magisterial lines? Do we see how he balanced *privation* with *pleasure*, and *fortitude* with *moderation*, and *fanatic* with *philosopher?* This is the device of parallelism. It figured heavily in Macaulay's style; it was not laid on afterward, but the device of parallel construction is just that—a device. It can be learned with practice.

To read Gibbon and Macaulay, among other great English stylists, is also to learn cadence. I have a notion, and pass it along to you, that a sure sense of rhythm is as vital to the writer as it is to the timpanist who makes a living on a kettledrum. This is because all life moves at an ordered pace—the planets turn, the moon swells and wanes, the tides move in and out, the waves have a cadence of their own. As human beings, we live by the beat of the heart, the breath of the lungs, the rhythms of menses and of copulation. The very air around us is filled with invisible waves of sound, traveling at rhythmic frequencies. We adjust subconsciously to this need for rising and falling, ebbing and flowing, and we come to attention when the rhythm breaks: We look up, listening: The clock's stopped, we say. The wind has changed. Isn't it time to feed the baby? We hear a knock in the motor.

So, too, I believe, with effective writing. It has to have cadence. By that, I do not mean metronomic regularity. I certainly don't mean that we should strive for a sing-song effect; for if you get to be self-conscious, if you strive for rhythm only, you will wind up getting dizzy, you will sound like Hiawatha. And I pray you, sirs, avoid it. No. I suggest only that we cultivate the inner ear. Let us listen to our sentences as they break upon the mind. With a little recasting—the substitution of an iamb for a trochee, the shifting of a foot here or there—it often is possible to gain cadence without sacrifice of meaning or exactitude. The rule of parallelism in construction is a sound rule; it is a rule of cadence, of order, of nicety in arrangement. The writer who learns the knack of balance or of deliberate imbalance; the writer who understands how to quicken his tempo with short words, quick darting words, words that smack and jab; the writer who learns to slow his composition with soft and languorous convolutions; the writer who practices the trick of sentence-endings, striving deliberately for syllables that are accented a particular way, for the long vowel sound or the short—such a writer is on his way toward mastery of a marvelous tool. Go to the poems of Housman. Go to Burke's *Reflections*. See how D.H. Lawrence did it. Dissect the Churchillian line as if you were exploring the anatomy of some laboratory frog. Cadence, alliteration, aspiration, the choice of consonants—these are not necessarily gifts of God, like perfect pitch; they may equally be the fruits of practice, like a racecourse run down the frets of a banjo.

One final word on this business of descriptive writing. The word is this: *Don't fake it*. Irving Stone, who usually does meticulous research on even the smallest details, once thought to inject a little color into his biography of Rachel Jackson. He put flocks of starlings into Tennessee in the early 1800s. He received hundreds of letters from bird-watchers who informed him that starlings hadn't been imported from Europe until the 1890s. The author of a book about prehistoric Europeans had his characters observing such North American animals as muskrats and skunks. Still another writer had a woodpecker "strutting" across a lawn—but woodpeckers' feet are made for hopping, not strutting. This same writer decorated his autumn woods in Ohio with red tulips. The tulips never happened.

Descriptive writers constantly are tempted to add just one more pretty brush stroke to the canvas of their prose. I blush to recall that forty years ago, in my early purple period, I turned out a lovely piece on 'coon hunting on a cold night in October. In my zeal to set the scene, I had the diamond-studded belt of Orion girdling the bare limbs of a mighty oak— only to be advised by a startled astronomer that on the night in question, Orion could not possibly have been where I put it.

Whether we are writing about murder trials, barrage balloons, spring flowers, or autumn colors, fake it not! Sticking to the facts not only deters remonstrances from knowledgeable readers; the rule also contributes to the integrity of whatever it is that we're writing. And whether we are writing fiction or non-fiction, in the end that is all we have to sell— the credibility and the integrity of the words we put together. Like Lee Smith's nine-year-old girl, we ought to look at that proposition very hard, so it will stay in our head for always.

4 The Things We Ought Not to Do

The presumptuous revisors of the Book of Common Prayer, who recklessly undertook a few years ago to improve upon one of the great works of English composition, at least left almost intact the old confession that is said at Morning Prayer. That confession contains a sentence of profound beauty: "We have left undone those things which we ought to have done, and we have done those things which we ought not to have done."

In this regard, writers are natural-born sinners. Every book on style or usage or grammar contains essentially the same admonitions and reminders: Don't do this. Do that. The trouble is, we forget. We wind up leaving undone those things which we ought to have done: We ought to have striven for clarity; we ought to have remembered the uses of simile and metaphor; we ought to have worked on the cadence of our prose. In the same fashion, we do those things which we ought not to have done: We forget to check a fact or to look up an uncertain quotation; we forget to keep a complex sentence in parallel construction; we do not take the time to rid our prose gardens of chickweed banalities.

What follows is a catalogue of a dozen things we ought not to do.

1. We ought not to use clichés.

Dr. Lois DeBakey, one of the top-ranking prescriptive linguists of our time, has made a one-woman crusade of teaching doctors how to write. (If we had a Lois DeBakey in law and academia, we would get better writing from lawyers and professors.) In an essay a few years ago for the International Journal of Cardiology, she dealt with the topic of clichés.

The word comes from the French *clicher,* meaning to cast from a mold. Such phrases are inherently trite, which comes from the Latin *terere,* to rub or to wear away. Such phrases are hackneyed, which comes out of Middle English; a hackneyed proverb was a proverb, says the OED, "worn out, like a hired horse, by indiscriminate or vulgar use."

Clichés, said Dr. DeBakey, "are the language of thoughtlessness," and indeed they are. They are poor, tired, but comfortable and familiar cubbyholes to which we retreat when imagination fails us. All of us recognize clichés. They fall like casual dandruff on the fabric of our prose. They are weary, stale, flat, and unprofitable. If we consider all the uses of our words, surely we can find something better than the bromide—for a bromide, by definition, is a chemical compound used as a sedative. Bromides put us to sleep.

I too have railed from time to time against clichés. So has Jack Cappon, the veteran newsfeatures editor for The Associated Press. In a homily for the Bulletin of the American Society of Newspaper Editors, he cited a few clichés so abysmal that no self-respecting writer would employ them in any context: *Selling like hotcakes, breath of fresh air, last but not least, shun like the plague, leave no stone unturned.* Fowler and Gowers, in *Modern English Usage,* cite such obvious specimens as *tender mercies* and *suffer a sea change.* These shouldn't be touched *with a ten-foot pole.*

Despite all the warnings, even experienced writers fall into sin. A couple of years ago Seymour Krim reviewed a book, *Last Rites: The Death of William Saroyan,* by Saroyan's son Aram. Krim is an old pro, a veteran reporter, editor, free-lancer, essayist; he has been teaching at writers' workshops since 1967. Aram Saroyan's story begins in April 1981, when Aram learns that his father is dying of cancer. "It concludes a month later," says Krim, "when the great-spirited singer of the American Depression bites the dust at the age of seventy-two."

Bites the dust! How could a professional writer write that sentence? There may have been a time, when Zane Grey was a boy, that dying Indians and wounded cavalrymen bit the dust as they fell from their horses, but in the context of Saroyan's death by cancer in a hospital the phrase is doubly offensive. It is woefully stale, for one thing, and it is garishly out of place.

Even the best writers occasionally fall into a slump for this reason: Bromides are handy. Every writer has racks and bottles of them on his office shelf. In Fowler's phrase, "They may be taken off the peg as convenient reach-me-downs.'' In the same week that Krim's offense appeared in The Washington Post, experienced journalists were telling us that a ruckus over a Reagan appointment was *much ado about nothing*, and that Senator Dole's tax bill, in a discouraging misquotation, was *a poor thing but his own*. The president was asking his supporters *to bite the bullet;* alas, Mr. Reagan faced *rebellion in the ranks*.

It is not only that clichés are handy; there is this further and more defensible explanation for their employment: They fit into our understanding like feet into old slippers; they ring little bells of memory and association. When we adapt Shakespeare or the Bible to contemporary illustration, we draw on great common reservoirs of allusion. Deftly employed, such quotations and adaptations add a nice polish to the surface of our prose.

The trick, it seems to me, is to use the old images selectively. Many times it is better to call up a cliché than to aim at originality and miss. ''Instead of expunging all clichés from our speech and writing,'' says Lois DeBakey, ''we should learn to use them consciously and aptly—to clarify or invigorate rather than to obscure and embellish. . . . Avoiding them entirely may lead to unidiomatic expressions and an awkward, unnatural, obtrusive style. When applied with restraint and judgment, clichés can add force and meaning, but indulged in mindlessly, they cloy.''

In his piece for the ASNE Bulletin, Jack Cappon said much the same thing: ''Clichés by definition are threadbare phrases that good writers try to avoid, but not all clichés are obnoxious to the same degree. . . . In many cases, no summary beheading is necessary. *Sour grapes, swing of the pendulum*, and *white elephant*, for example, are greatly worn. Yet each wraps up a rather complicated situation succinctly, and if your alternative proves labored and verbose, you're better advised to stick to the cliché.''

So, too, with Fowler. We would be needlessly handicapped, he observes, if we were denied the use of *feathering his nest* or *had his tongue in his cheek*. Fowler quotes the advice once given by J.A. Spender: ''The hardest worked cliché is better than the phrase that fails.''

I would say amen to all that, and add a warning: It is difficult to achieve a felicitous result by tricking up an old phrase in new words. It is like putting booties on a foxhound. ''A tumbling rock gathers no algae'' is ridiculous. Sometimes the stunt can be pulled off. Cappon cites the admirable flipside of a proverb: *Bedfellows make strange politics.* More often we get such strained and hollow echoes as, *looking a gift Ferrari in the carburetors.* There is indeed a *test of time,* and if a cliché has passed that test successfully, my advice is to stick with it.

With that word of caution, let me catalog a few clichés that I cheerfully would see abandoned for purposes of metaphor hereafter.

From the world of animals, birds, and insects: By winning his budget resolution only four months after taking office, Reagan demonstrated that it is *the early bird that gets the worm.* . . . The president accepted half his requested tax reduction on the theory that *a bird in hand is worth two in the bush.* . . . In badgering the Republicans on their request for an increase in the debt limit, the Democrats were saying that *sauce for the goose is sauce for the gander.*

In other instances, the newspapers have informed us that Mr. Reagan was *mad as a wet hen* at his budget director, that Senator Dole's tax bill was *a fly in the ointment,* that Democratic boll weevils were as welcome *as ants at a picnic,* and that the pending budget resolution was *a horse of a different color.* Thinking of horses, Mr. Reagan was advised *not to look a gift horse in the mouth.* In this same news story, dealing with the same bill, Minority Leader Bob Michel *smelled a rat.*

Other avoidable clichés of this genre: *chickens that come home to roost, dogs that have their day,* and *silk purses that can't be made from sows' ears.* Beware the *crooked snake,* the *catbird seat,* the *quiet mouse:* We have met all of them too many times before.

Clichés from the world of country living: *tough row to hoe, a country mile, get in a rut, to be in high cotton, put out to pasture, to be fenced in, needle in a haystack, slim pickings, grist for the mill, cut a wide swath,* and *make hay while the sun shines.*

Clichés from sports: *toe the line [mark], leap the hurdles, come down to the wire, go to the mat, throw in the towel, toss a hat in the ring, suffer a knockout blow, rock the boat, take hook, line, and sinker.*

Clichés from the sea: *ship of state, launch a campaign, at the helm, safely to port, any old port in a storm, off course, change course,* and *take a new tack.* We can find fresher metaphors than the stale *fire a broadside, fire a shot over the bow, get up a full head of steam,* and *walk the plank.*

Clichés from land warfare: *fire a barrage,* as in "The administration fired a barrage of statistics to jolt Congress into curbing civil service pensions." Others: *man the barricades, reach a truce, open fire, cease fire, roll out the big guns, drop a bombshell, beat a retreat,* and *take* or *hold hostages.*

No definitive list of clichés possibly could be compiled. Call them clichés, bromides, adages, proverbs, old saws, or hoary sayings, by any name *their name is Legion for they are many.* From the business world we get *bottom line* and *sea of red ink.* From gambling halls, *the die is cast* and *bet your bottom dollar.* From the arts: *paint on a broad canvas, finely etched.* From music: *play second fiddle, strike a responsive chord, harp on a theme, hit a sour note, sing the blues* and, most to be abhorred, *to orchestrate.* We find clichés everywhere along *the road to ruin, the primrose path, the straight and narrow path,* and a choice of *avenues to explore.* From mining we get *to hit pay dirt,* and *to find a few nuggets.* Among the most offensive clichés is *shot in the arm,* as a society columnist once employed the phrase in a piece about a socialite coming to her estate in the hunt country of Virginia: "If she spends the month of June at Oakwood, it will give this vicinity a shot in the arm."

Enough! Clichés spread like wildfire, they sell like hotcakes, and we do a land-office business in them. They are as numerous as flies in a cowbarn—and in most instances they are about as welcome. I pray you, when possible avoid them.

2. We ought never to fall into gobbledegook.

Maury Maverick, a congressman from Texas, generally is credited with inventing the term *gobbledegook.* He had in mind the image of an old turkey gobbler, strutting and preening, spreading his tail feathers, and going gobble-gobble-gobble. The image perfectly describes the kind of writing that is intended not to express a thought but rather to impress a reader. The impression that is left, unfortunately, is an impression of the incompetence and stupidity of the author.

A search of the works of early Greek and Roman authors surely would find denunciations of the gobbledegook of their time. In every era and in every tongue, verbosity has appeared—and verbosity has been condemned. In his essay on "The Abuse of Words," John Locke long ago spoke of the "affected obscurity" that is achieved "by putting words so together as may confound their ordinary meaning." The use of unintelligible terms, said Locke, keeps readers perpetually entangled in an endless labyrinth. Besides, he added, there is no better way to protect privileged sanctums, or to defend strange and absurd doctrines, than "to guard them round with legions of obscure, doubtful, and undefined words.''

In our time, valiant efforts constantly are made to suppress the gobbledegook that spreads like roadside kudzu, choking clarity along the way. Commerce Secretary Malcolm Baldrige had been in office only three months before the murk of departmental prose got to him. He dispatched a memo demanding ''short sentences and short words, with emphasis on plain English, using no more words than effective expression requires.'' Thus, for starters, he banned from departmental correspondence and papers such words as *maximize, institutionalize,* and *interface* (except when referring to communications systems). He banned *bottom line* and *serious crisis* and *material enclosed herewith.* He gave gobbledegook a good shot.

In 1980, U.S. News & World Report gave us some good news and some bad news about the efforts of state legislatures in this regard. The good news was that bills had been introduced in thirty states to require plain language in consumer contracts. The bad news was that in twenty-six states the bills had been voted down. Lawyers objected that old terms of contract law had been judicially construed so as to fix their meaning; they wanted no truck with newfangled clarity.

Not all lawyers are in love with obscurity. In Hartford City, Ind., attorney Max C. Peterson has been railing against ''syllabosity'' wherever he can find a forum. In an article in Res Gestae he once recalled that in 1941 the Indiana Legislature, in its wisdom and compassion, ''decided that thereafter no bastards should be born in Indiana, only 'children born out of wedlock.' ''

> Thus did that august body ban forever from Indiana law a beautiful old word of two syllables, going back to Middle English, hoary with respectability in Anglo-American jurisprudence, and substitute a phrase of five words and seven syllables.

> In 1973 another generation of legislators decreed six-syllable ''marriage dissolution'' as the successor to plain and simple two-syllable ''divorce.''

> ''Did your sister get a divorce?'' ''No, she got a marriage dissolution.''

Peterson's favorite target is *origination,* a squid word that swims in governmental waters. ''What is the difference,'' he fumes, ''between the *origin* of the loan and the *origination* of the loan? Why does my loan have to be *collateralized* with five syllables, rather than merely being *secured* with two?''

Why these eternal suffixes? What is the magic in *ation, ion,* and *ology?* By the rolling of Greek and Latin syllables do we charm ourselves into a belief in our own erudition and importance? Why *motivations* instead of *motives, medication* instead of *medicine, methodology* instead of *methods, stimulation* instead of *stimulus?*

Good rhetorical questions, all of them. And by his reference to ''magic,'' Mr. Peterson gets at the heart of gobbledegook. Knowingly or unknowingly, people who write this stuff are employing the arts of legerdemain. Instead of hocus-pocus-dominocus, the arcane words are polysyllabic invocations—*the implementation of a multifaceted and prioritized interface with varying parameters of communicative methodology.*

The discouraging thing—one discouraging thing—is that we find so many of these honeysuckle tangles in academic groves. If professors, principals, and school superintendents are incapable of writing clearly, how are their pupils to learn? In 1977 The Associated Press reported that the parents of a high school student had received a message from the school's principal about a proposed new program:

> Our school's cross-graded, multi-ethnic, individualized learning program is designed to enhance the concept of an open-ended learning program with emphasis on a continuum of multi-ethnic, academically enriched learning using the identified intellectually gifted child as the agent or director of his own learning. Major emphasis is on cross-graded, multi-ethnic learning with the main objective being to learn respect for the uniqueness of a person.

In the newsletter of the schools of Fairfax County, Va., this notice to parents appeared:

> Advanced graduate students who wish to broaden field experiences by interacting with other disciplines while diagnosing problems of the child with difficulty in symbolic functioning should inquire about a course starting Sept. 4 at George Washington University.

In 1982, the Ohio State University Press published a volume of criticism on Thomas Pynchon's *Gravity's Rainbow.* This was the publisher's blurb:

The last of the three novels, though almost immediately
acknowledged a masterpiece, has been found, nonetheless, to pose
particular difficulties for even the most enthusiastic reader caught
up—or perhaps preempted—by the novel's exceptional power.
Clearly, some guidance through the intricacies and complexities of
its structural convolutions and convulsive substantive shifts has long
been sorely needed, yet the work itself, in its bewildering if
deliberate multiformity, monumental erudition, narrative
eccentricity, and rhetorical innovation, has seemed almost to defy an
imposition of critical order, and to resist containment within the
smug categories of a necessarily expanded but still inadequate
literary taxonomy. Some, indeed, have even argued that any critical
intervention between the patient if bemused reader and the rich
imponderables and perplexities of the dense page that confronts him
is unwelcome, and serves but to dilute the force of the novel in a
romantic fragmentation of its author's imperfectly understood
intention.

Pause for a moment to examine that mush. The blurb comprises three
sentences. The first runs to thirty-six words, the second to sixty-five, the
third to fifty. (A fourth sentence, not quoted, contained another fifty-six
words, winding up with a statement that the volume "supplements the
artistry of the work it examines, and renders comprehensible its manifold
enigmas.") Notice the *-tion* suffixes: *convolutions, erudition, innovation, imposition, intervention, fragmentation, intention.* Notice the
squid phrases, spreading their inky murk: *intricacies and complexities of
its structural convolutions and convulsive substantive shifts.* Talk of the
"dense page that confronts" the reader! Physician, heal thyself!

The most fertile fields for the growth of gobbledegook are found in
government. In November 1975 Henry Kissinger proposed to create a job
in the State Department for a good friend. Henry himself is a superb
writer, possessed of clarity and grace, but he recognized that this was no
time to be clear. Thus he farmed out to a professional bureaucrat the task
of defining the new post of "consumer affairs coordinator." The
bureaucrat obliged. The coordinator "will review existing mechanisms
of consumer input, thruput and output." Moreover:

> The purpose of the department's plan is twofold: to confirm and
> reinforce the department's sensitivity to consumer rights and
> interests as they impact upon the Department and to take those steps

necessary and feasible to promote and channel these rights and interests with respect to the maintenance and expansion of an international dialogue and awareness.

The Washington Post examined all this carefully and came to a measured conclusion: "The whole job description is an onput." The Post's suggestion was that Henry and his colleagues "backput it to the drawing board."

We find rich lodes of gobbledegook in the military. A commandant of the Marine Corps once issued a memorandum:

It has been decisioned that some form of unit rotation may be a desirable objective. Detailed planning has been held in abeyance because of structural and manning level imbalances between WestPac and EastPac and other associated areas of concern. Recent CMV decisions have alleviated the major inhibitors allowing a fresh approach and revaluation of alternative methods of unit replacement of WestPac personnel. Preliminary staff analysis has concluded that a six-month TAD unit replacement appears to be an attractive possibility and should serve as the focal point for a full feasibility determination prior to development of any implementation procedures or recommendations.

Stop to examine this specimen also. Notice the passive voice: *It has been decisioned that . . ."* Notice the tentative phrases: *may be desirable, appears to be attractive.* Attend the mumbo-jumbo incantations: *alleviated the major inhibitors, focal point, full feasibility determination, implementation procedures.* This is magic! One wave of the commandant's baton, and meaning vanishes.

Congress does its bit to preserve the chickweed. This is from a conference report in 1975 on a bill intended to establish a national policy on energy. The bill would give the president

a substantial measure of administrative flexibility to draft the price regulatory mechanism in a manner designed to optimize production from domestic properties subject to a statutory parameter requiring the regulatory pattern to prevent prices from exceeding a maximum weighted average.

There is a certain genius here at work: We will craft a mechanism to optimize production subject to a statutory parameter that requires a regulatory pattern.

I do not mean to overlook the contributions of big business to the treasury of gobbledegook. These offerings are from IBM: "Meetings on equipment acceptance provide a severe test of our synchronized organizational parallel reciprocal monitored time-phased capability." . . . "The diversity nevertheless represents a burgeoning grass roots sort of pluralism discomforting only to those whose binary temperament eschews any evidence of ambiguity." By all means, let us eschew any evidence of ambiguity. Ambiguity ought always to be eschewed.

Debra Shore, who formerly taught English at Brown University, once gave her students a splendid assignment: They were asked first to take a passage of jargon and to translate it into English, then to take a passage of clear English and turn it into Doublespeak. The students succeeded brilliantly. Their papers, published in the Brown Alumni Monthly, included a prose translation by Dana Cowin '82 of the back of an Amtrak ticket. In the original:

> Time shown on timetables or elsewhere and times quoted are not guaranteed and form no part of this contract. Time schedules and equipment are subject to change without notice. Amtrak expressly reserves the right to, without notice, substitute alternate [they meant alternative] means of transportation, and to alter or omit stopping places shown on ticket or timetable. Amtrak assumes no responsibility for inconvenience, expense, or other loss, damage, or injury resulting from error in schedules, delayed trains, failure to make connections, shortage of equipment, or other operating deficiencies.

This was the translation:

> Amtrak schedules change and are sometimes wrong. Amtrak is not responsible for any problems resulting from changes in the schedule.

Another student, Mack Reed '81, provided this back formation from one of the best known passages of our English inheritance:

> At the inception of the primary fabrication time-phase, when the penultimate intelligence unit synthesized the geophysical locus and its concomitant gaseous hyperterrean coordinates, said mineral consolidation region failed to possess proper substance and volume reference points and displayed a lack of wave frequency vibrations in the specific imposition registers over the anterior surfaces of the

geotropic fault formation and with the aqueous gas-to-firmament interface destabilized by a major kineticizing meteorological manifestation. The previously discussed entitical sentience unit expressed a desire for increased wave frequency modulations and with the immediately subsequent amplification adjustment, registered his positive reactions.

Luckily, as Ms. Shore remarked, the translators of the King James Bible had not been introduced to the mysteries of twentieth-century jargon.

So let us positively avoid, and not merely eschew, lapses into gobbledegook. The remedy lies in short sentences, familiar words, and clear ideas to begin with. To be sure, if we are engaged in technical writing, we must use words of a particular technology. There is a place in mathematics for *parameter;* in a paper on computers, no objection can be taken to such verbs as *to interface* and *to access;* the writer who treats medical topics cannot simplify the vocabulary of medicine. This is understood. The lawyers doubtless have something on their side in contending that words of the law, however obscure they may seem to non-lawyers, are sufficiently clear to the courts. But the general rule is valid: Let us not be pompous. Let us not inflate a simple thought with gassy prose. When we let our prose go gobble-gobble-gobble, we turn out sentences that are turkeys.

3. We ought not to mangle our sentences.

The sin in prose composition that is known as the *mangle,* the *dangle,* or the *clunker* is related to the sin of gobbledegook, but though they achieve the same result the offenses are quite different. The shared result, of course, is confusion. Our reaction to gobbledegook is, What did he say? Our reaction to the mangle is, How's that again?

Most of the clunkers in my collection are the consequence of two blunders. One is the dangling participial clause; the other is the misplaced element. To speak of a ''dangling'' clause is not precisely accurate, for something that ''dangles'' must dangle from *something.* My dangles don't dangle from much of anything. They are orphans, wandering about in search of a proper subject to attach to. These are mangled dangles:

From the Newport News Daily Press, in a story on the launching of a ship: "After Mrs. Herbert C. Bonner smashed the stem of the 500-foot superfreighter, the newest thing in American maritime history, she entered the water at exactly 12:47 P.M."

From a commentary by Nicholas von Hoffman in The Washington Post: "Elected governor in an amusing upper-class tussle against fellow plutocrat W. Averell Harriman, Rocky's years in Albany could be charitably described as a fiasco. . . ."

From the letters column of a Western magazine: "After traveling widely throughout the world, Scotland is still my favorite place."

From the program notes of the Greenville (S.C.) Symphony: "Signed to an exclusive recording contract by RCA, Tedd Joselson's albums have consistently won critical acclaim."

From Al Burt's column in the "Tropic" supplement of The Miami Herald, in a piece about the Neuharth family of publishing fame: "After injuring his leg on the farm, Daniel Neuharth sold it and opened a creamery in Eureka."

From The Associated Press, reporting the auto race at Le Mans in 1983: "Racing to maintain the lead they held from the fifth hour of the race, smoke started pouring out of the exhaust two laps from the finish."

From a letter I received, complimenting me on a book of photographs for which I had written a narrative: "Being a Southerner, the photographs were wonderfully resonant."

From an ad in The New York Times Book Review: "Weighing nearly four pounds, with almost three times the content of his earlier work, the author enables you to manage your money. . . ."

From a squib in The New Yorker, taken from a science newsletter: "Long thought to be relatively flat and shaped much like huge Frisbees, the scientists have found that some galaxies are actually oblong in shape."

From the National News Council, after someone complained of a column I had written about lawsuits over Laetrile: "Although banned by the FDA, Mr. Kilpatrick noted that Judge Luther Bohannon had ruled . . ."

From the Tillamook (Ore.) Headlight-Herald, in a story about a calf with eight teats that was born to a heifer owned by Glenn and Pat Gallatin: "Normally adorned with no more than four teats, the Gallatins didn't have an explanation for the curious quirk."

These are examples of clunkers that materialize from modifying words or phrases that somehow get misplaced.

From the Youngstown Vindicator: "With seventeen rooms, eight fireplaces and three kitchens, Roberta 'Bobbi' Hahn was really counting on a zoning change to open a craft shop in her home."

From Reuters, about an earthquake in Peking: "A powerful earth tremor shook Peking early today, sending thousands of people rushing onto the streets, smashing windows and cracking walls."

From a Sunday supplement, in an article about police horses: "The horses are becoming desensitized to objects like grocery carts and nightsticks which will be carried by policemen."

From The Seattle Times, in a story about sex shops: "Before that arrest, the Kinky Korner had been viewed mainly as a shop dealing in novelties to police."

From the Monterey Peninsula Herald, in a story about a new telescope at the Monterey Institute for Research in Astronomy: "The 36-inch telescope will spend a significant proportion of its time on a systematic search for supernovas designed by astrophysicists from the Lawrence Berkeley Laboratory in Berkeley."

From a syndicated column by Dan Dorfman, having to do with an article in the Journal of the American Medical Association about threats of legal action against the manufacturers of epinephrine: "In fact, the prospects of legal action, I'm told, already have been raised by a few attorneys and families of patients who died in conversations with the co-author of the Journal article."

From the Greenville (S.C.) News: "An explosion and fire destroyed an apartment building in Boston's Chinatown, but a man sleeping on the fourth floor rode his bed to the ground as the building collapsed and walked away."

From United Press International, in a story about a prison employee killed in a riot: "Gunter was found with several stab wounds in the compound."

From The Miami Herald, in a report on current developments in the drug industry: "Upjohn Co. will test a new drug aimed at preventing asthma attacks later this year."

From the Chicago Sun-Times: "Illinois' current rape law says rape takes place when a male above the age of fourteen has sexual intercourse with a female who is not his wife by force and against her will."

From The Greenwood (S.C.) Index-Journal: "Barbara Warner reported that her husband had been attacked 'by a pack of dogs on a tractor.'"

From The New York Times, in a review of a play, *Moose Murders:* "Let's not review its climax here except to say that it was a comedy whose climax consisted of a gauze-wrapped quadriplegic rising from his wheelchair to kick a man wearing a moose costume in the groin."

From The Associated Press, in a story about a robbery in Rhode Island that was staged as Mrs. George Bush was eating next door: "Unaware of the robbery, Mrs. Bush finished a meal of chicken breast stuffed with crabmeat and strawberry shortcake."

From a newsletter to constituents of Senator Eleanor Lee in the thirty-third legislative district of Washington: "Citizens whose drivers' licenses are suspended under the implied consent laws in the past have been notified to quit driving by certified mail."

From The Associated Press, in a story about a retired sea captain in England: "Seventy rose bushes grow in a filled-in swimming pool rarely used by the family."

From an interview with the victim of an automobile accident: "My husband had just started up when he saw the guy coming out of the corner of his eye."

The writers of newspaper headlines are especially vulnerable to the construction of clunkers: "Body Found in House Up for Sale" . . . "Clinic Owner Is Arrested After Death" . . . "Judge Returns Home to Wife, Children."

Other clunkers come from eye-opening juxtapositions. From a Seattle suburban paper, in a story about a college teacher, Ellen Hofmann, who had been elected to a state commission: "While in Paris, she married her husband, Bill, who also teaches English at Highline College. The Hofmanns climbed the pyramids of Egypt on their honeymoon, and now have two children."

Still other clunkers are profoundly—well, profound. A top Washington reporter, writing about future economic trends, drew this sober conclusion: "Like most economic forecasting in recent years, these predictions may or may not prove out." The line recalls the wisdom attributed to physicist Niels Bohr: "Prediction is a very difficult art, especially when it involves the future."

One of the charming things about clunkers is that they often make a certain lunatic sense. Through its house organ, Think, the IBM company has been waging war against profoundly thoughtless sentences that turn up in office correspondence:

> After the system has been in operation for a time, the number of new subscribers will increasingly lessen.
> An urgent answer is required.
> You and your management team must assume the responsibility to place our posture in a superior position.
> The tendency to sidestep the issue continues full bore.
> I believe something has just occurred which may be concernable.
> Enclosed for your use are the following stuffs.
> Door is alarmed; do not use.

Anson S. Hosley of Hollywood, Fla., contributes an item from a police report: "The glass pane of the kitchen window was broken on both sides." From a column on marriage and the family: "If your parents never had any children, chances are you never will." From a novel he had read: "He walked across the room and kissed her where she sat." And from a dialogue he overheard, in which a husband complains to his wife: "You ruined the stew. You should have added less salt."

Dean Willard of Fort Hays (Kan.) State University was impressed by a TV commercial from the Grace Company: "At an alarming speed the American economy is slowing down."

Other readers offer contributions from radio and television. There was the traffic reporter who warned against "a stalled car going west on Sunset Highway." A TV anchorman informed us that "in the past ten years the divorce rate has increased 50 percent among married couples." There was the TV commercial that reminded us usefully that "anniversaries come but once a year." And there was something splendidly patriotic in this thought from a TV editorialist: "New Jersey *deserves* a national anthem."

Very well. Enough on mangles, dangles, and clunkers. The one point to be made by this tanglefoot parade of horrid examples is a point that never can be sufficiently emphasized: We must read our copy *critically* before we let it go. It is not enough to read for errors in punctuation, grammar, or spelling. We must read for the sense of it. If Rudolf Flesch had followed that rule, he would not have asked a rhetorical question: "Why do you sit down to write?" He thus invited a famous response from E.B. White: "Because, sir, it is more comfortable than standing up."

4. As a general rule, we ought not to use euphemisms.

The word *euphemism* comes out of the Greek for "word that sounds well." As such, the euphemism is a first cousin, once removed, from the words and phrases that constitute clichés, gobbledegook, Newspeak, and Doublespeak. There is no feasible way to write for publication, or to speak in public, without using euphemisms. They surely are not to be condemned out of hand, but when euphemisms can be avoided without giving needless offense, they ought to be avoided.

My own thought, which I trot out for inspection, is that most euphemisms may be classified under one of three headings: Euphemisms of Inflation, Euphemisms of Modesty or Taste, and Euphemisms of Deception. For a more definitive system of classification, let me recommend Hugh Rawson's delightful *Dictionary of Euphemisms and Other Doubletalk,* published by Crown in 1981. For the inveterate word-beagler— the person who loves to root around the hedgerows of language—this work of lighthearted scholarship offers hours of pleasant browsing.

To quote Rawson's definition, euphemisms are "mild, agreeable, or roundabout words used in place of coarse, painful, or offensive ones." They are "the outward and visible signs of our inward anxieties, conflicts, fears, and shames." They are the cotton candy expressions that dissolve at a touch and leave only a sticky residue behind.

Consider, if you will, some of the innumerable Euphemisms of Inflation. It is through this device that a *garbageman* becomes a *sanitary engineer,* a *janitor* becomes a *custodian,* and a *gambler* becomes a *speculator.* When he headed the Department of Health, Education and Welfare, Joe Califano had an *Assistant to the Secretary (Special Services).* This was his cook.

By this process of inflation, a *slum* becomes *inner city housing,* the *used car* a *previously owned vehicle,* and a *mechanic* an *automotive internist.* A few years ago in Dallas, *school buses* were known officially as *motorized attendance modules;* they were driven by *instructional facilitators.* Inflation pumps up a *graveyard* to a *memorial garden,* a *gym* to a *recreational facility* and a *library* to a *communications resource center.* A *house trailer* takes on new airs as a *mobile home.* Who would serve on a mere *committee* when he could serve on a *task force* instead? Given the unpleasant occasion, who would wish to be *fired* when he could be *selected out?*

Many of the euphemisms in Rawson's extensive collection come from the world of marketing and advertising. When a house is advertised as *adorable,* this means the house is small. In such products as toothpaste, one rarely finds tubes that are "small." They are *medium, large,* and *giant.* The promoters of Hadacol some years ago offered their product in the "hospital size." A coat of *Alaskan sable* is a coat of skunk fur.

Most of Rawson's engaging collection deals with Euphemisms of Modesty and Taste, and most of these have to do with bodily functions or with parts of the body. At one time *legs* in polite society were *limbs; breasts* were *chests* or *bosoms.* It was to avoid offense that chickens were butchered into *drumsticks* and *white meat.* When I entered newspapering in 1941, *social diseases* in print were just yielding to the boldness of *venereal diseases.* A few years would have to pass before syphilis and gonorrhea could be identified in the press as such. In those days none of a person's *private parts* could be acceptably spelled out; it was as if an airbrush had been taken to everything south of the navel. Over the years the buttocks have attracted a hundred euphemisms. President Reagan once gave new respectability to an old one: He was up to his *keister* in leaks to the press. Rawson devotes half a page to the euphemisms relied upon when we have to go to *the little boys'* or *little girls' room.* In this event, we have to *write a letter, consult Mrs. Jones, feed a dog, freshen up, give a Chinaman a music lesson, go feed the goldfish, shake hands with an old friend, wash our hands,* or *put some powder on our nose.* A *bathroom* (itself a euphemism) is *a cabinet, a facility, a head, a house of ease, a john, a latrine, a marble palace, a poet's corner, a throne room, a sanctum sanctorum,* or *a loo.*

Hundreds of euphemisms, not surprisingly, deal with sex. When we say that a man and a woman are *sleeping together,* something more than slumber is implied. The Bureau of the Census came up with POSSLQ to mean Persons of Opposite Sex Sharing Living Quarters; such persons are known as *good friends, roommates,* or *live-in companions.* The years have taken us far from the honest *whores* of the King James Bible; the softening folds of language have turned them into *ladies of the evening, call girls, streetwalkers, prostitutes,* or *filles de joie.* Rawson notes that scholars have counted 650 synonyms for *vagina.*

I venture no serious objection to most of the Euphemisms of Inflation. Some of them are funny, some are pathetic, but if it contributes to human happiness for a hairdresser to be a *beautician* or a *cosmetologist,* or an undertaker to be a *funeral director,* fine with me. Neither can I complain of most of the Euphemisms of Modesty; indeed I defend their usage. I may object to *pass on* and *loss* as substitutes for *die* and *death;* I may cringe at *pain in the tummy* for *stomach ache;* I would rather speak honestly of *constipation* than of *occasional irregularity;* but candor and plain speech are not always to be preferred to a gentler turn of phrase. Candor is a virtue, but courtesy, kindness, and consideration are virtues also. Except in writing for medical publications, nothing is gained by explicit terms for bodily functions. As a child I was taught that "horses *sweat,* men *perspire,* but ladies merely *glow.*" Speak to me not of *fat!* In my book Jackie Gleason is *portly* and Elizabeth Taylor is no more than pleasingly *plump.*

It is the third class of euphemisms that gives pause. These are the Euphemisms of Deception. Some of them are mild. Members of Congress insist that they do not take *vacations;* they take *district work periods.* They do not go on *junkets;* they engage in *foreign oversight.* When Mr. Reagan agreed to an increase in the tax on gasoline, he was not seeking an increase in taxes; he was asking for *revenue enhancement.*

The danger arises when matters of serious substance are coated with a film of washable words. A poor family lives in poverty, not in *a low-income status.* Nothing is gained by calling malpractice a *therapeutic misadventure.* President Carter's laudable attempt to rescue hostages in Iran was a fiasco; it was not, as the White House described it, a *limited success.*

We ought strenuously to resist the camouflage beloved of the military. A *payload* is in fact a *bombload.* The bombs that fall by error on schools and hospitals are something more than *incontinent ordnance.* We can make a joke of the army's definition of a shovel as a *combat emplacement evacuator,* but we become accessories to disinformation when we write of a bombing as a *protective reaction strike.* Professor William D. Lutz of Rutgers, who is as indefatigable as Rawson in collecting euphemisms, has said with much truth that politicians—and generals, and industrialists, and the operators of nuclear power plants— have no right "to misrepresent, mislead, or lie by omission."

For some years Lutz has been actively fighting Euphemisms of Deception through the Quarterly Review of Doublespeak. I am indebted to him for some ominous examples of the art. Note how the New Jersey Division of Gaming Enforcement lent a certain social respectability to gangsters of the Mafia: They were *members of a career offender-cartel.* In the nuclear power industry, an explosion is an *energetic disassembly.* A fire is *rapid oxidation.* A reactor accident is *an abnormal evolution* or *a normal aberration.* It is in such areas as these that euphemisms must be examined with great care: Here we are being bamboozled. Here we ought not to speak of *implements for digging;* here we ought to call spades what they are: *spades.*

5. *We ought not to pile up nouns as adjectives.*

An annual report floated across my desk early in 1983 from an outfit I happen especially to admire, the Washington Legal Foundation. The author of that report fell into one of those constructions so beloved in this age of the bumper sticker. He said that one of the foundation's purposes is to protect the rights of *violent crime victims.*

Perhaps nothing was seriously wrong with the phrase, for its meaning was immediately clear, but this business of drafting nouns to serve as adjectives gets to be a slovenly habit. We could define it, if we were so inclined, as the leaving the socks on the floor habit, or even the leaving the socks on the floor by the bedside habit.

In the phrase that provoked my irk (the irk phrase?), nothing of importance would have been lost by writing of *victims of violent crime.* It would have been two letters longer, but the gain in euphony would have been worth the trouble. Most of the time, in my observation, the addictive use of nouns as modifiers may be cured by a dignified recourse to the prepositional phrase. For a while, the country heard much talk of *the five-cent per gallon gasoline and diesel fuel tax increase bill.* What we were talking about was *the bill to increase the tax on gasoline and diesel fuel by five cents a gallon.* The Consumer Product Safety Commission once reported on its *expansion and utilization plans for its product and hazard specific injury data system.* I might have gleaned a better inkling from *plans to expand the commission's system of obtaining data on specific products and hazards.*

Some years ago, The Washington Post carried in its Sunday book supplement a delightful piece on the subject by Bruce D. Price, president of Word-Wise Advertising in New York City. He continues to crusade against what he denounces as the modifier noun proliferation increase.

He writes modifier noun proliferation increase articles. When he is really wrought up, he writes modifier noun proliferation increase article protests.

"What's happening," says Price, "is that nouns are being strung end to end in mindless litanies, and the beauty that was Samuel Johnson and the brevity that was Oscar Wilde go down the drain."

As Price willingly concedes, there is nothing wrong with such familiar constructions as *deer crossing*, or *toothpick holder*, or *street musician*. We need not become so obsessed with avoiding the noun-adjective that we write of *crossings for deer* and *holders for toothpicks* and *musicians who play on the streets*. This is not the problem.

The problem arises when we elect to dress a noun in spats and striped pants in the thought that we are achieving something spiffy. A columnist tells us that the president sought to provoke a *confrontation situation*. A trade association holds a seminar on *management controls expansion*. U.S. Law Week reports on a case involving the admission of *past sexual behavior evidence*. Even the respected Wall Street Journal falls into discourse on *economic policy management shortcomings*. When we are told about an *increased labor market participation rate*, we are meant to understand that more people are working.

Notice, again, how these ill-wrought sentences could have been remedied by a simple recasting: *a seminar on expansion of management controls, evidence of past sexual behavior, shortcomings in the management of economic policy.*

We fall into what Price calls Nounspeak out of some frenetic compulsion to save space or time. It is the instant bumper sticker addiction, or the headline writer compression fixation, that afflicts us. (And, yes, Little Eva, the foregoing sentence was writ deliberate.) Whatever the reason, we ought to watch these things. Sir Ernest Gowers, mentor to us all, once remarked that "It has been widely said that the adjective is the enemy of the noun." When nouns are press-ganged into service as adjectives, we have fratricidal warfare.

My thought is that by curbing the use of Nounspeak, we gain not only in clarity but in cadence also. In 1982, a top Washington correspondent was reviewing a study of Reagan's social legislation. It appeared that in each year of his presidency, Reagan hoped to repeal a decade of previous domestic policy. This was the correspondent's cracker: "If he were given two full terms to operate, by the time he left the White House he would have moved things back just about to the time of his own boyhood in the William Howard Taft administration.'' Notice how that sentence could have been improved, and given a nice smack of finality, simply by speaking of *the administration of William Howard Taft*.

One more example of the process: A writer in The Washington Post developed a story on a controversy in the Pentagon over sidearms. One faction wanted to retain the .45-caliber automatic; an opposing faction wanted to switch to a 9-millimeter Luger. A congressman thought that some of the army spokesmen who were defending the Luger weren't really in favor of it. He thought, said the writer, ''the army munitions men were closet .45 fanciers.'' Much better, it seems to me, to say *the army munitions men were closet fanciers of the .45*. That way, you wind up with a short word and a long vowel, and the sentence has at least the good crack of a .22.

Nouns are the solid building stones of our structure. When we plaster them with stucco—''Jane Fonda is perhaps the country's most publicized civil rights and arms reduction advocate''—we lose sight of both form and meaning. Let us limit our employment of modifying nouns to those occasions that naturally demand them: *drama criticism, automobile license, newspaper editor.* And let us join Price in his crusade. If we succeed, he promises one day to write about the modifier noun proliferation increase phenomenon article protest campaign success story, but he doesn't expect to write the piece any time soon.

6. We ought not to coin words wantonly.

Webster's III offers us a vocabulary of some 450,000 words. With that many words to work with, the question may be asked: Do we really need any more? And the answer, of course, is of course. If our language ever should fail to grow, it will wind up a dead language.

That having been said, much more remains to be said, for not all coinages have a good ring. A publishing house in Pennsylvania is pushing a book on the law of real estate; the work contains ''forms to assist in the obtention of information during title research.'' *Obtention?* In Chicago, a TV critic mourns the absence of Dick Cavett: He contributed ''grace and dignity to a medium where mediocracy usually suffices.'' *Mediocracy?* The Associated Press tells us that in Richmond, Va., ''the city government is administrated by a city manager.'' *Administrated?* In Saturday Review, we read of a plot to present low appraisals of Brooklyn's collection of primitive art ''so that the museum board would deaccession them at fractional values." *Deaccession?*

Some of the most offensive coinages result from the melting down of adjectives and nouns to mint them into verbs. "The B-1 bomber *will obsolete* the B-52." "Professor Hargrove *has authored* six other volumes." Senator Schmitt said he was "tired of *ad hocking* on education." "Union Carbide *is officed* in Danbury." "The committee *decisioned* a dividend increase." "William Powell and Myrna Loy have *eternized* Nick and Nora Charles." "Hellman has laid proprietary claims to the *biographizing* of poor Hammett." "There was the usual *strategizing* over issues yet to be confronted." "They are *parenting* three children." "Some women went *cowboying* or homesteading."

Sportswriters and sportscasters have made their contributions, for good or ill. During a telecast of a basketball game between North Carolina and Villanova, Al McGuire spoke enthusiastically of a player who *uptempoes* the game. In 1982, "the Redskins consistently *outyardaged* the opposition." We also learned that the Redskins *outstatisticked* their foes. This was because they *defensed* so superbly, and perhaps because their quarterback knew how to *audibilize* his signals.

The jargon of politics provides words to which only insiders are privy. Senator Armstrong "has won his battle *to sunset* the Credit Control Act," which is to say, the senator has succeeded in fixing a date on which the act will expire. Senator Long objected "that if the bill came to the floor next week, it would be *christmas-treed.*" He meant that it would be hung about with amendments. My brother pundit Jack Germond once saw no way "*to molasses over*" the culpability of the Carter White House." In state capitols, lawmakers are prone *to grandfather* their bills.

Al Haig, former secretary of state, provided rich lodes of neologisms: "I'll have *to caveat* my response to that one." He could not answer a question from Senator Glenn "in the way you *contexted* it." He spoke of "*nuanced* and fundamentally sharp departures." He had trouble "*definitizing* an answer."

Most of the foregoing coinages strike me as abominable, but lovers of the language always will disagree on the utility or permanence of new words or forms of words. I once got into an argument with William Safire over *to obsolete,* which I scorned and he embraced. After all, he said, "if we can sweeten our coffee and blacken a reputation, why can we not obsolete a bomber?" Let Safire obsolete his own bombers; I will make mine get that way on their own.

7. We must not break the rules of grammar.

Thomas Middleton, who ordinarily is among the mildest of men, once lost his temper thoroughly in Saturday Review. He erupted against "probably the most distressing misusage in American English today." His target was, *between she and I*. Huzzah! Over the years Middleton's essays on language have provided some of the wisest and wittiest commentary to be found anywhere. In attacking "The Tarzan Theory" of pronouns, he pounced upon a truly offensive target.

The ape-man, you may recall, supposedly met his lady and said, "Me Tarzan, you Jane." (In point of fact, when the two met, Tarzan spoke fluent Ape, fair Lion, and a smattering of Elephant; he could read and write English, but could not speak it. His first words to Jane, many months later, probably were, "Bonjour, Mademoiselle Porter," for what he had learned to speak was French.) Never mind. "Me Tarzan, you Jane" lives on. And there are times when it is right to be deliberately wrong. Vermont Royster, who spent many brilliant years as editor of The Wall Street Journal, has recalled the time a reporter accurately quoted an incident at a police lineup. The victim of a holdup, seeing the woman bandit in the line, cried out, "It's her!" A finicky copy editor primly changed it to read, "It is she!"

In his piece in Saturday Review, Middleton cited some horrid examples: "It was a bad week for he and his family." "This is the crucial time for he and his teammates." I once received a thank-you note from a colleague high in the ranks of newspapering. He had come to a luncheon and wanted to thank us "for inviting my wife and I" to the party. We were indeed glad to have she and he.

An endless parade could be marshaled of *it's* for *its* and *its* for *it's*. The Reader's Digest once quoted a woman whose husband had found an interesting old magazine: "Where'd you get that? Who's attic you been in?" The Peoria Journal Star quoted Dick Williams on a tight race in the National League: "Pennantwise, it's going to depend on whose got the best pitching."

Even professionals have trouble with matching subjects and verbs. The Birmingham News once hung a jarring headline over one of my columns on the writer's art: "Flotsam and jetsam bobs on the ocean of language." An annual report of the Wickes Companies told stockholders, "Your continued cooperation and support is appreciated." In The New York Times, "The smuggling and distribution of cocaine, officials say, is largely controlled by Colombians and other Latin Americans." The Supreme Court falls into error. Justice White: "The agency's fears . . . is expressly dependent." Justice Rehnquist: "The panoply of statutes and regulations . . . are more extensive."

We ought to get straight on *either* and *neither.* A food columnist says of an Argentine restaurant that "Neither price nor menu description are a fair guide." The UPI says that Dan Rather and David Brinkley have covered more politics "than either of them care to remember." A small paper in Tennessee provides a large headline: "Neither Johnny nor his teacher have mastered the art of writing." Comparatives give trouble. Even Tom Wicker nods: "The House, long the most conservative of the two bodies . . ."

Well, all of us know better than to confuse nominative and objective pronouns, and all of us know better than to impose singular verbs on plural subjects. We just get careless. Let us strive to be careful instead.

8. We ought not to write dialect or slang unless we are certain of both our ear and our audience.

So you have this impulse to write in dialect? You want to write jus' like people talk? Very well. Let me venture a word of sound advice: Lie down until the impulse goes away.

Writing good dialect is among the most difficult of the prose arts. It demands, for one thing, uncanny skills in spelling. How do you reproduce phonetically, one letter at a time, the sounds of accented speech? Such writing demands a keen ear for the cadence of language. Can you echo the beat exactly? Dialect demands consistency. If your fictional character is saying he's *gonna git it jus' right* on your first page, he had better be gittin' it jus' right on the last page, or the phoniness will cause you embarrassment.

This is Negro dialect:

(1) I was a-listenin' to all de talk, en I slips into de river en was gwyne to shove for sho' if dey come aboard. Den I was gwyne to swim to de raf' again when dey was gone.

(2) No'm, de cow ain' daid. Din' you know? She done have a calf las' night. Dat why she beller so . . . An' ain' no use quarrelin' wid blessin's, cause dat calf gwine ter mean a full cow an' plen'y buttermilk for de young Misses, lak dat Yankee doctah say dey'd need.

(3) One day we wuz gwine along a road . . . We didn't know we wuz so close to whar de fightin' was gwine on 'twell we walked on to a bridge and come right on a whole regiment of Germans, swimmin' in de river. Dey seed us about de same time we seed dem and div under de water.

The first example comes from Mark Twain, in *Huckleberry Finn;* the second from Margaret Mitchell, in *Gone With the Wind;* the third from William Faulkner, in *Sartoris*. One heard *gwyne,* the other two heard the same vowel sound and spelled it *gwine*. Mitchell heard *an'* and Faulkner heard simply *and*. Mitchell's *din know* was closer than Faulkner's *didn't know.* Twain spelled it *was,* Faulkner *wuz.* Why did Twain spell out *aboard?*

This is Irish dialect:

(1) A dhirty man goes to clink for a weakness in the knees, an' is coort-martialled for a pair av socks missin'; but a clane man . . . may, spakin' in reason, do fwhat he likes and dhrink from day to divil.
(2) This here wave iv rayform that's sweepin' over th' counthry, mind ye, is raisin' the divvle. I've seen waves iv rayform before. Whin the people iv this counthry gets wurruked up, there's no stoppin' thim. They'll not dhraw breath until ivry man that took a dollar iv a bribe is sent down th' r-road. Thim that takes two goes on th' oomity iv th' wave iv rayform.

The first comes from Rudyard Kipling, in a short story about soldier Mulvaney; the second, of course, is from Finley Peter Dunne's tales of Mr. Dooley. One heard it *av,* the other *iv.* Kipling was content with a simple *the;* Dunne always knocked it down to *th'*. Kipling heard *divil* and Dunne heard *divvle*. Dunne was satisfied in other passages, not quoted here, with *queen* and *clean* and *what,* but Kipling had to Irish-up *quane* and *clane* and *fwhat*. James Joyce in *Dubliners*, incidentally, didn't spell in Irish at all.

Some of our most acclaimed writers have had trouble in maintaining a decent consistency in their dialectal writing. D.H. Lawrence failed woefully in the speech he put in the mouth of his famous gamekeeper. In the midst of the same conversation, with no reason ever suggested for change, we find Oliver saying *you, yo', tha, ter,* and *yer.* Stephen Crane, in *The Red Badge of Courage,* had one of his soldiers saying *the* about half the time and *th'* the other half. Some writers suppose they can write dialect merely by spelling *was* as *wuz* and *of* as *uv,* but there is more to the art than phonetic orthography. James Fenimore Cooper, as Twain noted, never learned this.

Successful dialect demands an intimate knowledge of the vocabulary—and of the nuances within the vocabulary—of the speech one is attempting to duplicate. Leo Rosten is a master, I am told, of Yiddish speech. (I say, "I am told," because I could no more recognize perfect Yiddish than I could recognize perfect Russian.) In his preface to *The Joys of Yiddish,* Rosten touched upon the difficulties inherent to the writer of dialect:

> Jews had to become psychologists, and their preoccupation with human, no less than divine behavior made Yiddish remarkably rich in names for the delineation of character types. Little miracles of discriminatory precision are contained in the distinctions between such simpletons as a nebech, a shlemiel, a shmendrick, a shnook; or between such dolts as a klutz, a yold, a Kuni Lemmel, a shlep, a Chaim Yankel. All of them inhabit the kingdom of the ineffectual, but each is assigned a separate place in the roll call.

One of my correspondents, Robert G. Lundergan of Camp Hill, Pa., passed along a prescient thought on this whole matter: "Whenever one hears a thick dialect, it is usually from a character who is not too literate. He is therefore steeped in the mores, superstitions, and traditions of his ethnic background. This background should be a part of the way he speaks.

"I remember reading a chapter years ago of a book written in Irish dialect. The brogue was as thick as peat moss, but more importantly I could get the feeling of his Irish life style. By little bits here and hints there, I could sense the values and beliefs of that particular culture. An Irish blessing comes to mind: 'May ye haf t' take ahf bawth y'r shoes t' count ahl y're blessin's.' By implication it's understood that the whole known world is mathematically illiterate."

Lundergan resolved that before he ever wrote a paragraph of dialect, he would live at least six months in that particular ethnic group. I doubt that six months would suffice. I have lived more than sixty years in the South, and unless I were overcome with a spirit of reckless adventurism I would never attempt to write Southern. The years have taught me that eastern and western Tennessee have wholly different patterns of pronunciation and syntax. There is one accent in Mississippi, an entirely different accent in parts of Louisiana and Alabama. Experts in geographical linguistics, like Henry Higgins of Shaw's play, can identify regions by what we call the container we use for bringing groceries home—a *bag,* a *sack,* or a *paper sack.* In some areas the time is *two-thirty;* in others it's *half past two.* It's a *quarter of* the hour in some places, a *quarter to* the hour in others.

I have no ear at all for Yiddish dialect, and only a tin ear for Indian and Mexican and Swedish dialect, but I am certain the problems are as difficult in any tongue. My only suggestions, if you insist on having a go at dialect, are to listen intently—really *intently*—and to be consistent in your spelling. As I say, if your stage Irishman says *fwhat* the first time, you'll have to *fwhat* him every time thereafter. It will drive your editors to dhrink.

Some of the same admonitions apply to writing slang, for slang is a kind of dialect of its own. Don't fake it! Be consistent! Know your character, and know your audience. Writing for Playboy is one thing; writing for Reader's Digest is quite another. In the Digest people say, "Scram!" In Playboy the imperative is something else.

But the problems of slang, unlike those of dialect, are primarily problems of taste. Over the years our society has become increasingly tolerant of slang, profanity, and obscenity in print, but for popular writing at the level of a community newspaper I offer this advice: Don't err on the side of boldness. Err if you must on the side of prudence instead. Some years ago I used what seemed to me a mild and harmless expletive, *zounds!* Reproachful letters came from readers reminding me that *zounds* is a spin-off from *God's wounds* and hence blasphemous. I am cautious about even *helluva.* In a moment of total exasperation about the poor quality of our public education, I blamed the condition upon the indifference of the people. "They don't give a damn," I wrote. One of my editors changed *damn* to *hoot.* Several readers wrote me tut-tut letters. This is a sensitive business.

We ought not to get so oversensitive, however, that we deny ourselves the zest and flavor of speech that is slangy or colloquial. Earlier I mentioned President Reagan's exasperated remark that he had had it "up to my *keister*" with leaks to the press. In the process he gave new respectability to an old euphemism, and he set in motion some trains of thought on changing words and changing mores. Crowell's *Dictionary of American Slang* defines *keister* with admirable brevity. It is "the human posterior."

Slang words abound for the stern end of our anatomy. The interesting thing is that just about all of them have won some sort of social acceptance in this generation. The New York Times, with no evident hesitation, has printed *fanny*, a word that was banned by the Keith Circuit vaudevillians as recently as 1929. Such words as *behind, backside, bum, caboose, derrière, duff, gluteus maximus, rump, rumble seat, tail, rear end*, and *tushie* (to cite Hugh Rawson's scholarship) now cause only the mildest offense. Despite President Carter's promise, as to Senator Kennedy, that "I'll whup his ass," I don't believe *ass* has yet made it to the family paper, though as *arse* the word dates back to at least 1000.

A final word about writing in dialect or slang: Cultivate a keen sense of doubt about using it, and when in doubt, don't.

9. *We ought not to be redundant.*

A redundant word is an unnecessary word. Considering the high price of newsprint and book stock, we ought to watch for redundancies and pluck them from our writing as if we were plucking ticks off a dog's back. Redundancies, like ticks, suck the blood from our prose.

Dr. Lois DeBakey, whom I have quoted before, has used a different metaphor: Redundancies are "verbal deadwood." They provide no shades of meaning; they serve only to detract from the main branches of a sentence. She provides some examples:

"When someone says *appears to be suggestive of the possibility that*, he means only *suggests* but has used seven unnecessary words to say it. *In close proximity to* means *near; has the capability of* means *can; produce an inhibitory effect on* means *inhibit; in short supply* means *scarce; it is the opinion of the author* means *I believe; present a picture similar to* means *resemble; in the majority of cases* means *usually;* give *consideration to* means *consider;* and *serves the function of being* means *is*—nothing more. In language, as in mathematics, the shortest distance between two points is a straight line; remembering that principle will make our speech and writing not only more direct but more forceful as well."

Redundancies abound. They appear in advertising: Every new depositor at a bank will receive a *free gift* or even a *free complimentary gift*. The Johnson Wax people make an insecticide that *kills garden bugs dead*. Redundancies appear in writing about the law: "Earlier the witness had filed *a sworn affidavit*." "The murder victim *died of fatal* wounds to the chest." A witness has a "good reputation for *truth and veracity.*" Redundancies are weeds; they crop up everywhere. Don't pull them *out!* Just pull them!

Richard Cohen, one of the bright stars of The Washington Post, once mused about redundancies:

> This is only me, myself, talking. In my own mind, I hear redundancies. I see them in visual observation and hear them in oral conversations. I see them in close, personal contact and feel completely surrounded by them on all sides. I guess this is because of my past experience or, as the police say, my past record. My future plans are to avoid them. (My future record has been misplaced.)
>
> Stories are totally fabricated and buildings completely destroyed or, worse yet, razed to the ground. People are strangled to death in senseless murders and Washington is full of close, personal aides. They are the ones with new initiatives who get prior approval to sign off on a preplanned ongoing process with an ink pen. The president promises to personally testify, which is all right because Ronald Reagan promises a new beginning.

Some redundancies are large: *At this point in time* means *now,* and *at that point in time* means *then.* Other redundancies are small: We learn that higher spending in one area of the government will *cancel out* higher revenues from new taxes. We *revert back* to prior examples. The reduced size of the public sector, says a budget message from the White House, "will *free up* the resources for a strong, rapidly growing private sector." Margaret Aspegren of Burr Oak, Kan., says we *up* almost everything: A rider saddles up, a writer types up, vacationers close up, children clutter up, maids fold up and make up, and in the bathroom we wash up. We warm up leftovers, finish up a day's work, hunt up a lost item, muss up our hair, lock up a store, start up a car, burn up waste paper, and fatten up a herd of cattle. Such upmanship should be pruned up.

I have belabored *component parts* in my Glossary of Crotchets, but would add a low growl here. The Bulletin of the American Society of Newspaper Editors, of all publications, has written of the newspaper of the future: It would be "custom-designed for Everyman's *component parts.*" In The Washington Post, a small electronics manufacturer is "selling *component parts* for home earth receivers." One of the National Rifle Association's concerns has to do with laws that "control the importation of all firearms and their *component parts*." An architectural design was conceived "with all *component parts* related."

Single most is another pet peeve, but let us not be tautological. In my personal opinion, there being no other kind of opinion I could hold, redundancies are pimples on paragraphs that otherwise might be pretty. We ought to get rid of them.

10. We ought not to use words that have double meanings.

Let me revert to an analogy I was using earlier. A writer is a kind of forest ranger, leading his readers like a troop of tenderfoots along an unfamiliar trail. If the guide does a good job, his charges will not stumble over strange words or awkward clauses; they will not lose their way in an underbrush of ambiguity; as readers, they will not suffer those almost imperceptible flickers of uncertain understanding that diminish their pleasure.

One way to ease the hike is to avoid words that have double meanings—words that compel a reader to make an instantaneous choice of one meaning or another. By way of example: *since.* I know that all the dictionaries authorize its use in the sense of *because.* But in my experience, nine times out of ten *because* is a better choice than *since.* The problem arises because *since* telegraphs an instant connotation of time passing. The ear receives a sentence beginning, *Since he entered the priesthood,* and the ear tunes itself for a principal clause that will relate some happenings over a period of years. The ear is thus affronted when the sentence concludes, *he could not marry.* The reader has stumbled; he may not have stumbled seriously, but small stumbles are still stumbles.

From The New York Times: "Since the Mozart Quintet comes close to being a horn concerto, Mr. Tuckwell's performance was the most conspicuous." Wouldn't *because* have been better? From Time magazine: "Since prosecutors and litigious Californians flood the court with more than 220,000 cases annually, and since criminal matters have priority, it takes more than four years for the average civil jury suit to reach trial." I would have preferred *because* in both instances. From the old Washington Star: "In a second term, Carter might have moved the course of government toward the left, but since Reagan won the election the nation's political movement has been toward the right instead."

If our intention is to state a causal relationship, it seems to me better to write, *Because it rained last night, we will not have to water the lawn today,* than to write, *Since it rained,* and so forth. In this fashion *since* can be reserved for a context of time elapsed. *Because* is a fine, honest conjunction; that is all it is; it puts on no airs; it cannot be misunderstood. But *since* can function as a preposition and an adverb as easily as it can serve as a conjunction.

While we're on the subject, watch out for *while.* It has much in common with *since.* Its first meaning also has to do with time: "While I was asleep the mail arrived." To use *while* in the sense of *although* can trip you up: "While he was a married man, he was a notorious woman chaser." If you mean to say *although* or *whereas,* put *while* away for a while and use the better word.

For another example: *due to.* It can mean *scheduled to,* e.g., "The plane is *due to* arrive at 4 o'clock." It also can mean *owing to* or *because.* If we write, "Due to his plane's late arrival, he missed the dinner meeting," we risk creating one of those imperceptible hesitations we should be anxious to avoid. If we employ *owing to* in such a sentence, we risk pretentiousness, but at least we are clear.

Another word that occasionally gives trouble is *last.* Its first meaning, unmistakably understood, is *final, terminal, ultimate.* But *last* also can mean "most recent." If we fall into a sentence involving *the last few months* or *his last book,* we may cause a flicker. By contrast, *past* admits no confusion in a context of time: *the past few months.* Instead of *his last book,* I would suggest *his latest book.*

These are small points, I grant you, but small points have a distressing way of adding up to large confusions. The word or sentence that may be absolutely clear in your own mind may not be nearly so clear to a reader. After all, you know the trail; he has never been down it before.

11. We ought not to write portmanteau sentences.

Early in 1983 a reporter for United Press International filed a story from Tel Aviv: "The 16-1 vote followed a grenade explosion in a crowd of Peace Now protestors outside the Cabinet meeting that killed a paratrooper who friends said fought in the Lebanon invasion and injured nine others who demanded Sharon be fired." That is a portmanteau sentence. The reporter tried to pack everything he owned into a single traveling bag, and he left ties, socks, and shirttails sticking out.

Here is another portmanteau sentence, this one from a story in the Los Angeles Times. The story had to do with a former professor at the

University of California Santa Barbara who had opened a restaurant. "Banished after eight years by UCSB's English department, by 'an anonymous committee—and I was too proud to find out who, or why,' Brandts turned his attention to The English Department, the dusty, dusky bar he founded dead opposite the Goleta Transit Station—just minutes from the sandy, sunny campus of UC Santa Barbara."

Here is yet another, from The Greenville (S.C.) News: "'I am furious and shocked,' Community Council's executive director said Wednesday in reaction to Appalachian Health Policy and Planning Council president's statement Tuesday that he is not attempting to obstruct Community Council's efforts to start implementing plans to constitute the Community Council as an agency to aid cooperation of social service groups in Greenville."

And yet one more, from The Washington Post's man in London. He remarked that The Times, once England's premier newspaper, no longer is regarded as the best periodical in the English language. He thought that distinction had passed to The Economist. He continued: "Founded in 1843—and edited later in the century by Walter Bagehot, the period's most famous English journalist of democratic politics and capitalist economics—the weekly's circulation has doubled to about 200,000 over the past decade."

Still another, from the Birmingham Post-Herald: "She was shot through the right lung after confronting a woman married to her ex-husband inside the Food World Store on Bankhead Highway shortly before 1 P.M."

These dreadful specimens of prose composition exhibit many faults, but chief among them is the authors' ambition to say everything at once. When I went into newspapering in 1941, I too was afflicted with the portmanteau syndrome. Charles H. Hamilton, who was then city editor of The Richmond (Va.) News Leader, dispelled the affliction in a note he left on my desk:

Kilpo:
    I have something for you:
    ....
    Those interesting objects are called periods. They are formed by the second key from the right on the bottom row of your typewriter. Please put them to good use.

                                                   CHH

A judicious application of this Hamiltonian wisdom would have saved the UPI reporter in Israel. By my own count, he was trying to jam ten facts and one unintended implication into his horrible sentence; the implication was that the Cabinet meeting killed the paratrooper. The sentence about the banished professor would have been improved not only by a few periods, but also by a complete recasting. Nothing can be done to salvage the sentence from Greenville.

Notice that in two of the examples, the writer's troubles were compounded by a thought set off between dashes. I confess to a great fondness for the dash. Properly used, the device can add an air of spontaneity to our writing; it helps us to echo speech, which ordinarily is filled with digressions, afterthoughts, and interruptions. But in the piece from Santa Barbara, the writer forgot to end one pair of dashes before sprinting into another. The Post's man in London got so lost in his fog of dashes that he wound up with the weekly's circulation being founded in 1843.

This is not to say that you never should construct a long and complicated sentence. As I propose to say in a few minutes, there are times when we want to "write slow." The deliberately extended sentence is a device toward that end. But Charlie Hamilton's general rule is sound: Locate that interesting key on your typewriter; and then use it.

> *12. We ought not unintentionally to give offense*
> *by sexist words or phrases, but we ought not to*
> *be intimidated either.*

Over the past few decades, the sexual revolution has won revolutionary changes not only in mores, politics, and the economy, but also in the English language. In the midst of this revolution, I count myself a Tory. The kind of clumsy alchemy that converts *waitress* or *waiter* into *waitperson* strikes me as absurd. In my book, *chairman* is a common noun; it identifies an office and not the sex of the person holding it. The efforts that periodically are made to rout "sexist" terms from the Bible are a form of vandalism. The notion that *manpower* should be abolished in favor of *human resources,* which the Pentagon decreed in 1978, is a notion as feeble as the intelligence of those who persist in clinging to it.

Yet there is a case to be made for the advocates of a unisex vocabulary, and fairness demands that I state that case as well as I can. Let me borrow from an essay on "Sex and the Word" by Geraldine Hammond, a professor of English at Wichita State University. The essay appeared in the university's magazine in the fall of 1977.

"The scientific truth of the matter," she writes, "is that language not only describes but tends to limit and direct thought and attitudes as well. It is possible, therefore, to increase awareness of old limitations and of new possibilities through changes in language and language usage."

Dr. Hammond asks us to reflect upon such words as *man-hours, take it like a man*, and *separate the men from the boys*. The subtle implications suggest that the hours of a woman's work are not as important as the hours of a man's work; that women have no courage or stamina worth remarking; that women are unable to face hard challenges as men face them.

"It becomes a little more than obvious that much of our language, our terminology, and presumably our thinking is sexist. Why this is so is not as important now as why it should not be so, for sexist language has consequences—in the lives of men and boys as well as in female lives. . . .

"The exclusive and excluding use of *man, mankind*, and *the race of man* to mean all humanity not only is no longer necessary (if it ever was) but is potentially damaging in subtle ways to human value scales in our society, especially for children trying to understand how things really are. When children are struggling to understand and establish their own identities it is confusing to both girls and boys to learn, or try to learn, that when people say *man* they mean girls and women too, except, of course, when they don't."

Dr. Hammond's complaint is that when we use *men* and *man* so consistently and persistently, when alternatives are available "that are just as good or even better," we make it quite clear that our scale of human values puts women in second place.

These are rational and persuasive arguments, and all of us who practice the writing art should be sensitive to them. We ought constantly to be aware that a substantial number of our readers are offended by what they perceive as sexist slurs or put-downs. Instead of writing that "every student has an obligation to do *his* duty," we may write with equal clarity that "all students have an obligation to do *their* duty." With a little thought, and without damage to style, we can avoid many occasions of offense—and it is important that we avoid them. One of our purposes presumably is not to irritate the reader we are attempting to inform, to persuade, or to amuse. The sexual revolution surely has raised my consciousness in these matters.

But it has not raised my consciousness enough to make me write a paragraph such as this one, from a textbook on economics:

> Since the only way he or she can sell more units of the product is by lowering the price, the marginal revenue he or she receives from selling an additional unit is less than the average revenue or the price he or she receives. . . . If a monopolist had no variable costs at all, he or she could sell no units of the product. He or she could then see what happens when he or she charges successively lower prices. He or she would travel down the marginal revenue curve as he or she did this. . . .

That is bilge. It is indefensible in the name of women's liberation or anti-sexism or in any other name. Such self-conscious efforts to avoid chauvinism leap from the page; we hear the author shouting, "Look how virtuous am I!"

I venture this guess, that at least as many persons of taste and sensibility are offended by the stilted employment of *he or she* as are offended by the traditional usages of grammar and terminology. Not all women, going off to college, want to be known as *freshpersons*. (If you suppose I made that one up, kindly consult a manual prepared by Montclair, N.J., State College in 1981 "to streamline the introduction of freshpersons.") Surely many widows must wince at the thought that officially they are *surviving spouses*. The Defense Department has promulgated guidelines under which *brothers* and *sisters* would disappear from personnel records, to be replaced by *siblings*. I doubt that more than a handful of extremists would see an improvement.

I am bolstered in that view by an incident that occurred in 1979. The National Office of Fisheries, an offshoot of the Department of Commerce, became embroiled in a bitter semantic conflict. Juanita Kreps was then secretary of commerce. In a futile effort to appease the militants of that day, she decreed that henceforth *fishermen* were to be known officially as *fishers*.

It didn't take. Out on the West Coast, infuriated members of the Pacific Coast Fishermen's Wives Coalition erupted in anger. They let Ms. Kreps know, in words that gave no room for misunderstanding, that their husbands were not *fishers*, they were *fishermen*, and they were damned proud of it. The bureaucrats hauled in their sails. The offensive *fishers* sank without a trace. Today the office deals with *fishermen* and *watermen,* and if a few Tugboat Annies object, too bad. My thought is that except for a vociferous minority of militant feminists, public opinion supports the fishermen's wives.

Linguistic history stands behind the essential neutrality of *man.* Unlike other languages, which link modifiers to nouns by gender, English knows no genders. *La table* and *le livre* are *table* and *book* to us. When we speak of *mankind,* we speak of all humanity, without the slightest implication that the word applies only to the male of the species. Who is foolish enough to complain that *man does not live by bread alone* is a sexist aphorism?

Obviously some persons are that foolish, because sporadic efforts sputter along to clean up the Bible. A Methodist Task Force on Language Guidelines has proposed to wipe out *Lord* and *King* when referring to God. The word *Lord* "carries on the assumption created by other male-gender words that God has male characteristics." As for *King,* the task force would substitute *Ruler.* Under these proposed guidelines, the Ruler's Prayer would survive—but only by a divided vote: "There are those for whom *Father* in reference to God is no longer acceptable. It carries sexist connotations. Other persons, while they acknowledge that *Father* is not entirely suitable, question whether there is an adequate substitute. . . ."

For the writer, this whole business of sexist language presents a dilemma: On the one hand, he wants to write gracefully and smoothly, and not awkwardly or jerkily; on the other hand, he wants to avoid wounding the sensibilities of the waitperson faction. The dilemma is more apparent than real. When gender-neutral terms may be employed, without significant sacrifice to style, we do well to employ them. But we ought never to be so intimidated by the militants that we let our writing be wrecked on the shoals of *his/her* and *she/he.*

13. *We ought not to make mistakes in spelling.*

This final admonition is so elementary that ideally it could be left unsaid. Every editor in the land, and every personnel director, would testify that ours is not an ideal world. Americans are terrible spellers.

Part of the problem derives from the inherent disorder of our mother tongue. Other languages are neat and tidy. English is a teenager's bedroom. It is almost impossible to misspell a word in Spanish.

Swedish, Danish, and German are obedient to a few simple rules. The Italian and Turkish alphabets are orderly affairs; each of them nicely matches letters and sounds. Russian is an orthographer's delight. French is a little more difficult, for it contains some non-phonetic trickers, but these are consistent trickers; they always trick the same way.

English, by contrast, offers the reckless challenge of a poker game played with twenty-one wild cards. Our twenty-six letters express at least forty-one sounds, and according to a pair of Michigan scholars, these sounds have at least 561 spellings. Ayb Citron and Charles Kleber, the two linguists, note that the sound of *eye* can be spelled in twenty-seven ways—for example, as *aisle, sign, aye, sty, high, indict, pint,* and *seismic.* They find at least twenty ways to represent the *sh* sound of *ship: sure, issue, conscience, moustache, suspicion,* and so on. No orderly language would permit such rhymes as *chaff, calf, laugh, giraffe,* and *epitaph.* What is an immigrant to make of *plane, pain, reign,* and *champagne*? How is a child to master *brier, buyer, choir,* and *dire*?

The self-evident fact is that most of our schoolchildren never master these mysteries at all. The Wall Street Journal once quoted an executive of a major insurance company: More than 70 percent of the company's correspondence has to be retyped in order to correct errors in spelling. Courses in remedial English, concentrating on elementary spelling and grammar, are a staple part of the curriculum at every college in the country.

The lamentable thing is that the people who ought to be the best spellers—the people who write for a living—often are wretched spellers. It ought to be no trick to get proper names right. Such convenient reference works as *Who's Who in America* and the Garraty-Sternstein *Encyclopedia of American Biography* are usually close at hand, but even experienced writers often fail to use them. That venerable tycoon, statesman, and diplomat, Averell Harriman, spent eighty years wincing at the indignity of Averill. General Joseph Stilwell suffered from Stillwell throughout World War II. It's not Jeanne Kirkpatrick; the ambassador's first name is *Jeane*. The great historian was a one-*r* Morison. The great pundit was a two-*n* Lippmann. The senator from Indiana was a Beveridge; the secretary of commerce under Reagan was a Baldrige. The nineteenth-century writer was not Edgar Allen Poe, for heaven's sake. He was Edgar Allan Poe.

Many professional writers not only get careless with proper names. They also stumble over the spelling of words in common use. I discovered this at first hand a few years ago, when I was serving on the board of the Fund for Investigative Journalism. The fund exists to award modest stipends to professional journalists who need a little financial help in digging out difficult stories. The board's task is to review the applications that come in. These letters of application are formal papers, prepared with care. It is a reasonable assumption, given the nature of such competitions, that the applicants seek to make the best impression they can make.

The first batch of applications given to me for review provided a melancholy experience. One hopeful reporter came up with *similiar, knowlingly, favortish, in-laid,* and *effecting* (for affecting). Another applicant wrote of *comperability,* of things that are *comperable,* of things, indeed, that are *numberous.* He spelled the state *Louisana.* A young woman who identified herself as a graduate of a top-ranked college delivered herself of *elegible, jockying, supercede,* and *franchize.* Her story, as a matter of fact, had to do with franchises. Fourteen times she spelled it *franchize.* A middle-aged reporter from the Midwest applied for a grant to help him expose wrongdoing in the grain markets; he spelled it *commodoties* twenty-two times. In other letters of application, my eye caught *publically, volontary, dependance, occured, Hawaiin, inadvertantly,* and *curruption.* And these letters, mind you, came from professional journalists who wanted to impress us with their competence and skill.

To describe the affliction is not to prescribe a cure. Proposals for wholesale reform of English orthography have been advanced for centuries. Ben Franklin, Noah Webster, Andrew Carnegie, Theodore Roosevelt, Bertie McCormick, and George Bernard Shaw have had a go at it. Thomas Jefferson favored some plan of simplified spelling but despaired of ever seeing reforms accomplished. In a letter to John Wilson in 1813, Jefferson recalled attempts to banish the letter *d* "from the words *bridge, judge, hedge, knowledge,* etc., and to write them as we write *age, cage, sacrilege, privilege.*" Wilson had sent Jefferson the manuscript of a plan for such modest reforms as to standardize the plurals of words ending in *y* or *ey.* Jefferson thought this might be a step forward, but he sent the manuscript back:

> My opinion being requested I must give it candidly, that judging of the future by the past, I expect no better fortune to this than similar preceding propositions have experienced. It is very difficult

to persuade the great body of mankind to give up what they have once learned, and are now masters of, for something to be learned anew. Time alone insensibly wears down old habits, and produces small changes at long intervals, and to this process we must all accommodate ourselves, and be content to follow those who will not follow us. Our Anglo-Saxon ancestors had twenty ways of spelling the word "many." Ten centuries have dropped all of them and substituted that which we now use. I now return your ms. without being able . . . to encourage hope as to its effect.

If our bizarre orthography is not to be reformed, we are stuck with it and must do the best we can. The only advice I can offer my brothers and sisters (siblings?) is to cultivate an eye of uncertainty. If a word *looks* wrong, look it up. There are dictionaries specially devised for poor spellers. A little while ago, working on this chapter, I mentioned the Rutgers professor who so industriously collects euphemisms. I said he was indefatigible. The more I looked at that word, the more it looked wrong. And it was.

5   The Things We Ought to Be Doing

"We have left undone those things which we ought to have done." Few persons who write for a living, or who write merely for their own amusement or for purposes of casual correspondence, ever are wholly satisfied with their products. Looking back at our work, we almost always can see some little change—or some major change—that would have improved the composition. We recognize the deficiencies, but now the piece has been printed or the letter has been mailed. It is too late to do what we ought to have done.

These rueful reflections never can be eliminated, but they can be minimized by a firm adherence to some of the fundamental rules of the writing art. All of us know what we ought to be doing.

1. *We ought to master our tools.*

What tools? I am speaking here of those devices of prose composition that are the writer's equivalent of the carpenter's chisel and miter box. To recur to an earlier theme: Words are our building materials. The tools are what we put them together with. For simple tasks, a hammer and saw may suffice; almost anyone can nail together a string of declarative sentences. But enough has been said about writing that is simple and clear. Let us move on.

We ought to work on our *similes*. Effectively used, good similes can light up a paragraph as a smile lights up a face; the image comes alive. The first rule is that similes must be accurate. The things compared or equated have to be genuinely alike. We ought not to lead the reader around:

Hamlet: Do you see yonder cloud that's almost in shape of a camel?
Polonius: By the mass, and 'tis like a camel, indeed.
Hamlet: Methinks it is like a weasel.
Polonius: It is backed like a weasel.
Hamlet: Or like a whale?
Polonius: Very like a whale.

Shakespeare liked to see things in clouds. In *Antony and Cleopatra,* the deceived and desperate Antony speaks to Eros of the signs he has seen.

Sometimes we see a cloud that's dragonish;
A vapour sometime like a bear or lion,
A tower'd citadel, a pendent rock,
A forked mountain, or blue promontory
With trees upon't, that nod unto the world
And mock our eyes with air . . .

Good similes depend upon close observation. They depend also upon brevity and wit. William Gass, writing in The New Republic, spoke of the style of Ford Madox Ford: Themes are packed into paragraphs "like fish in tins." Ford set his scenes "in the slow deliberate way posts are sunk in concrete." Jerry Adler, reviewing a spy story for Newsweek, described 630 pages of clandestine maneuverings "as opaque as a chocolate milkshake."

A good many years ago I happened to be covering some hearings on labor racketeering. Among the witnesses who took the Fifth Amendment was one especially repulsive fellow, dressed in a suit of bilious green. He was short and fat and his vocal cords had been smoked in the gas of ten thousand cigars. I wrote that he sat at the witness table "like a frog on a lily pad, dripping hostility from hooded eyes, and repeatedly croaking 'duh privilege.'"

It struck me as a pretty good simile.

One more thing about similes: They have to fit in context. A woman's hair may be as fine as a spider's web, but the hair ought not to gum up her lover's mouth. The writer who spends a thousand purple words in rich and glorious description of an afternoon on the desert should pause before he employs a nice simile in the wrong place: "And so the sun, like a fried egg, slipped into the black skillet of the night." It's all very well to write that the sun looks like a fried egg, for sometimes the sun does look like a fried egg, but let us have the simile in a context of baking heat and toasted sand.

Metaphors are the icing on the pound cake of ordinary prose. Metaphors also are a touch of brandy in the sauce of style. A literary cook can get too heavy with the icing, or too heavy with the booze. Metaphors can be overdone, as I am overdoing this one, but used judiciously, metaphors are marvelous devices.

For the record: In the metaphoric phrase, we are not saying that something is *like* something else; we are saying it *is* the something else—icing, or brandy, or whatever. By definition (not an especially felicitous definition), a metaphor is "a figure of speech in which a word or phrase literally denoting one kind of object or idea is used in place of another to suggest a likeness or analogy between them." That definition comes from Webster's Collegiate, whose editors could think of no better example than "The ship plows the sea."

Very well. That is not the freshest metaphor ever coined, but it suffices. Speaking literally, tractors plow and horses plow; fields are plowed and gardens are plowed; but only by analogy does a ship plow the sea. Let us not labor the point.

What are the rules for using the tool of metaphor? The first rule is to keep metaphors short. Metaphors are rope-slung bridges over Andean gorges: They are fragile affairs, incapable of bearing great weight. If you ask a metaphor to carry you across a long sentence, you are likely to get flipped over the edge of folly.

Justice John Paul Stevens once took a tumble. He was concurring in *Schad* v. *Borough of Mount Ephraim*. That was the case in which the Supreme Court said a small town could not absolutely prohibit nude dancing in an "adult" bookstore in the name of property zoning. Said Justice Stevens:

> Even though the foliage of the First Amendment may cast protective shadows over some forms of nude dancing, its roots are germinated by more serious concerns that are not necessarily implicated by a content-neutral zoning ordinance banning commercial exploitation of live entertainment.

Justice Stevens is capable of writing some snappy stuff, but here he lost his point in the foliage, the shadows, the roots, and the germination.

Here is a more egregious example of the disasters that result when a metaphor is too long extended. It comes from a speech by a lobbyist for the coal industry:

The steam coal explosion of the past three years is witness that the American ship of state is traveling in new energy waters. We are riding the crest of a new energy tide which already is lapping at the shores of Europe and steadily rising toward those of the Pacific Rim nations. Over the past 10 years, the peoples of the free world have been little more than passengers on an energy ship set adrift in the ever-changing currents of OPEC pricing and production decisions. These days soon can be at an end if we fire our energy ship with American coal—if we join together and keep a steady hand on the energy policy helm. For with expanding coal markets overseas, we have the choice of charting a new and more certain energy, economic and political course, leaving the oil crisis far behind in our wake.

Sunk! Sunk! Sunk!

The first rule is to keep our metaphors short. The second is to keep our metaphors internally consistent. If we fail to sustain a metaphor, we get into what has been termed a mixaphor. Thus, in Jacksonville, an editorial writer found that Florida's system of criminal justice "is bogged down by a stranglehold of delays and logjams." The Washington Post once gave us a vivid description of the president's budget director: "Stockman's high-wire performance, conducted at a hectic pace hip deep in leaks that gave him political soundings as he progressed . . ." A television newscaster: "The mayor has proposed yet another tack to add money to the city's sagging coffers." I happened to be in California on election night in 1976, when conservative Republican S.I. Hayakawa had been elected to the Senate and liberal Democrat Ron Dellums had been re-elected to the House. A local TV announcer provided a fascinating vision: "California voters," he said confidently, "have today dipped their toes into a mixed bag." Maybe California breeds the mixaphor. Former Governor Jerry Brown once was quoted in the San Francisco Chronicle with a lively criticism of President Carter: "The president has been riding the waves of his current saber-rattling, but his balloon is about to be deflated."

These blunders happen everywhere. In New Jersey, a sportscaster once reported that when it came to their first draft choice, "the Patriots are playing their decision close to the vest right down to the wire." A thoughtful politician had some sound advice for his fellow Democrats: "If the Democratic party would put its shoulder to the wheel, we could get it off the launching pad.'' The Associated Press recalled ''the sick stock market of 1977 which reached an unpleasant milestone with the Dow-Jones industrial average teetering at the 800 level for the first time in more than two years.'' Lawrence Harrison, who served in the State Department in the early 1970s, collected these things: ''He threw a cold shoulder on that idea. . . . He deals out of both ends of his mouth. . . . Let's do it and listen to how the shoe pinches. . . . He's trying to get his foot in the tent. . . . This project is going to pot in a hand basket. . . . The issue is on the back burner in a holding pattern.''

In these instances, the metaphors collapsed from the weight of the clichés in which they were fashioned: *strangleholds, logjams, high wires, dipped toes, rattling sabers, mixed bags, milestones, launching pads, cold shoulders, back burners* and *holding patterns*. So the third rule for metaphors is to make them like breakfast biscuits, fresh every morning. Forget that steady hand at the helm of the ship of state. If we can find nothing fresher than that, let us write, ''The president seemed in firm control of his budget bill,'' and let it go at that. But we ought to keep trying at metaphors. When we fail even to try, we are leaving a thing undone that we ought to have done.

Here is a third device in our tool box, the device of *repetition*. I am not talking now about repetition to avoid a foolish effect, as in the case of the fellow at the Times who wrote *oil* three times and then called it the *lucrative liquid*. I am talking about repetition for deliberate effect. It can be a formidable tool.

Over a long lifetime, I have wondered, how many speeches will a reporter hear? The mind boggles. In person, on the tube, or on recordings, a journalist will listen to thousands. Only a handful are truly memorable, and in each of them we hear the device of repetition. Do you remember Churchill at the onset of war? ''We shall fight on the seas and oceans . . . we shall fight on the beaches, we shall fight on the landing grounds, we shall fight in the fields and in the streets, we shall fight in the hills; we shall never surrender.'' Douglas MacArthur's farewell at West Point turned on his invocation to ''the corps . . . the corps . . . the corps.'' Martin Luther King, Jr., was a master of the art.

The greatest speech I ever heard was delivered by Charles Malik, former president of the United Nations, before a small audience in the reconstructed colonial capitol at Williamsburg. This was late on a perfect afternoon of June 1960, with the sun sending shafts of dusty light into the shadowy room. Malik's grand theme was the life-and-death struggle between international communism and the Western world. What would be the outcome of that struggle? On the debit side, he said, we must face a series of depressing facts.

> Communism started from zero forty-three years ago and today it rigidly controls one-third of mankind and has penetrated and softened up in varying degrees the remaining two-thirds: *was this phenomenal development inevitable?* The victory of Communism in the late forties in China means that the largest compactly homogeneous mass of humanity, numbering some 600 million people, are now sworn enemies of everything free and Western: *was this development inevitable?* The Korean War, despite all its heroic exertions, ended in a draw: *was this outcome inevitable?* In Southeast Asia there has occurred during the last ten years an advance of Communism and a retreat of freedom: *was this advance and retreat inevitable?* Whereas international Communism was effectively absent from the Middle East ten or fifteen years ago, and in the consideration of Middle-Eastern problems Communism was treated as though it did not exist, international Communism enters decisively today into the determination of every Middle-Eastern problem: *was this development inevitable?* Whereas ten or fifteen years ago Communism was effectively absent from Latin America, today it is visibly present: *was this development inevitable?* The Communist Party, receiving orders directly from Moscow, is certainly more active and influential today in Asia and Africa than ten years ago, and several responsible United States officials said recently that the Communists have markedly intensified their activity in the United States: *was this penetration inevitable?*

Malik hammered that word *inevitable* into our heads as if he were driving railway spikes. Granted, this was a speech, not an essay, but the principle is the same. I remember an editorial in the midst of the war in Vietnam, though I cannot cite the publication, in which each sober paragraph of a grim recital ended with a single question: *Is it worth it?* It was a marvelously effective device.

Beware the tool of *alliteration*. It must be used with extreme care. If we put it purposely to work in every paragraph of our prose, we probably will not prompt our patient readers into palpably protracted panegyrics. Keep in mind that two things are going on whenever we read: We are seeing the words with our eyes; we also are hearing them subconsciously through our inner ears. This is what a musician does when he is reading, but not actually playing, a score: He reads the notes in silence, but he hears the sound in his head. Used softly and subtly, and without calling attention to itself, alliteration often can lend vitality to a humdrum passage. We ought to use this tool more often than we do.

The same suggestion applies to the device of *onomatopoeia*. It is like one of a woodcarver's tiny gouges; the occasions for its use are few, but its usefulness belies the infrequency. If our bells do not merely *ring*—if they *clamor, clatter, jangle, tingle,* or *tinkle*—we may add a vivid touch. Our language has loud words and soft words; it has words to convey the shrillness of a siren, the racket of a jackhammer, the swish of a quiet surf. But here again, as in every other instance, the rule for onomatopoeia has to be obeyed: Listen *intently,* and do not fake it. Sometimes an axe, cutting into a tree, goes *thud;* sometimes it goes *whack;* it depends upon the sharpness of the axe, the kind of tree being cut, the skill of the woodsman, and the heaviness of the air. In our house we have two wind-up clocks. One goes *plink,* the other goes *bong.* If our purpose is to transcribe sound, or to evoke the memory of sound, let us go at the task with care—but let us try.

Back in Chapter 3, in speaking of the style of Gibbon, Macaulay, and Burke, I touched upon the uses of *antithesis.* Let me return to the topic here. It is among the most effective devices of prose style. Skillfully employed, a touch of antithesis impinges on the ear with the same solid satisfaction that one gets from hitting a clean forehand or closing the door of a Mercedes-Benz.

Webster's defines antithesis as ''the rhetorical contrast of ideas by means of parallel arrangements of words, clauses, or sentences.'' Technically speaking, the element of contrast ought always to be present, but less precisely, the art of antithesis is the art of parallel construction in a compact form.

Familiar examples spring to mind from the world of politics. All of us will recall John F. Kennedy's inaugural: ''Ask not what your country can do for you, but what you can do for your country.'' Many of us will remember the explosion that followed Barry Goldwater's famous line at the Republican convention of 1964: ''Extremism in the defense of liberty is no vice! Moderation in the pursuit of justice is no virtue!'' There was John Mitchell's gung-ho slogan: ''When the going gets tough, the tough get going.''

The translators of the King James Bible delighted in antithesis: ''The harvest truly is plenteous, but the laborers are few." . . . "He that findeth his life shall lose it, and he that loseth his life for my sake shall find it." . . . "What God hath joined together, let no man put asunder." . . . "Render therefore unto Caesar the things which are Caesar's; and unto God the things that are God's."

My own nominee for the greatest contemporary master of antithesis would be G.K. Chesterton (1874-1936). Not long ago I came across his brief biography of Robert Browning and counted fourteen neat sentences in the first fifty pages. These are instructive examples:

On Browning: "His work has the mystery which belongs to the complex; his life the much greater mystery which belongs to the simple."

"His intellect went upon bewildering voyages, but his soul walked in a straight road."

"He was not unintelligible because he was proud, but unintelligible because he was humble."

"He was not vain of being an extraordinary man. He was only somewhat excessively vain of being an ordinary one."

"With him, as with all others, the great paradox and the great definition of life was this, that the ambition narrows as the mind expands."

On "Pippa Passes": "A man's good work is effected by doing what he does, a woman's by being what she is."

On the difficulties of producing a play based upon the lives of Charles I and Mary Queen of Scots: "Within the minute limits of a stage there is room for their small virtues and no room for their enormous crimes."

On medieval philosophers: "It is not only true that they never discovered the steam engine; it is quite equally true that they never tried."

Notice, if you will, the balance in the contrasting clauses: "Not only true" is balanced against "quite equally true." "Small virtues" carries the same weight as "enormous crimes." Verbs match verbs, adjectives match adjectives. Try your hand, and improve your style.

Now and then a touch of irony may add a spark of life to a passage we are working on. One of the devices toward this end is the *oxymoron*. It comes out of the Greek for pointedly foolish. It is "a combination of contradictory or incongruous words." The usual example is *cruel kindness*.

In 1983 National Review entertained submissions from aficionados of the oxymoron. Some lovely entries came in. One was from a professor on leave, whose title was *professor in residence in absentia.* Another contestant proposed *covert aid to Nicaragua.* A third offered *efficient bureaucracy.* My own favorite was *common sense.* Actress Ali McGraw turned up in Washington for a promotional appearance, but alas, she had left her regular hairdresser behind and had to draft a local fellow to get her properly coiffed. The press asked the fellow what style he had contrived. "Elegant messy," he said.

The nation's capital has fostered a couple of oxymoronic phrases. One is *negative support,* which is what Jimmy Carter had a good deal of in 1980. Another is *negative income,* which means *loss.* The 1983 arms control talks produced the *build-down.* From the Greenville (S.C.) *News,* a reader clipped a story having to do with a fusion test reactor: "Pessimists wonder if the technology will ever be mastered in a way that will be expensive enough to use commercially."

I suspect that last example is a poor one, because oxymorons ought to be deliberate and not accidental. They are jack-in-the-boxes that pop out of our prose, grinning and bobbing. They add a touch of surprise, sometimes a touch of mordant wit. They are good fun. We ought to do more with them.

Some of my more pedantic correspondents quarrel with me on the propriety of this last device: They mistakenly suppose that the rules of grammar forbid the *sentence fragment.* Humbug. Nonsense. No way. Our purpose in writing is to convey thought. No rule says that thought *always* must be conveyed on the parlor cars of a proper subject and a proper predicate. There are times, especially when you have subjected your readers to a string of long and complex sentences, sorely taxing their concentration, when a sentence fragment comes as a welcome relief. No fooling. Like other tools in the box, it is a device to be used sparingly and in keeping with the tone of a composition. If we are being light and sprightly, a sentence fragment can bounce into a paragraph as prettily as a child's balloon. If we are composing a Letter to the Shareholders, it's probably better to stay sober.

2. We ought to pay more attention to cadence.

Some years ago I lectured on the writing art at a journalism school down South. I have forgotten which one, or I would tell you. A month before the engagement I invited the students, if they wished, to let me have two samples of their work. I asked for (1) an editorial on some contemporary topic of their choice, and (2) a sonnet on the love affair between Richard Burton and Elizabeth Taylor.

To my sorrow, a mere handful of students accepted the invitation. Several of them sent editorials only, along with apologetic notes: "I'm no good at writing poetry." The few sonnets that arrived were mostly dreadful, and the editorials that accompanied them were lackluster also.

But I recall one sonnet that fairly burbled with passion. Burton and Taylor were "like two moths consumed in common flame." The sonnet was properly rhymed. All the feet were in step. The poem had a beginning; it also had an ending. I turned to the student's companion piece, and aha! The editorial was great. Excelsior! I cried, or something to that effect: *This girl can write.*

I tell the tale by way of suggesting to all of you who want to write: Write verse. It is the finest discipline ever devised for writers who would hone their skills with language. Mind you, I am not talking about writing free verse. It was Robert Frost who once defined free verse as playing tennis with the net down. Free verse is to prosody as drip-and-dribble is to painting. I am not even talking about blank verse—unrhymed iambic pentameters—though this would be better than nothing.

I am talking about verse that adheres to precise and familiar patterns of rhyme and meter—limericks, if you cannot think of a form more interesting; or sonnets, or rondeaux, or quatrains in the fashion of Housman, or odes in the fashion of Horace. Try the Japanese haiku, if you would learn to detect a single syllable out of place. I used to fill yellow tablets with ballads that imitated the works of Robert W. Service: "The chamber stills as a man named Mills strides to the center aisle." It was doggerel, not poetry, but we learn even from the writing of doggerel.

The best writing—the writing that is quotable, that zings and stings and packs a wallop—depends on many elements. It depends on having something to say and on saying it clearly; it depends upon fresh metaphors and lively similes, and of course the grammar and syntax and spelling have to be right. But when all those elements have been raked and weeded and watered, our prose gardens demand something more: *cadence.*

We ought never to be embarrassed, in the privacy of our chambers, to "sound out" a sentence. Fingers were made to count feet. As Barbara Tuchman has said, "An essential element for good writing is a good ear: One must listen to the sound of one's own prose." If a sentence lacks cadence, the sentence collapses like an overcooked soufflé.

Let me try to describe how we search for cadence. The example that follows most certainly is not offered as an example of deathless prose. I offer it solely for the purpose of demonstrating how an opening paragraph is crafted. It was close to Christmas, some years ago, and I wanted a column keyed to a festive holiday. It snowed, and it occurred to me simply to write about the snow. I began a first draft along these lines:

> The first snow of the winter began falling a little before 2 o'clock on the morning of Sunday the 16th. By Colorado's standards it was no snow at all—three inches, maybe four—but a brisk wind made scallops of whipped cream and we awoke on Monday to brilliant sunshine, snowbound in beauty.

It wasn't right. It had the air of understatement that I wanted, but the two sentences didn't pull well together. Besides, I wanted to get into a particular metaphor, and I wanted this in my first paragraph.

> The snow that fell on Rappahannock County Sunday night was typical of those that come our way. It was no big deal.

This was better. Now I had the iambic cadence going. I changed *those* to *snows,* to gain the advantage of alliteration, and kept going.

> In Boston or in Boulder it would have been no snow at all.

That alliteration was forced; it was too obvious. Boston and Boulder would not do. The *no snow at all* followed too closely upon *no big deal.* I liked the *It was no big deal* because it broke an iambic rhythm that might get sing-songy if I didn't watch. Forget Boston and Boulder.

> The snow that fell on Rappahannock County Sunday night was typical of snows that come our way. It was no big deal. It began a little after two, borne by a hard north wind. It slacked; at dawn it stopped, and magically a canopy of clouds gave way to brilliant sunshine. We awoke to a wedding-cake morning.

Still not right. In the last sentence I had shifted from iambic to dactylic. The *brilliant sunshine* wasn't fresh.

> The snow that fell on Rappahannock County Sunday night was typical of most December snows that come our way. It was no big deal. The storm began a little after two, borne by hard north winds.

At four it slacked; at dawn it stopped. A bright sun pulled its way across the eastern ridge, and we awoke to find the farm a wedding cake.

The garden's wall of stone had disappeared, lost in mounds of icing. The cutting stump was frosted like a petit four. At the crest of White Walnut Hill, in white mustache and dark and formal posts, the summer house stood like a stiff and aging groom. . . ."

And so on. In the final draft I got rid of *petit four,* citing the rule against unfamiliar words, and I replaced the alliteration of *four* and *frosted* with a *c*-alliteration: *The cutting stump, cake-frosted, stood with firewood cookies.* This gave me two *stoods* butting heads; one had to go. *The cutting stump, cake-frosted, shared its plate*—no, too much, the metaphor is getting out of hand—*shared its place with chips of firewood cookies.*

Let it go. Nothing immortal here, but I believe the piece improved with each recasting. It gained *cadence.* The first draft had lacked that quality altogether: *The first snow of the winter began falling a little before 2 o'clock on the morning of Sunday the 16th.* That was a perfectly okay sentence; nothing was wrong with it syntactically. But the rewritten sentence began to tap iambic feet, and if you were to complain that I changed *a little before 2 o'clock* to *a little after two,* I would respond by saying that *after* gave me an accented syllable where I needed one, and this wasn't a meteorological essay anyhow.

Everett Allen, a venerable New England editor who is known in newspapering as "the iambic man," once described his gentle art to the National Conference of Editorial Writers. Cadence, he remarked, isn't a province of "pretty writing" only. It is just as easy to write from City Hall, *The mayor cast the lone dissenting vote* as it is to write, *The mayor cast the only dissenting vote.* The meanings are identical, but *lone* falls more trippingly upon the ear than *only.*

A word of caution: Deliberate resort to cadence can be overdone, of course, as any other device of composition can be overworked. Too much of *ta-DUM, ta-DUM, ta-DUM* gets to be a bore. But ordinarily the fault lies in the other direction. So practice on poems. Most of them will be awful—I know, because you send them to me—but even the awful ones will help you on the way to better prose.

> *3. We ought to pay closer attention to the arrange-*
> *ment of our words and clauses.*

In the summer of 1968 William F. Buckley, Jr., wrote a long piece for Esquire about "The Politics of Assassination." This was his lead paragraph:

> Robert F. Kennedy had a way of saying things loosely, and it may be that that is among the reasons why so many people invested so much idealism in him, it being in the idealistic (as distinguished from the analytical) mode to make large and good-sounding generalities, like the generality he spoke on April 5 after the assassination of Martin Luther King, two months exactly before his own assassination.

That paragraph drew a raspberry from Bill's close friend, Professor Hugh Kenner of Johns Hopkins, who sent him a note chiding him for "filigree syntax." Kenner agreed that the sentence parses, "to say which is to say that a chicken coop does not collapse," but he commented that it "resembles less a tensioned intricacy in the mode of M. Eiffel than it does a toddler's first efforts with Tinkertoy."

Bill thought it over. He still liked his lead. He queried Kenner: "Surely you are wrong about that lead sentence? I reread it, found it springy and tight."

The ensuing correspondence between these two writers has achieved a classic status. Bill has permitted me to reprint it here, with the elision of a few passages that were clear enough then but may not be clear now. This was their disputation:

HK to WFB:
"Springy and tight" my foot. Those aren't springs, they're bits of Scotch tape. Have your syntactic DNA checked for mutations; it just isn't governing the wild forces of growth as of yore.

WFB to HK:
Come on, now, you are a goddam professor of English, so stop name calling and get to work. . . ."

HK to WFB:
. . . Okay, that sentence:
One way of putting the problem is that it's not discernibly heading anywhere; it ambles along, stuffing more and more odds &

ends into its elastic bag, until it simply decides to sit down. . . .

I revert to the concept: something, something corresponding to tension and relaxation, to the turn of the key and the swing of the door, to departure from and return to the tonic, makes us willing to accept the necessity of a long sentence being one sentence and not three spliced by mispunctuation.

Back to the exhibit: if there were a period after "loosely" no one would feel that a flight had been arrested in midcourse. Or after "him," or after "generalities." I think one test of the long sentence is that if it's stopped before it's over the reader should sense the incompleteness. This is sometimes a matter of formal grammar: if we start with "because" the reader won't accept a full stop until he's been accorded a principal clause. It's sometimes just a matter of promising in the opening words or by the opening cadence (a device of Gibbon's) some amplitude of concern the reader expects to see implemented. But here the offer to develop the proposition that RFK had a way of saying things loosely creates no syntactic expectation because it's capable of standing as a sentence by itself; nor does it retrospectively command the rest of the sentence, because the sentence has managed to end not with an amplification of RFK's looseness but with a triplicated irrelevancy about the date.

"Robert F. Kennedy had a way of saying things loosely: large and good-sounding generalities which being in the idealistic (as distinguished from the analytical) mode help explain why so many people invested so much idealism in him—generalities like the one Martin Luther King's assassination prompted him to utter on April 5, just two months, as it happened, before he was assassinated himself."

A possible improvement, if one *must* include all those components. The main difference is that by putting the colon after "loosely" one gives notice that the opening clause will preside over the remainder, not simply join to the next section of track. Then, repeat of "generalities" to hitch the peroration to the second member. And rearrangement of terminal items keeps the mention of King and l'affaire Sirhan from sounding like doodles irrelevantly prompted by "April 5." I do not offer the improved version as anything but an exercise; I wasn't writing the article and haven't in my blood the points you anticipated making, so all I can manage is a piece of engineering. . . .

In my suggested version I've avoided "that that," "reasons why" (your ear had told you to eschew yet a third "that"), and "it being." These all have rhetorical uses, as colloquialisms bounced off girders, but strung along in a row like old peanut shells they suggest WFB just plain improvising while he awaits a glimpse of daylight, and suggest to les Dwight Macdonalds that the Scrambled Egghead Method is to talk till one figures out what one is saying. This method is of course frequently necessary, and inoffensive, viva voce, say on TV, but its appearance should be avoided in print.

WFB to HK:

. . . I worry about that confounded sentence, as one worries upon failing to appreciate something which one is prepared to postulate as good, to wit your criticism of it. I shan't even apologize for belaboring the point, because I know that you will know that by talking back, I am proving that I have not put you to such inconvenience merely for my own amusement.

"Robert Kennedy had a way of saying things loosely" followed by the colon you suggest means to me that I am about to demonstrate my allegation, or give an example of it. Followed by a period, the lilt of the sentence is, it seems to me, self-consciously dramatic, as in "John F. Kennedy had a way of seducing women." Followed by a comma, I thought it to be leading rather gradually to a point I did not want for a while yet, until the mood set in, to crystallize: whence, *"and it may be that that is among the reasons why so many people invested so much idealism in him"*—again, if the period had come here, I'd have attempted, or so it strikes me, a stolen base, and the reader would have been annoyed by the intimation that I have proved my point; or that I infer that the reader will merely permit me to asseverate it. When, i.e., by way of further explanation, begging the reader's indulgence so to speak, *"it being in the idealistic (as distinguished from the analytical) mode to make large and good-sounding generalities"*—department of amplification, not without— yet—the example I am about to furnish, and spend several hundred words confuting, *"like the generality he spoke on April 5, after the assassination of Martin Luther King"* surely writing about what Kennedy said about another man's assassination a few days after Kennedy's own assassination (which is when I wrote this article), gives a certain spooky suspense, which is ratified, Robert-Louis-Stevenson-wise, with the adverbial clause, *"two months exactly*

before his own assassination. " That last I take to be a fair substitute for "two months exactly, as it happened, before his own assassination." Seems to me that, although the sentence is long it is not impossibly long, and that although the commas appear somehow to be loose and thoughtless linkages they are justified by their meiotic contribution to the plot I am contriving. Hell, it merely disturbs me that while I *understand* your generic points, my ear does not grant them a preemptive relevance in this instance; and I repeat that I worry because undoubtedly you are right and I wrong. Anyway, I shall remember the generic advice. Believe. Me. Pal.

HK to WFB:

. . . Not to wrangle, I'd make a final suggestion: that your inability to relate my comments, which you follow, to the sentence, the intentions of which you expound convincingly, is perhaps based on this, that you're not reading the printed sentence but hearing yourself speak it. By pause, by suspension, by inflection, by variation of tone and pace, you could make the "little plot" you speak of sing. The written language provides no notation for such controls, and your intention as graphed by printed words leaves the reader too much to supply, and too many options for supplying the wrong tacit commentary, e.g., that WFB is standing in an open space scattering peanut shells.

We have no such public style as Pope could posit, and vary from minutely, in an aesthetic of microscopic inappropriatenesses. We have instead the convention that the writer creates his operating conventions de novo. "Robert Kennedy had a way of saying things loosely." Followed by a hypothetical period, you say, its lilt is self-consciously dramatic. Yes, but those are the very first words of a long essay; we are just tuning in to station WFB; his eschewal of the self-consciously dramatic is not yet an operative principle; and one of the options open to us is to suppose that a dramatic opening was intended but muffed by a fault of punctuation. I think your rebuttal to my statement that the sentence could be terminated by a period at several points without creating a sense of incompleteness consists in an appeal to nuances of taste: it would make nuanced differences to cut it off here or here. So it would. But the reader hasn't yet a feel for the governing structure of taste in the piece before him. *Especially* in an opening, the reader would be well served by a syntactic tension, as inevitable as gravitation on an included plane, which makes it essential that the sentence incorporate, as it proceeds, the members it does, or else fall down. . . . *Mais passons.*

Unrepentant, Bill inquired of readers of National Review, *Who's right?* Kenner was right; of course he was right. My beloved brother Buckley had created syntactical pasta, and as Kenner observed, spaghetti should be cut into shorter sentences where natural stopping places occur. It is not necessary that *all* our sentences be bite-sized; we can take into our hands a sentence as gooey as a cheese and pepperoni pizza, and chew the mess with some degree of pleasure, but the rule is sound: Let us arrange our words and clauses as tidily as so many knives and forks in the silver drawer, so that they will be where we expect them to be. In any event, I reprint the Kenner-Buckley exchange mainly to suggest how good writers—writers who dearly love the language—can find so much fun in the parsing of a single sentence.

Failure to guard against misarrangement can lead to trouble. From The Birmingham News: "Mrs. Pardue finally learned from one of the wives of a man at her husband's company that the Mountain Brook schools were closed." . . . From United Press International: "A Common Pleas jury also convicted Cecilia M_____, 45, of conspiracy on Saturday." . . . One of my readers often wonders why so many persons in the news have names taken from days of the week: "Harriet Jones Wednesday signed a contract." . . . "Robert Medley Friday was named vice president."

On this matter of arrangement, one more word might be said about two shibboleths. The notion that infinitives *never* should be split is a notion that ought to be discarded, but I persist in believing that the parts of a verb ought never to be separated needlessly. The notion that we ought *never* to end a sentence with a preposition is a notion that had no merit to begin with; it is far better to write that *We will see what the Congress comes up with* than to fall into the contortions of *We will see up with what the Congress comes.*

We have talked before about the bad business identified as the noun modifier proliferation phenomenon. Let me return to the topic by recalling one of the most remarkable men I ever met, Douglas Southall Freeman. He is best remembered as a biographer; in his works on Lee and Washington he left standards of scholarship for other historians to steer by, but I knew him in the 1940s when he was the editor of The Richmond (Va.) News Leader and I was a general reporter. Dr. Freeman was a meticulous writer—not an especially graceful or felicitous writer, for his sentences often rolled with the sound of tumbrels rumbling—but he took his writing seriously. In the 1920s he prescribed "The News Leader's Fundamental Rules of News Writing." I have excerpted ten of them that are as sound today as they were when Dr. Freeman handed them down from his editorial Sinai more than sixty years ago:

(1) Shun the employment of nouns as adjectives; it is the lowest form of careless English. There always are better ways to condense than to pile up nouns before a noun and pretend they are adjectives.

(2) Do not change subject in the middle of the sentence unless there is (a) definite antithesis or (b) no possible way of avoiding the change of subject. If you must change subject, always insert a comma at the end of the clause that precedes the one in which you make the change.

(3) Do not end sentences with participial phrases. Beware such sentences as, "The Mayor refused to discuss the subject, *saying* it was one for consideration of the Council."

(4) Do not change the voice of a verb in the middle of a sentence. If you start with an active voice, keep it active. It is sloppy to say, "He went to Hopewell and was met by . . ."

(5) Seek to leave the meaning of the sentence incomplete until the last word. Add nothing after the meaning is complete. Start a new sentence then.

(6) Make every antecedent plain: Never permit "it" or "that" or any similar word to refer to different things in the same sentence.

(7) When you write a clause beginning with *which,* do not follow it with one that begins *and which.* Never write a sentence such as, "The ordinance which was considered by the finance committee and which was recommended to the Council," etc.

(8) In sentences where several nouns, phrases or clauses depend on the same verb, put the longer phrase or clause *last.* For instance, do not say, "He addressed the General Assembly, the members of the Corporation Commission, and the Governor."

(9) In conditional sentences, seek to put the conditional clause *before* the principal clause. An *if* clause at the beginning of a sentence is better placed than at the end, unless the whole point of the sentence lies in the *if*

(10) Try to end every story with a strong and, if possible, a short sentence.

Violation of Freeman's Rule One can cause serious damage. "The city hall has a soccer-field-sized conference hall." . . . "There is a tendency to cast opponents of public school sex education into the same bag as book-burners, creationists and religion-in-school advocates." Surely the former sentence could better have been recast to read, *a conference hall the size of a soccer field.* To my eye and ear, the latter could have been improved: *There is a tendency to cast opponents of sex education in the public schools into the same bag with book-burners, creationists, and advocates of religion in the schools.*

Notice the dividend that is achieved by such a rearrangement: We benefit from the effects of Freeman's Rule Ten. We get a strong ending to the sentences. We end one sentence with *field,* which has a long vowel and a good post-dental stop; this surely is better than ending the sentence with *field-sized conference hall.* We end the other sentence with the short word *schools;* this surely is better than *religion-in-school advocates.*

In the journalism schools, the professors teach the writing of leads, and good leads of course are important: If you do not capture your reader's eye with your opening sentence, all your wit will have been wasted thereafter. The reader's eye will have wandered away. But I wish the same emphasis put upon writing leads were put on the writing of crackers also. In any piece of writing—and especially in a short piece of writing—the last sentence is at least as important as the first. A good cracker has the snap of a mousetrap. It sums up. It makes a final point. Then it stops. I like to end my own stuff, when feasible, with an accented word or syllable that contains a strong vowel or diphthong. These are not the best examples, for they breathe too heavily, but they will make the point: "Action must be taken, and action must be taken *now.*" . . . "The deficits must come *down.*" . . . "In their indifference to the consequences, the Soviets play with *fire.*" On my desk as I write are a couple of copies of The Wall Street Journal. It is not by accident, but by design, that the four editorials in the two editions end with *life, flow, vice,* and *days.* Bill Polk, a great North Carolina editor, once said that no self-respecting bee would sit down without leaving a sting. He was right.

*4. We ought to keep in mind that words have
nuances; words carry connotations, and words
that may be appropriate in one context may not
be appropriate in another. We ought constantly to
search for the right word.*

A long time ago, when I was struggling through my fourth year of
college French, I asked a woeful question of the Parisian woman who
was then serving as our visiting professor: How long would it take me to
learn to speak French "like a native"?

She was too kindhearted to say that with my Southern accent I never
on this earth would learn to speak French like a native, but her answer
was to this effect: Anyone can learn the conjugation of irregular verbs;
anyone can master the mechanics of inflection; anyone, with hard work,
can unravel the French subjunctive. But it would take a lifetime, she
said, for me to grasp the nuances of her beautiful language.

"Zee shades of meaning," she added. "Zat ees what makes zee
deefairahnce."

Shades of meaning matter greatly in every language. Let me take
Fernald's *Handbook of Synonyms* from the shelf, and let it fall open at
random to the entries under *encourage*. Among the listed synonyms are
*animate, arouse, cheer, embolden, excite, hearten, inspire, promote,
reassure*, and *stimulate*. I will let the handbook fall open again, this time
to *inquire*. Among the synonyms: *ask, examine, interrogate, investigate, question*. It is apparent at a glance, which is why we glance so
frequently at Fernald, that the suggested synonyms cover a wide range.
To encourage a young writer is not necessarily to arouse him; to inquire
of a telephone operator is not to interrogate the operator.

Words move restlessly in penumbras of meaning. Let us suppose that
a young lady has gone to a wedding reception. She happens to dislike
champagne, but she wishes to be well-mannered. Thus she exclaims
with every appearance of enthusiasm over the champagne put before her.
This is a *pretense*. Let us see what Fernald offers as synonyms: *affecta-
tion, assumption, cloak, color, disguise, excuse, mask, pretension, ruse,
seeming, subterfuge, trick*, and *wile*.

None of the synonyms fits exactly. The young lady's effort surely was
no *trick* or *wile*; it was not an *excuse* or a *mask*. How about *sham?* Or *put-
on?* We must keep looking for the right word until we find it.

A gentlewoman in Dunkirk, Ohio, once inquired of me about

remember, recall, and *recollect:* Any difference? I'm not at all sure I provided a correct answer, for I doubted I could identify the nuances. I think I would *remember* when I fell in love; I would *recall* the vote on a tax bill; and I would *recollect* where I filed the bank statements.

In the spring of 1983 an overblown controversy arose about a manifesto of the Catholic bishops. For days the clerics wrangled over a single word: Should the U.S. government be urged to *halt* or to *curb* the deployment of nuclear arms? Now, *to curb* means *to restrain* or *to control,* and *to halt* means *to stop,* but manifestly a halting is also a curbing. In the end, the manifesto was so long that almost no one but the printers and theologian Michael Novak read the whole of it, but I recall the incident to make a useful point: We ought to pray incessantly over the *right* word.

I am not speaking here of the embarrassment that accompanies the dropping of an infield fly. John Connally of Texas, a first-rate orator, once looked back sadly on the days before Vietnam: "In the early sixties," he said, "we were strong, we were virulent." Washington's greatest morning daily once explained that Ambassador Habib's mission was to diffuse tensions in the Middle East. That wry logomachist, J.T. Harding, collects such specimens in his monthly Editor's Revenge: Here we meet the railroad magnet Cornelius Vanderbilt, the squads of police in plane clothes, the bails of marijuana that are seized, the woman who had her arm strapped to her waste. In Florida, a fireside cook clacks long metal tongues around fat oysters. At a restored castle, rushes are spread upon stone floors to cut down on chill blains, which doubtless are more uncomfortable than warm blains. Whether these are true malapropisms or merely misspellings, they are no more than irresistible digressions from the thought at hand.

Let me get back to the thought at hand. Many words have nuances that we comprehend more by osmosis than by conscious effort. Almost any interest in politics is by definition a special interest; there's nothing "special" about the interests of labor or business or the medical profession. But when we write of a senator who is in league with the *special interests,* we have put a little spin on the ball. The linkage carries a pejorative connotation. In diplomacy, "to make concessions" carries one connotation; *to appease* carries another. One nuance darkens *union boss,* another lightens *union leader.* In the vocabulary of desegregation we come across *forced busing* and *court-ordered busing,* and to the extent that a court may compel obedience to its orders, the two phrases may appear to mean the same thing; but they have different connotations abroad, and they are not the same thing.

Back to the Catholic bishops. When they had finished their revisions of a first draft, they informed the press that "certain sections have been nuanced differently." Webster's III sanctions *nuance* as a transitive verb, but American Heritage, Random House, and the OED do not. The word comes out of the root for *cloud,* and we see the meaning throughout the afternoons of summer—black clouds, white clouds, thunderclouds, and fluffy clouds. They differently affect the very air, and they cast different shadows on the land below. So it is with language. As a young reporter in Virginia I learned quickly to distinguish the friends and enemies of Senator Harry F. Byrd, Sr. To the senator's friends, it was "the Byrd Organization." To his enemies, it was "the Byrd Machine."

As we go word-hunting across the heaths of language, it often is not sufficient to hunt merely for the *right* word or even for the *exact* word. Good writers also keep in mind the *appropriate* word. Let me repeat this admonition, because it is vital to a mastery of effective communication: We ought to keep a steady eye on the audience we are addressing. Slang has its place; idiom has its place; the easygoing colloquialism has its place, and even profanity has its place, but their places are not always the same places. If we mean to shock our audience, or to offend sensibilities, by all means let us have at it; but let us shock deliberately; let us offend knowingly. Bess Truman had a friend, so the story goes, who wished Harry would clean up his act. Couldn't he be persuaded to say *fertilizer* instead of *manure?* "My dear," Mrs. Truman is said to have said, "you have no idea how long it took me to get him to say manure." The element of taste is important. Keep it in mind.

Another kind of inappropriateness should concern us. The Washington Post's garden columnist once wrote about the clematis. He delighted in watching "this graceful little creature as it waddles up a white post on the front porch." *Waddles?* A sportswriter said of admiring fans that they *girdled* the winning quarterback, by which he meant that the fans pressed tightly around him, but *girdled* was not the word he wanted. Even the most skilled writers can err in this regard. Annie Dillard, in *Pilgrim at Tinker Creek,* turned out a naturalist's book of poetry in prose, but she had a way of breaking her mood with the intrusion of the word *pizzazz:* "The Creator loves pizzazz. . . . The point of goldfish is pizzazz. . . . The landscape of the world is given with pizzazz. . . ." It was as if a beautiful woman, immaculately gowned, superbly coiffed, subtly scented, suddenly had belched.

If we are to cultivate the use of words that are right words, exact words, appropriate words, we must use all the help at our command. A good thesaurus, half a dozen dictionaries, a sensitive ear—all these play a part. We must listen for the lead-nickel word. Professor C. Ray Wylie of Furman University once sent me a clipping from Parade magazine. The story had to do with what a federal prosecutor had described as a *blatant* violation of the pure food laws. "It seems to me," Mr. Wylie remarked, "that while selling ground-up umbrella handles as Parmesan cheese is surely a *flagrant* case of food adulteration, the last thing the perpetrator wants is to be *blatant,* i.e., 'noisy' or 'conspicuously obtrusive' about it." Precisely so.

So let us love words, and let us treat them with tender loving care. Shades of meaning matter greatly; exactitude matters greatly. Empathy for our audience matters greatly. When we give attention to these considerations, we are doing those things we ought never to leave undone.

5. We must keep our instrument properly in tune.

This is Rule One, I suppose, for the concert violinist. If the "A" on his instrument is not vibrating at the same frequency as the "A" in the string section, he is in for a bad evening. By extension the rule applies to writers also. We have to stay in pitch.

I remember a moment, back in the spring of 1949, when I had just begun writing editorials under the steel-framed eyes of Dr. Freeman. I brought him a change-of-pace piece about the Lee House down on East Franklin Street. The piece began with a lyric sentence, in which the ghost of the South's noblest figure still lingered in the shadowed rooms, etc., etc. The piece ended, I am embarrassed to recall, with a sentence that wasn't quite as bad, but almost as bad, as "Things ain't what they used to be." Dr. Freeman sent the editorial back to my desk with a note in his eight-point script:

Mr. Kilpatrick—
    If you start purple, finish purple.
                    DSF

That is the key element of what might be called "mood writing." The mood has to be sustained. If our mood is angry, let us be like the fellow who was known as the even-tempered man: He *stayed* mad. Once I was on the receiving end of an absolutely splendid piece of invective by a West Coast columnist, Jack Cady of The Port Angeles (Wash.) Daily News. He had read one of my wise, reasoned, temperate, and sagacious columns, and he had found it the merest claptrap. He set out to give me a hiding, and he did a superlative job of it. He began by identifying me as a "crap artist." He continued by remarking upon my capacity for "psychopathic right-wing hatred." My brain, he happily surmised, "would look like a dog's breakfast." And so forth. He started out fortissimo and he finished fortissimo. If your purpose is to castigate someone, this is how it should be done.

More often we write in sorrow, not in anger. If your memory of air disasters is good, you may recall the crash of an Air Florida plane as it was taking off from Washington's National Airport in January 1982. The tragedy was relieved in part by the heroism of an unidentified passenger. Roger Rosenblatt wrote an essay for Time magazine, "The Man in the Water."

As disasters go, this one was terrible, but not unique, certainly not among the worst on the roster of U.S. air crashes. There was the unusual element of the bridge, of course, and the fact that the plane clipped it at a moment of high traffic, one routine thus intersecting another and disrupting both. Then, too, there was the location of the event. Washington, the city of form and regulations, turned chaotic, deregulated by the blast of real winter and a single slap of metal on metal. The jets from Washington National Airport that normally swoop around the presidential monuments like famished gulls are, for the moment, emblemized by the one that fell; so there is that detail. And there was the aesthetic clash as well—blue-and-green Air Florida, the name a flying garden, sunk down among gray chunks in a black river. All that was worth noticing, to be sure. Still, there was nothing very special in any of it, except death, which, while always special, does not necessarily bring millions to tears or to attention. Why, then, the shock here?

Perhaps because the nation saw in this disaster something more than a mechanical failure. Perhaps because people saw in it no failure at all, but rather something successful about their makeup. Here, after all, were two forms of nature in collision: the elements and human character. Last Wednesday, the elements, indifferent as ever, brought down Flight 90. And on that same afternoon, human nature—groping and flailing in mysteries of its own—rose to the occasion.

Of the four acknowledged heroes of the event, three are able to account for their behavior. Donald Usher and Eugene Windsor, a park police helicopter team, risked their lives every time they dipped the skids into the water to pick up survivors. On television, side by side in bright blue jumpsuits, they described their courage as all in the line of duty. Lenny Skutnik, a 28-year-old employee of the Congressional Budget Office, said: "It's something I never thought I would do"—referring to his jumping into the water to drag an injured woman to shore. Skutnik added that "somebody had to go into the water," delivering every hero's line that is no less admirable for its repetitions. In fact, nobody had to go into the water. That somebody actually did so is part of the reason this particular tragedy sticks in the mind.

But the person most responsible for the emotional impact of the disaster is the one known at first simply as "the man in the water." (Balding, probably in his 50s, an extravagant mustache.) He was seen clinging with five other survivors to the tail section of the airplane. This man was described by Usher and Windsor as appearing alert and in control. Every time they lowered a lifeline and flotation ring to him, he passed it on to another of the passengers. "In a mass casualty, you'll find people like him," said Windsor. "But I've never seen one with that commitment." When the helicopter came back for him, the man had gone under. His selflessness was one reason the story held national attention; his anonymity another. The fact that he went unidentified invested him with a universal character. For a while he was Everyman, and thus proof (as if one needed it) that no man is ordinary.

Still, he could never have imagined such a capacity in himself. Only minutes before his character was tested, he was sitting in the ordinary plane among the ordinary passengers, dutifully listening to the stewardess telling him to fasten his seat belt and saying something about the "no smoking" sign. So our man relaxed with the others, some of whom would owe their lives to him. Perhaps he started to read, or to doze, or to regret some harsh remark made in the office that morning. Then suddenly he knew that the trip would not be ordinary. Like every other person on that flight, he was desperate to live, which makes his final act so stunning.

For at some moment in the water he must have realized that he would not live if he continued to hand over the rope and ring to others. He *had* to know it, no matter how gradual the effect of the cold. In his judgment he had no choice. When the helicopter took off with what was to be the last survivor, he watched everything in the world move away from him, and he deliberately let it happen.

Yet there was something else about the man that kept our thoughts on him, and which keeps our thoughts on him still. He was *there*, in the essential, classic circumstance. Man in nature. The man in the water. For its part, nature cared nothing about the five passengers. Our man, on the other hand, cared totally. So the timeless battle commenced in the Potomac. For as long as that man could last, they went at each other, nature and man; the one making no distinctions of good and evil, acting on no principles, offering no lifelines; the other acting wholly on distinctions, principles and, one supposes, on faith.

Since it was he who lost the fight, we ought to come again to the conclusion that people are powerless in the world. In reality, we believe the reverse, and it takes the act of the man in the water to remind us of our true feelings in this matter. It is not to say that everyone would have acted as he did, or as Usher, Windsor and Skutnik. Yet whatever moved these men to challenge death on behalf of their fellows is not peculiar to them. Everyone feels the possibility in himself. That is the abiding wonder of the story. That is why we would not let go of it. If the man in the water gave a lifeline to the people gasping for survival, he was likewise giving a lifeline to those who observed him.

The odd thing is that we do not really believe that the man in the water lost his fight. "Everything in Nature contains all the powers of Nature," said Emerson. Exactly. So the man in the water had his own natural powers. He could not make ice storms, or freeze the water until it froze the blood. But he could hand life over to a stranger, and that is a power of nature too. The man in the water pitted himself against an implacable, impersonal enemy; he fought it with charity, and he held it to a standoff. He was the best we can do.

I have read Rosenblatt's beautiful piece a dozen times. Two years after it appeared, I cannot reread it without a lump in my throat. It ran to only nine hundred words, but it was a jewel. Rosenblatt succeeded so brilliantly for this reason: He set out in a mood of objective understatement, and he sustained it perfectly. Given an occasion of great drama, he wrote undramatically; he wrote in a minor key for muted strings.

Look back at Rosenblatt's lead. It was almost conversational: "As disasters go, this one was terrible but not unique." In that simple sentence, he set up the contrast he would develop between the crash, which had few unusual elements, and the heroism of the Sixth Man, which moved a nation. In his second paragraph Rosenblatt broke a "rule." He employed two sentence fragments, and with careful deliberation he introduced each of them with *perhaps*. Look back at the amplifying *after all* in that paragraph. Rosenblatt intended to observe the tragedy as if he were a Greek chorus commenting upon the action. This is how Greek choruses speak. Notice his verbs: They are subdued verbs— *saw, rose, brought down*. Rosenblatt never sawed the air or rent his garments. When he began his essay, he knew how he meant to end it. His piece came off because he set a tone and held it.

Let me offer another example in this genre. This was a column I wrote in January 1968 under my dateline of Scrabble, Va. It was titled, "Death of a Helpin' Man."

They buried Charlie Settle last Wednesday at the Baptist Church in Woodville. He was the last man on earth you would have picked as a prospect for a heart attack, but it hit him Sunday and that was it. He came from a vanishing breed, Charlie did, a whooping crane of a man, and I write of his death in sorrow.

Charlie was an Independent American. They are rare birds in our time. He stood just under six feet tall, slim as a snap-bean, with a long sad face that always looked as if he'd slept in it. His teeth were terrible, half of them missing and those left dark-stained, but you forgot it all when he smiled. It was the happiest smile you ever saw.

We first met Charlie in the spring in 1966, when some work had to be done on the place. The problem was presented to Mr. Burke, the patriarch of Scrabble District, who runs the store and Esso station at Woodville. He gave us our first lesson in country manners. We had said respectfully that we wanted to "hire" someone to get a few things done.

"You look up Charlie Settle," said Mr. Burke. "He's working on a wall down the Slate Mills road. But don't you say you want to 'hire' him. You ask if he'll help you."

So we drove down the Slate Mills road, sun-drenched in an April morning, the dogwoods white and the streams cut-crystal, and sure enough, Charlie was working on the wall. He didn't look up, just kept laying stones. It took twenty minutes of irrelevant conversation—the winter past, the spring present, the art of building walls, the hopes of the Baltimore Orioles—before the delicate subject of employment could be approached. But finally, "yep," said Charlie, he would come on a Tuesday and see what he could do.

As it turned out, Charlie could do anything. He could paint a house, frame a door, pour concrete, patch a roof. He could lay bricks, spread linoleum, run a wire, prune a tree. He could plow a garden, build a fence, ditch a road. There is an art to splitting logs; Charlie knew it. There is a way of rolling stones, using the weight of the rock against itself; Charlie knew it. He could kill a hog, tend bees, set a trap, put poison in a groundhog hole. He could spread gravel, move dirt, mow weeds, make a motor run. He was a master at building walls of stone. But where he had taken his Ph.D. was in springs.

A city boy has no real measure of his ignorance until he undertakes to fathom the working of a spring. You have to have a sixth sense of how water moves, deep in the earth; how it finds a spring rock, and how it lies under the spring rock; and then you have to know—carefully, carefully—just how to free the water, guide it to a reservoir, bring it to a pump. Now in winter, and the fields frozen, the mind's eye turns to Charlie in the summer, shin deep in mud, his shovel like a magic wand, gazing with pure intensity at the slow trickle that became a steady stream, thick as your wrist. "Theah she is," he would say. "Theah she is."

Charlie fixed his own wages. Two dollars an hour, flat. It was too low, we said. He would not be budged. If he made more money, he'd start to worry about it; he'd get tied down to property; pretty soon he'd be borrowing and get in debt. Then he'd *have* to work. Damned if that was any life for a man. So Charlie fixed his hours, too. He would show up for three or four days, then go fishing, or putter around his own place, or work for someone else in greater need. He was a free man.

He used to rattle around Rappahannock County in an ancient pickup truck, with a devoted mutt named Ringo at his side. He knew every hollow, every house, every still, every covey of birds. Once he showed us the tiny schoolhouse where he got his rudimentary schooling. His education, you might say, was not extensive; he could read the things that mattered. There it stopped. Late on Saturday evenings, over a can of beer, we would settle up on his weekly hours: "Two eights," he would say, "one four-and-a-half, and one nine-and-a-quarter." It sufficed. He knew the higher mathematics of moons for hunting 'coon and stars for planting corn.

Well, it's goodnight, Charlie, and sleep well in the hills. We will hire city people now, from Culpeper and Front Royal and Warrenton, competent men with power tools and bill forms and numbers in the Yellow Pages, and the work will get done, but it won't be the same. Down at the foot of the hill, close by the stream, is a spring house of stone. It is, in its way, a work of art, perfectly proportioned, built for the ages. The cement cap bears a proud inscription: "C. Settle, 1966." Michelangelo never did anything better.

Let me make the point and pass on: If you would write emotionally, be first unemotional. If you would move your readers to tears, do not let them see you cry.

Mood writing has something in common with long-distance running. The key element is a sense of pace—the business of knowing when to slow down, and when to speed up. The guidelines for "writing fast" and "writing slow" apply not only to the writing of fiction, where they are seen most commonly, but also in the drafting of business letters, fund-raising appeals, and many other communications. To be sure, if your purpose is to draft a manual for assembling a Christmas toy, you want a nice even pace—something at about the level of "Insert Tab A in Slot B." Often we want something more.

One of the most gifted writers of suspense stories today is Ken Follett. In *The Key to Rebecca,* he spins a wonderful yarn involving a heroine, Elene; a villain, Wolff; and a hero, Vandam. This is how Follett writes when he wants to write fast:

Elene jumped out of the car. She still had the broken-off gear stick in her hand. She saw Wolff bring back his arm, ready to slash at Vandam once more. She rushed up behind Wolff, stumbling in the sand. Wolff struck at Vandam. Vandam jerked sideways, dodging the blow. Elene raised the gear stick high in the air and brought it down with all her might on the back of Wolff's head. He seemed to stand still for a moment. Elene said: "Oh, God." Then she hit him again. She hit him a third time. He fell down. She hit him again. Then she dropped the gear stick and knelt beside Vandam.

From the same work, this is how Follett writes when he wants to write slow:

The great and ancient caravan route, which Wolff had followed from oasis to oasis across the vast empty desert, led through a pass in the mountain range and at last merged with an ordinary modern road. The road was like a line drawn on the map by God, for on one side were the yellow, dusty barren hills, and on the other were lush fields of cotton squared off with irrigation ditches. The peasants, bent over their crops, wore galabiyas, simple shifts of white cotton, instead of the cumbersome protective robes of the nomads.

The two passages are of substantially equal length, but the differences are instantly apparent. The first has fourteen sentences, the second, only three. When he writes fast, Follett uses fast verbs: *jumped, slash, rushed, jerked, hit,* and so on. For slow writing, he wants slow verbs: *led, merged, bent, wore,* the parts of *to be.*

John D. MacDonald, author of the delightful tales of Travis McGee, uses the same technique. In between the bash-'em-up, track-'em-down passages, he intersperses philosophical asides. Dick Francis, another craftsman of the mystery story, moves smoothly from the trot to the canter to the dead run.

Sentence length is one of the elements of pace. Syllabication is another. Follett, writing fast, gives us only 120 syllables in 112 words. Follett, writing slow, spreads 132 syllables over 94 words. Voice is another element—active in the one case, passive in the other. Simple sentences make a sprint; compound and complex sentences serve the mile run. We can dash, or we can peregrinate, but we can't achieve both effects with the same style.

Whatever the mood may be that we are seeking to achieve, we ought to go at our task with this elementary reminder in our heads: We will not overwrite. We will not add mustaches to our Mona Lisas. This is the kind of thing that happens when we let ourselves be swept away by the excitement of a moment:

OAKMONT, Pa.—In the end, when the multitudinous voices that had railed against the strangling fairways and decried the carnivorous greens were long dispatched, discouraged or otherwise silenced, it was a putt destined for mythology that won the rain-interrupted 83d United States Open yesterday morning.

That was from The Washington Times in June of 1983. A golfer named Larry Nelson had won the tournament with a 62-foot putt.

One trick of conveying mood is to let the action itself do the work. "Place yourself in the background," E.B. White has urged us. "Write in a way that draws the reader's attention to the sense and substance of the writing, rather than to the mood and temper of the author." Once we sense that the author is trying to tell us how we should feel, we no longer are alone with our book or our paper; the anxious writer is peering over our shoulder, worrying that we may not see what he wants us to see, and he is trying too hard. I once bought a paperback mystery by a gentleman named Brown. Somehow I thought I was buying a story about the detective Father Brown, but no matter. My investment proved to be at once regrettable and instructive. This was a wholly abominable book, but we learn from abominations. We learn about things not done, and about things that are left undone.

The trouble was not with the author's paper characters nor his improbable plot nor his off-the-rack size 42-regular sex. These could be forgiven. The author of this wretched work could seldom be content with "I said" or "she said" or "he said." No, indeed. On page 8, the heroic detective "snarls." He continues to snarl. He snarls on page 22, and again on pages 23 and 24. He snarls at page 30, page 49, and page 51. He snarls eight times thereafter, and this is not a long book. When he is not snarling, he is gritting, barking, grunting, growling, or croaking.

The good guys, the bad guys, and the voluptuous women of Mr. Brown's contrivance could not say things simply to one another. They spoke *warmly, coolly, coldly,* and *icily.* They spoke *firmly, flatly, evenly, tersely,* and *tautly.* They spoke *doubtfully, dubiously, tentatively,* and *a little uncertainly.* They spoke *darkly, demurely, disdainfully, disgustedly, earnestly, easily, encouragingly, finally* (though they did not speak finally soon enough). They spoke *forlornly, frantically, generously, genially, gently, gratefully, gravely, grimly, happily, harshly, heavily, helpfully, hoarsely, humbly, idly, impatiently, incredulously, innocently, interestedly,* and *irritably.*

Good writers do not litter their sentences with adverbial garbage. They do not hold up signs reading "laughter!" or "applause!" The content of dialogue ought to suggest the mood. Is a conversation warm, cold, tense, casual, or crisp? We should know this without being told. If you budding novelists would hold a reader's attention, do not slug him with two-by-fours. Do I say this firmly? You'd better believe it.

If you would study a master at work, read any of the essays of E.B. White, and do not miss his "Death of a Pig." You will find it in *The Second Tree from the Corner.* Here White set out to tell a story that fairly may be described as both sad and sentimental. He succeeded memorably, because he did not write sadly and he did not write sentimentally. This was his introspective lead:

> I spent several days and nights in mid-September with an ailing pig and I feel driven to account for this stretch of time, more particularly since the pig died at last, and I lived, and things might easily have gone the other way and none left to do the accounting.

None of us is likely ever to match E.B. White in the realm of the mood piece, for he is beyond dispute the best of our generation, but we can learn by example. We can learn, or at least admire, his simplicity, his sense of flow, his economy of style. Let us read his essays, and breathe a small sigh of envy, and get back to work.

> *6. We ought to remember that life is not entirely serious, and therefore we should pay some attention to humor.*

Every newspaperman who writes a syndicated column sooner or later gets the same inquiry: It comes from a reader who asks, "What does it take to get a job as a reporter?" Or, more to the point of these immediate reflections, "How can I get to be a columnist?"

Ordinarily I answer the first question with a long disquisition on the necessity for an academic grounding in the liberal arts, with a major in whatever subject one proposes to write about—politics, business, law, science, nutrition, the theater, whatever. Sometimes I field the second question with a question in return:

"Can you write funny?"

My thought is that "writing funny" is the toughest of all areas of popular writing. My first city editor, Charlie Hamilton, thought I had the gift. He would come across some clipping that suggested treatment as a *brite,* which was how the AP spelled it, and he would drop the clipping on my desk: "Hey, Kilpatrick," he would say, "be funny." At that instant humor curled up and died.

It is no trick at all, I can tell you, to write regularly about Social Security reform, or about the recurring federal deficits, or about an approaching election. Any pundit of even moderate paunch can instruct the Israelis and the Arabs on achieving peace in the Middle East. But to write funny—to write pieces that consistently produce the chuckle or the haw-haw—requires genius of a high order. The writer who has the gift of laughter, and can put that gift on paper, can write his own ticket.

What is the secret of writing funny? If I knew, I would write my own ticket. But I venture this thought: The art begins with a sense of sadness. This is the clown's gift. Early in 1983 the country went through a national celebration marking the last episode of the TV series *M*A*S*H*. The show had broken every record for nighttime viewing; it had won every award the industry offers; it had made millionaires of the cast. Why had it endured? What lifted it so memorably above other situation comedies that vanished after a couple of years? It was the dark side of *M*A*S*H* that was always just beyond the laugh lines.

Shakespeare knew the trick. The second scene of Macbeth's second act is a scene of terrible apprehension and remorse; the murders have been committed; Macbeth wonders madly if great Neptune's ocean will wash the blood clean from his hand. He and his lady exit—and who at once enters? It is the drunken porter crying, "Knock, knock, knock!"— and the tension snaps in laughter. We see the same device in Hamlet. Ophelia has just drowned, and we are moved to tears; then follows the graveyard scene with the two soused clowns and their jesuitical exchange. Mark Twain's marvelous essay on Tennessee journalism is the funniest short piece I ever read; it deals with editors who shoot each other. Twain's piece on French duelists is cast from the same black comedy. Ring Lardner had the gift; he was a wonderfully funny writer, but his best stuff evokes not only a laugh in the belly but a lump in the throat as well.

The literary anatomist hasn't been born who could precisely dissect the anatomy of humor. I can suggest some things that humor is not. Humor ceases to be humor when it gives grievous offense to unoffending readers; once it may have been possible to write funny about race, but race isn't funny any more. Twain wrote some hilarious pieces about religion; I wouldn't try that if I were you. Cancer is nothing to joke about. Physical and mental handicaps are beyond the humorist's range—

as Interior Secretary James Watt discovered to his sorrow. The best wit follows the rule of the Gridiron Club: It is wit that singes but never burns.

If you would write funny, you ought first to read the masters of funny writing. What were Twain's tricks of construction? What were his devices of style? Exaggeration was one. Repetition was another. Mock seriousness was a third. In Twain's little stage box of properties (his phrase) was the carny's Kewpie doll and rubber ball; Twain would set up a proposition in one sentence and knock it down in the next. In *Deerslayer,* said Twain, James Fenimore Cooper violated eighteen of the nineteen rules governing literary art. The rules require, among other things:

> That a tale shall accomplish something and arrive somewhere. But the *Deerslayer* tale accomplishes nothing and arrives in the air. . . .
>
> They require that the personages in a tale shall be alive, except in the case of corpses, and that always the reader shall be able to tell the corpses from the others. But this detail has often been overlooked in the *Deerslayer* tale.
>
> They require that the personages in a tale, both dead and alive, shall exhibit a sufficient excuse for being there. But this detail also has been overlooked in the *Deerslayer* tale.

And so on. I have read "Fenimore Cooper's Literary Offenses" at least twenty times, and held my sides every time, and wiped away tears of laughter, and marveled at Twain's technique. Charles Neider assembled Twain's funniest material in *The Comic Mark Twain Reader.* If you would write funny, read it.

It is natural, I suppose, that when we think of comic writers, we think of writers who have gone before: Aristophanes, Juvenal, Molière, Swift, Shaw. Gibbon once remarked the universal tendency among men to exalt the past and to deprecate the present. Not long ago I came across a slim volume of the essays of Joseph Addison, and for an hour or two I fed upon his pleasant observations of the eighteenth-century world in which he lived. His stuff stands up. It wasn't the stuff of ho-ho-ho, but it had charm and wit.

Addison was a columnist. We link his name with his colleague and editor, Richard Steele, and venerate the two of them as masters of the journalistic art form. Most of Addison's pieces ran to fifteen hundred words or less. He wrote about every topic under the London sun—

politics, law, hairdressing, lady orators. He followed the army's apocryphal Rule Six: He took none of them too damned seriously. Nearly three hundred years have passed since his essays appeared in The Tatler and The Spectator, and still his name and fame endure.

But a nice thought: Unless my judgment is badly awry, we have in our own time and in our own press a number of light essayists whose work is every bit as good as the work of Addison and Steele. It rarely occurs to us that in such gentle humorists as Art Buchwald and Russell Baker, we have two Addisons of the twentieth century. Two hundred years hence, the best of their stuff will stand up too.

What giddy fantasies lie in Buchwald's bag of tricks? A kind of drunken sobriety is among them. Buchwald calls on that great American patriot, Harvey Ripplemyer, and solemnly interviews him on his achievement, which is—to make so much money that he pays no income taxes. This is top-grade satire, combining truth and malice and comedy. Buchwald's art is the art of the funhouse mirror. He starts with a truth: Many rich people do indeed shelter so much money that they pay no taxes. Given that ironical fact, his imagination leaps. He comes down with the clown's achievement, the gravedigger's spade in one hand, the skull of Yorick in the other.

We think of American humorists of the twentieth century, and we think of such familiar names in journalism as Finley Peter Dunne, Westbrook Pegler, Damon Runyon, Ring Lardner, Erma Bombeck, Calvin Trillin, Art Buchwald, and Russell Baker, but there are some very funny writers not so well known—the late Jim Dance of The Miami Herald, for one, and Charles McDowell of The Richmond Times-Dispatch for another. Let me nominate two others who dwell in the boondocks: Paul Walker of The Harrisburg (Pa.) Patriot-News, and Dick Swank of the nearby Duncannon Record. In the summer of 1982, having nothing better to do in their columns, the two aging editors fell into reverie on the proper answer to an engrossing question that somehow had been posed in the news: "What do you hold onto when you're putting on your pants in the morning?"

Walker wrote his disquisition first, suggesting that after sixty neither men nor women hold onto anything when putting on their pants. They sit on the edge of the bed. Then Swank got into the act:

For the past several years I have been holding either to the arm of a chair or have been seating myself on a low structure and pulling my pants over both feet before standing up and adjusting my belt. I have not thought about it, have just gone and done it because it had to be done.

Walker suggests that one foot might go in before the other. He brought an unthinkable and, up to now, unimportant, matter to the surface. This morning I stooped with one hand on the bedpost and the other near the floor where my trousers dragged dolefully—and I was unable to get up enough nerve to pull the damn pants up to my hips. *I had forgotten how.*

Within the time I ordinarily take to pull on my pants and a sweatshirt, to slide my feet into loafers and to dash a bit of water in my eyes, I wasted that entire five or so minutes staring down into the crotch of those pants, undecided whether my left foot went in the right hole or the left. And when I did get the feet in I took a step and fell to the floor.

Swank, by this time wholly disconcerted, went on to discover that he could not remember how he began to brush his teeth. ''I stopped to think whether to start at a left molar and go right, or to start at the remaining eye tooth and go left.'' He could not remember how to part his hair. Did he polish his glasses, right lens first or left lens first? His was a funny piece, light and crisp as a good meringue. Why did it click? For one thing, he wasn't making fun of anyone else; he was making fun of himself. For another, he was dealing with a universal human experience. All of his readers, at some point in their lives, had pulled on a pair of pants. For the few minutes it took to read his column, he had all of us standing in our underdrawers; and in a small Pennsylvania weekly we had a touch of the human comedy.

Those of us who practice the writer's art are subject to insidious temptations, and to our credit we succumb to most of them. One temptation is to throw in an occasional pun; the other is to write satire. I cheerfully commend to you both vices—but with a few reservations.

Time and Newsweek magazines have whole stables of punsters. Peter S. Prescott of Newsweek once wrote about authors who turn their backs on their places of birth: ''You can always trust a writer to bite the land that breeds him.'' A writer in Time spoke of Hugh Hefner's daughter as the hare-apparent to the Playboy empire. In his delightful *Joy of Lex,* Gyles Brandreth offers a whole bakery of hot-crossed puns: ''Puberty is a hair-raising experience.'' . . . ''Absinthe makes the tart grow fonder." . . . "A white lie is aversion of the truth."

Puns are like baseball games; there is no such thing as a truly bad one. Short puns are clean singles; triple or quadruple puns are better yet. There was the one about the deposed tribal chieftain who learned to his distress that people who live in grass houses shouldn't stow thrones. There was the one about the Indian housewives and the animal skins, which taught us that the squaw of the hippopotamus is equal to the sons of the squaws on the other two hides. And of course there was the one about the custodian of the sultan's aquarium and zoo, who died in discovering that one should not cross state lions for immortal porpoises.

If puns are sins at all, they are forgivable sins. Satire is a riskier business. The perils in satire are three in number. If the satire is too broad, it loses the cutting edge of wit. If the satire is too obscure, it serves not to amuse but merely to mystify. If the satire is just right, it will be taken seriously.

An authority on this topic, often cited, is the late Jonathan Swift. He once defined satire as "a sort of glass, wherein beholders discover everybody's face but their own." Back in 1729 he delivered himself of a work that he titled, "A Modest Proposal for Preventing the Children of Ireland from being a Burden to their Parents or Country."

> I have been assured by a very knowing American of my acquaintance in London that a young healthy child is at a year old a most delicious, nourishing, and wholesome food, whether stewed, baked or boiled, and I make no doubt that it will equally serve in a fricasse or a ragout.

It was deadly satire, and hence subjected Swift to peril number three. People thought he meant it. To the end of his days—he died in 1745— Swift was fending off cries of "monster!" and "cannibal!"

The literary hoax, a first cousin to satire, involves the same risks. A few years ago my brother pundit Bill Buckley got himself into a serious picklement. He devoted an entire issue of National Review to some purported "Pentagon Papers" that supposedly supplemented the real Pentagon Papers. His bogus letters and memoranda were masterpieces of the hoaxer's art. Carefully studied, they raised a dozen warning flags to signal intentional deception, but for several days serious people took the Buckley Papers very seriously indeed.

I have been in trouble myself. Just before Christmas in 1976 I scooped

my brothers of the press with an exclusive column under a dateline of
Ann Arbor, Mich.

In an effort to "give the nation a lift," President Ford two years
ago attempted to stage an elaborate Yuletide production on the
White House lawn, but the project had to be abandoned for want of
an acceptable environmental impact statement.

This was disclosed today when the first of Mr. Ford's presidential
papers were deposited with the Eritas Memorial Library of the
University of Michigan. Franz Olegna, the library's chief archivist,
said he saw "no valid reason" to keep the papers any longer under
wraps. "Let the chips fall," he said.

From the records made available to reporters, it appears that Mr.
Ford conceived the project late in September of 1974. The country
then was suffering high inflation, high unemployment, and the
trauma of the Nixon pardon. The President's "WIN" campaign had
flopped. Mr. Ford reasoned that a pageant based upon "The Twelve
Days of Christmas" might boost the national morale.

Carlton Foops, a White House aide put in charge of the venture,
ran into difficulties almost at once. The Environmental Protection
Agency, getting wind of the project, demanded that all the agency's
"impact" rules be strictly observed. "It would be unthinkable,"
wrote Administrator Russell E. Train, "to insist that others fill out
forms we are unwilling to fill out ourselves."

Seeking to comply with Train's directive, Foops solicited
opinions and assistance from other government agencies that might
be involved. When it became evident that the necessary impact
statement could not be submitted in time for Christmas 1974,
"Operation True Love," as it came to be known, was carried over
to the following year. Eventually a staff of 172 had to be employed.
Olegna said he had turned up no record of the cost. The Office of
Management and Budget declined comment.

The Fish and Wildlife Service, according to the Foops files,
balked at providing 12 partridges. While there is no quail season in
the District of Columbia, quail are hunted in neighboring Virginia
and Maryland. The Service took the view that live partridges could
not be made available between Christmas and Epiphany without
arousing a protest from sportsmen. The Museum of Natural History
said it had only eight stuffed partridges and saw no reason to
increase its inventory.

The National Arboretum advised Foops that it would provide a dozen pear trees, provided the pageant were rescheduled for either March or November when the trees could be appropriately planted. In a heated exchange, Foops refused the alternate dates and the arboretum withdrew its support.

The discouraged director tried a Washington pet shop for the required 22 calling birds, but he never was satisfied with what the birds called him. Earl Butz, who served as secretary of agriculture in this period, apparently did his best to cooperate.

"Am requisitioning for Operation True Love 30 French hens, 42 swimming swans, and 40 fresh Jersey cows," Butz wrote the director. "Also 33 bum jokes. Please advise disposition."

Unfortunately, as it turned out, Butz's colleagues in animal husbandry refused to go along until acceptable barns, ponds and laying houses could be designed. A special program had to be devised for inspecting and grading goose eggs, of which the administration soon had a surfeit. The impact of the cows upon the White House lawn created insoluble problems. The Occupational Safety and Health Administration got into the act with a demand that special facilities be provided for the 40 maids a-milking. An OSHA administrator also balked at "the predictably intolerable noise levels" that would be produced by 12 drummers and 22 pipers.

Even the State Department gave trouble. Secretary Kissinger said that he could foresee no difficulties with Her Majesty's government in making available 36 ladies dancing, but to provide "30 leaping Lords would involve the most delicate negotiations." When Foops pressed the point, Kissinger threatened to resign. Meanwhile, the British pound collapsed.

So did Operation True Love. The final environmental impact statement ran to 12 volumes and 15,000 pages. When this was returned by the EPA in October, 1975, for "additional supporting data," Foops resigned and the staff went mad. Nothing remains of the ill-fated project but the records filed with the Eritas Library here.

Now, you would not believe that any grown-up of even minimal perception could have been taken in by that nonsense, but you would be wrong. The column produced fifty letters in which readers fired off in all directions. Some were indignant that President Ford should have proposed any Christmas pageantry at the White House. Some complained of the waste of money. Most of the readers were furious at the thick-wittedness and pettifoggery of the bureaucracy. I heard from a former congressman who had been defeated for re-election in November of 1976: He had known of Operation True Love in 1974 and 1975, he said, and he wanted me to know he had supported the venture.

A former bureaucrat with the Environmental Protection Agency went through the same experience. This was Nancy Maloley, who at the time was editor of a publication called the EPAlog. In an unguarded moment she reported that agency scientists were speculating that "burping cows must rank as the number one source of air pollution in the United States." It was estimated, she said, that cows "annually burp approximately 50 million tons of hydrocarbons into the atmosphere.

There presently exists no available technology for controlling these emissions. However, the Department of Agriculture has suggested that perhaps a gas mask might do the trick if such masks can be designed to allow cows to eat grass while wearing them. It might even be possible to recover the natural gas generated by these cows, which would perhaps increase the supply by ten percent. Rest assured the EPA will take every measure to see that this significant source of hydrocarbon emissions is substantially reduced.

The immediate aftermath was that Representative John B. Ashbrook, R-Ohio, warned his rural constituents to keep a close watch for EPA inspectors carrying emission control devices. He charged the agency with "going overboard in their attempt to purify the environment." As the roof fell in on Ms. Maloley, she was heard to say: "I never thought anyone would take it seriously."

That's what they all say. Walter Shapiro of The Washington Post set out to advise President Reagan where $3 billion could be cut from the federal budget. Nearly $900 million a year could be saved, he suggested, by abolishing the wine and cheese stamp program. Another $1.4 billion in loan guarantees would be saved by ending the Federal Home Library Assistance Corporation. At the risk of offending the labor vote, the president could press for repeal of the Bolling-Long-Thompson Act, amending Davis-Bacon, which provides for free lunches for union workers on federal projects. Alas, members of Congress on both sides of the aisle leaped to denounce these extravagances and to call for an end to the outlays.

By this time, my own Operation True Love, Ms. Maloley's burping cows, and Mr. Shapiro's wine and cheese stamp program have entered the archives of the Eritas Memorial Library. Founded in 1923 in Colorado Springs, this modest institution was transferred in 1970 to Ann Arbor under a grant from the National Endowment for the Humanities. The library's small but dedicated staff devotes itself to discovering and recording those bubble-fantasies of our journalism that otherwise might perish in the noonday sun. Among its treasures is a full account of Ben Franklin's Polly Baker, who gave birth to five illegitimate children and defended unfettered motherhood. There, too, is H.L. Mencken's scholarly article on the first bathtub in the White House, installed at the direction of President Fillmore in 1851. The library houses the original manuscript of Norman Cousins' editorial on Representative A.F. Day, whose bill to abolish golf courses was analyzed in Saturday Review on April 3, 1971.

At the risk of further immodesty, I may add that one of my own editorials is included in the Eritas collection. This was a piece in The Richmond News Leader of May 14, 1958, under the caption of "Notes on an Ancient Game." It dealt with the history and current play of tiddlywinks in the British Isles. Here I reviewed the references to the noble game in Chaucer, Shakespeare, and Marlowe. I described the chased ivory winks and silver cups to be seen in the great museums of Europe.

One tends to get swept away. I reported the precise dimensions of the ivory winks, the approved cup, and the ring, or "pale," around the cup. I covered the etymological aspects; the game, I said, had enriched our language with such phrases as beyond the pale, in the cups, tiddly, flipped, quick as a wink, and forty winks. The piece ran on and on—*and it was taken seriously.* Indeed it was. It was taken seriously by, among others, one sportswriter, two instructors in physical education, and the publisher's cousin.

"Doesn't everyone," asked Ms. Maloley, "have a sense of humor?" Alas, it is not so. The Eritas Memorial Library is itself an enduring reminder, in brick and stone and glass, that only a thin cover of skepticism conceals man's inner core of credulity. We want to believe. We are chagrined when the loaded cigar of satire suddenly makes its presence known. But gullible's travails can rarely be avoided. The best rule, when temptation cannot be resisted, is to add an italic line at the end: *The foregoing artickle was writ sarkastick.*

7. We must copy-edit, copy-edit, copy-edit!

This is the last reminder under the heading of the things left undone that we ought to have done, and it is perhaps the most important of all. We must check our writing right up to the moment of deadline.

Twenty centuries ago, more or less, Horace made an observation that has given comfort to writers ever since. *Quandoque bonus dormitat Homerus.* Sometimes even good old Homer nods. Most of us who write for a living have our snoozy moments. We don't take the time to correct a misspelling or to untangle a tangled antecedent. We report that something has occurred in seven states, and we set out to list them but list only six. It is the finishing process that separates Tom Chippendale from Jack the jackleg—the scraping, the sanding, the waxing, the rubbing.

I have nodded, God knows I have nodded. I have confidently identified Al Smith as "the onetime mayor of New York City." He was in fact the onetime governor of New York. In a moment of metaphorical fantasy about acrobatic swallows, I put Baron von Richthofen in a Messerschmitt, not a Fokker. I once undertook to quote Mr. Pope without bothering to check the quotation. "A little knowledge," I said, "is a dangerous thing." Well, of course it is a little learning that is a dangerous thing. True, how true!

Misquotation is a peril that we ought to avoid. Hamlet never said, "Alas, poor Yorick! I knew him well." What Hamlet said was, "Alas poor Yorick! I knew him, Horatio." Touchstone, in *As You Like It*, did not describe his country wench as "a poor thing, but mine own." The wench was "an ill-favoured thing." Winston Churchill never exhorted his countrymen to endure "blood, sweat, and tears," though it would have been a better line than the "blood, toil, tears, and sweat" of his wartime address. The biblical reminder is not that "pride goeth before a fall" but that "pride goeth before destruction, and an haughty spirit before a fall." Cromwell did not implore the elders of the Church of Scotland to consider it possible they might be wrong; he asked them to consider it possible they might be mistaken. Mark Twain did not originate the saying that "everyone talks about the weather but no one does anything about it." The epigram ought properly to be attributed to Charles Dudley Warner, associate editor of The Hartford Courant. Edmund Burke may have said that "the only thing necessary for the triumph of evil is that good men do nothing," but scholars cannot find the aphorism in his published works or letters. Humphrey Bogart did not say, "Play it again, Sam." General Pershing did not say, "Lafayette, we are here."

Check, check, check! This is what dictionaries, books of quotations, encyclopedias and other reference works are for. Use them!

It is sometimes imagined, by people who do not write for a living, that writers are not really *working*. There is a popular notion that we ink-stained wretches of the press are having a larky time of it—that compared to law or medicine or teaching, the business of writing is a pretty easy life. Those who are thinking of careers in writing should not be misled. Writing is work. It is often hard work, demanding work, exhausting and frustrating work. Every writer has endured the agony of writer's block, when a piece won't cohere and the right words can't be found. There come times when the composition of a single paragraph is like walking through three feet of snow. The words trudge heavily, one slow-footed phrase after another. "I am irritated by my writing," Flaubert once complained. "I am like a violinist whose ear is true, but whose fingers refuse to reproduce precisely the sound he hears within." All of us have shared the experience.

Yet writing is also pleasure, and when we are writing on some topic *con amore*, writing is among life's greatest pleasures. Whether we are writing news articles, editorials, essays, magazine pieces, novels, advertising copy, or speeches for the boss, we are creating; we are combining whatever wit and skill and experience we have into a product that did not exist an hour before. To borrow Ma Bell's famous slogan, we reach out and touch someone. Ninety-nine percent of what we write is written on sand or in the air. The world of publishing and broadcasting is a minotaur that must constantly be fed; it must be fed words, millions of words, and almost any old words will do. But when a writer looks back after a week's hard labor, and finds that he has written *one good sentence*, that satisfaction is enough to keep him going. He willingly will cook up more scraps for the minotaur.

So we write, edging our way across the minefields of language, and we do not apologize for practicing the writer's art. It is a way of life to be proud of. For the past thirty years, I have ended all of my talks to journalism students and newspaper colleagues with the same quotation from Alexander Woollcott. It ought to be engraved in the hearts and minds of all of us in the press:

"I count it a high honor to belong to a profession in which the good men write every paragraph, every sentence, every line, as lovingly as any Addison or Steele, and do so in full regard that by tomorrow it will have been burned, or used, if at all, to line a shelf.''

6   The Tools
        We Live By

Of the making of books, said the Preacher, there is no end—and certainly there is no end to the number of books about words and usage and style. Every professional writer possesses eight feet or nine yards or, for all I know, whole furlongs of shelf space filled with such books. They are the tools we live by.

The list that follows is not intended to be comprehensive. I doubt that a truly comprehensive list ever could be compiled. My thought is only to catalog a few of the books in my own reference library that have been most helpful to me.

DICTIONARIES

From the time of its appearance in 1961, *Webster's Third New International Dictionary* has been roundly denounced. It rarely has been defended, and this is grossly unfair. The Third is in many ways an admirable work—indeed, an almost indispensable work—for any person who hopes to use the English language accurately.

The scorn arises from the decision deliberately made by editor-in-chief Philip B. Gove to provide "meanings in which words are in fact used, not to give editorial opinion on what the meanings should be." This is not a decision I would have made; my thought is that writers need all the help they can get, and the opinions of professional lexicographers would be useful. But never mind. The Third is intentionally descriptive, not prescriptive, and it must be accepted on the editor's terms.

Copies of *Webster's Second,* which appeared in 1934, are not easy to come by. The work is now fifty years out of date, but it is nonetheless a volume to be cherished if not often consulted.

I like the *American Heritage Dictionary*, edited by William Morris, precisely because it is in part prescriptive. Morris and his panel of experts on usage do not flinch from offering opinions on what is good, better, or best—or for that matter, on what is bad, worse, and worst.

Another useful work is the *Random House Dictionary*, though I use it less frequently than I use the others. The *Oxford American Dictionary*, which appeared in 1980, is still on probation, but there is much to be said for a dictionary that quotes a sentence, *Hopefully, we shall be there by one o'clock*, and adds stiffly, ''Many people regard this use as unacceptable.''

The dictionary of my everyday choice, if I could afford but one compact volume for constant use, would be *Webster's Ninth New Collegiate Dictionary* of 1983. The work is set in a typeface so small—smaller than agate—that the font might be identified as Surgeon General Bold. Even so, it is the best of the compacts.

The dictionary for my luxurious taste, of course, is the justly famed *Oxford English Dictionary* (OED). For lovers of the language, few pleasures match the pleasure of browsing through its pages. The monumental work began as a gleam in the eye of the Dean of Westminster in 1857. The Philological Society took up the idea, expanded the dean's concept, and began accumulating words and citations. It was to be a wholly new dictionary. In 1878 the project began to get rolling, and the first volume covering *A* through *Ant* appeared in 1884. The last of the ten original volumes came off the press in 1928. By that time five million excerpts from English literature had accumulated, and 1.8 million passages actually had been quoted. The whole thing ran to 15,487 pages.

In the 1960s, the Oxford University Press commissioned a series of four supplements intended to bring the masterwork up to date. The first of these, covering new words from *A* through *O*, appeared in 1972; the second, going from *H* through *N*, came out in 1976. The third, taking us from *O* through the first part of the letter *S*, appeared early in 1983. The supplements don't come cheap. The first two were priced at $90 each, the third at $125.

Several years ago, thanks to advances in the technology of printing, Oxford produced a splendid two-volume edition of the original ten volumes. These two volumes are in microprint, a greatly reduced typeface that must be read with a magnifying glass, but no matter: The publishers thoughtfully provide a good glass with the set, and the whole works can be had for a reasonable price.

In addition to these dictionaries of general reference, I might suggest a few dictionaries of special use:

Dictionary of American Slang (Crowell, 1960), compiled by Harold Wentworth and Stuart Berg Flexner. It let me down on *hickey*, which to my sexagenarian surprise no longer means a mere pimple, but generally it has proved reliable.

Brewer's Dictionary of Phrase and Fable (Harper & Row, 1970), revised by Ivor H. Evans.

Safire's Political Dictionary (Random House, 1978), by William Safire.

A Dictionary of Euphemisms and Other Doubletalk (Crown, 1981), by Hugh Rawson.

Morris Dictionary of Words and Phrase Origins (Harper & Row, 1977), by William and Mary Morris.

Webster's Biographical Dictionary (G. & C. Merriam, 1971).

Everyman's Dictionary of Shakespeare Quotations (Dent & Dutton, 1953), compiled by D.C. Browning. The work is miserably indexed and has some startling omissions, but it is useful even so.

The Oxford Dictionary of Quotations, Third Edition (1979).

Bartlett's Familiar Quotations, Fifteenth Edition (Little, Brown, 1980).

A New Dictionary of Quotations (Knopf, 1962), selected by H.L. Mencken. Here the quotations are arranged topically, a tremendous help to the columnist or editorial writer who needs a couple of ribbons and bows to dress up his copy.

New Rhyming Dictionary and Poets' Handbook (Harper, 1957), by Burges Johnson.

Dictionary of Foreign Terms (Crowell, 1975), by C.O. Sylvester Mawson, revised by Charles Berlitz.

AUTHORITIES ON USAGE

The writer who takes his writing seriously will begin with Henry Fowler's *Modern English Usage*, as revised by Sir Ernest Gowers (Oxford, 1965). The work has this in common with an American Express card: We ought never to go to work without it.

The idea for an authoritative guide to English usage originated in the minds of the brothers Henry and Francis Fowler in 1909. They proposed "to assume a cheerful attitude of infallibility," and they did just that. The work had to be put off while the brothers completed their *Concise Oxford Dictionary* in 1911. In 1914 they enlisted for World War I, but the war broke Francis's health. He died in 1918.

Henry set to work on *Modern English Usage*. After eight years of loving labor, the work appeared in 1926. It swiftly became the classic, ultimate authority, and it remains the classic, ultimate authority to this day. Sir Ernest Gowers, in 1965, was the ideal choice to bring Fowler's original work up to date. He was just as didactic, just as prejudiced, just as cheerfully assured of his own infallibility as his illustrious predecessor. Without a careful, entry-by-entry comparison, it is hard to tell where Fowler ends and Gowers begins. A paperback edition of Fowler/Gowers appeared from the Oxford University Press in 1983.

My own copy of *Modern English Usage* lives on a shelf about three feet from my typewriter. The work is valuable not merely for purposes of reference, but also for a quality rarely found in books that deal with grammar, syntax, and semantics: It is great good fun to read. Unlike Dr. Gove and his lexicographers of Webster's III, Fowler was not at all concerned with descriptive analysis. He was nothing if not prescriptive. He snorted. He fumed. He denounced. He scorned. He derided. But he also teased and poked fun, and he talked good sense.

Fowler's little essay on "Preposition at End" is a typical gem. Here he traces the "superstition" that prepositions must never appear at the end of a sentence. The controversy goes back at least to Dryden and to Gibbon, both of whom tended to translate their English into Latin and the Latin back into English. Fowler had no patience with writers who struggle to avoid the sentence-ending preposition.

"That depends on what they are cut with," said Fowler, "is not improved by conversion into, *That depends on with what they are cut,* and too often the lust of sophistication, once blooded, becomes uncontrollable, and ends with, *That depends on the answer to the question as to with what they are cut.* Those who lay down the universal principle that final prepositions are 'inelegant' are unconsciously trying to deprive the English language of a valuable idiomatic resource."

Fowler's lecture on "Love of the Long Word" is another jewel: "It is a general truth that the short words are not only handier to use, but more powerful in effect; extra syllables reduce, not increase, vigour."

Very well. We must have Fowler's *Modern English Usage* close at hand. We must also have Wilson Follett's *Modern American Usage* (Hill and Wang, 1966), if only to read and reread Follett's opening three essays, "On Usage, Purism and Pedantry," "On the Need of an Orderly Mind," and "On the Need of Some Grammar." In themselves, these constitute an excellent small textbook for the writer, but Follett's work is useful in a hundred ways. His brief appendix on punctuation is a first-rate guide for all of us to follow.

In addition to Fowler and Follett, I rely upon anything—well, almost anything—by the late Theodore Bernstein, of The New York Times. He was one of the great copy editors of all time, a man who regarded language as "a precision instrument," to be kept sharp and not to be used carelessly. In the course of a long and productive life (he died in 1979 at the age of 74), Bernstein wrote six books and edited 389 issues of Winners and Sinners, the occasional in-house memoranda he prepared for members of the Times staff.

Bernstein had a thing about *who* and *whom,* and he labored both incessantly and futilely to keep reporters and editors straight on the correct usage. From the respected columns of the Times he plucked all kinds of errors—*peddled* for *pedaled,* and *who's* for *whose,* and *Marquis de Queensberry* for *Marquis of Queensberry.*

In an obituary on Bernstein, Charles B. Seib of The Washington Post recalled that Bernstein, like Thoreau, valued simplicity. "When a Times story said that a man died one year and his wife expired the next, Bernstein commented: 'Why the fancy word *expired?* Do away with monologophobia and repeat, *died.*'" Seib recalled that Bernstein collected mixed metaphors, and once cited as "possibly a record" this remarkable sentence: "Hope for a resumption of Arab-Israeli negotiations is hanging on the slimmest of threads, but two developments of recent days flash the signal that the door remains at least ajar for the kind of diplomatic footwork that can forestall the outbreak of war."

Bernstein's books include one that I consult regularly, *The Careful Writer: A Modern Guide to English Usage,* and one that often provokes a choleric reaction, *Miss Throttlebottom's Hobgoblins,* in which Bernstein indulged all his permissive impulses. He was not nearly as crotchety as I am about a misplaced *only,* and he brushed aside the distinction between *such as* and *like* as mere nitpicking. When a writer is stuck for a word, another Bernstein book worth having at hand is his *Reverse Dictionary* (Quadrangle, 1975). It includes a table of creature terms, from which one can learn that a group of bears is a *sloth,* a group of herons is a *siege,* and a group of peafowls is a *muster.* Hummingbirds and finches come in *charms,* sparrows in *hosts,* and nightingales in *watches.* A she-polecat is a *jill.* But I digress.

The *Harper Dictionary of Contemporary Usage* (Harper & Row, 1975), compiled by William and Mary Morris, is an excellent guide through the thickets of English. I turn frequently to *Words on Words* (Columbia University Press, 1980), by John Bremner. Yet another useful reference work is Roy Copperud's *American Usage: The Consensus* (Van Nostrand, 1970), in which he tallied the votes of Fowler, Follett, Bernstein, and others on disputed points. For both pleasure and instruction, William Safire's *On Language* and *What's the Good Word?* are good fun. In the same vein, Edwin Newman's *Strictly Speaking* and *A Civil Tongue* will delight the careful writer.

These several authorities are often in passionate disagreement. In this regard, they are like the nine justices of the Supreme Court, who are at their best and most vigorous in denouncing the wrongheadedness of one another. My advice is to read all of them and then, after reflection, decide which authority you prefer. We ought never to follow Fowler slavishly, or to swallow everything that Follett and Bernstein prescribed. When it comes to words, nobody has the last word.

BOOKS ON HOW TO WRITE

This category can be dealt with briefly. Whether you classify yourself as amateur or professional, if you could acquire but one book on how to write, that one book incontestably would be William Zinsser's *On Writing Well* (Harper & Row, 1980). Zinsser is an old Herald-Tribune hand, former columnist for Life magazine and The New York Times, for nine years a teacher of writing at Yale. At $8.95, his book is the best bargain since Bill Seward bought Alaska. It's available in paperback also.

One of Zinsser's best chapters has to do with the litter that clutters our copy—the little words that add nothing and serve only to take up space. "He is a *personal* friend of mine." Or, "Let us open *up* the discussion." Zinsser's sound theory is that "writing improves in direct ratio to the number of things we can keep out of it."

E.B. White, in his superlative *Elements of Style* (Macmillan, 1959), makes the same point. His particular war is upon such qualifiers as *rather, very, little,* and *pretty.* "These are the leeches that infest the pond of prose, sucking the blood of words.'' White's book developed as the outgrowth of a much earlier text on writing that had been prepared by William Strunk, Jr., who was among White's professors at Cornell some sixty years ago. Every writer who aspires to improve his prose should be commanded to reread Strunk/White at least once a year. It teaches us just about all we really need to know.

I recommend Zinsser as first choice only because *On Writing Well* covers more ground than Strunk/White. Zinsser has instructive things to say not only about writing in general, but also about writing in such specialized fields as travel, humor, sports, criticism, and science. An especially useful chapter deals with ''Writing in Your Job,'' in which he suggests that office managers and corporation executives should learn to impart information ''clearly and without pompous verbosity.'' (I have a notion, but do not insist upon it, that *pompous* is clutter in that sentence. To be verbose is almost inherently to be pompous.) In 1983, Zinsser produced still another useful book, *Writing with a Word Processor.* It's a most reassuring work for those of us whose mechanical skills end with changing a light bulb.

An alternative to Zinsser, pitched more closely to the needs of the absolute beginner, is *Writing with Precision* (Acropolis, 1978) by Jefferson D. Bates.

BOOKS ON WORDS

For those whose interests tend toward etymology, which involves (among other things) the tracing of words to their earliest use, Henry Mencken's *The American Language* offers a happy pasture to romp in. Mencken's purpose was not to update Sir William Craigie's four-volume *Dictionary of the American Language.* His purpose was to have a wonderful time with words. He loved words in the same way that a philatelist loves stamps and a vexillologist loves flags. He was a great stylist, an excellent reporter, and the finest non-professional student of linguistics ever to come along.

Another book that is nice to have around is *English English* (Verbatim, 1980), by Norman W. Schur, in which the differences between American English and English English are neatly catalogued. In the United States, political parties have *platforms.* In the U.K., they have *programmes.* Our *string beans* are their *French beans;* our *truck* is their *lorry,* and so on.

A third useful work, though it suffers for want of a better index, is *American English* by Albert H. Marckwardt, as revised in 1980 by J.L. Dillard (Oxford). Of primary interest to scholars is the *Linguistic Atlas of the United States and Canada.*

BOOKS TO HAVE FUN WITH

Somewhere in this broad land there may be a writer who detests crossword puzzles, anagrams, double-acrostics, and the like, but I have never met such a writer and I would approach his work with a skeptical eye. Writers cannot work all the time at their tasks. They must have time not only to work with words but also to play with words.

Eugene T. Maleska's *A Pleasure in Words* (Simon & Schuster, 1981) is just that—a pleasurable book about words by the crossword puzzle editor of The New York Times. Another book that is fun to browse through is Gyles Brandreth's *The Joy of Lex* (Morrow, 1980). Willard Espy's *Almanac of Words at Play* (Potter, 1975) will provide hours of delightful reading.

BOOKS ON SYNTAX AND GRAMMAR

Professor George Curme's two-volume work, *A Grammar of the English Language* (Verbatim, 1977) is the classic in its field. One volume deals with parts of speech, the other with syntax. Once you figure out Curme's system of references and cross-references, the work provides a clear road map to correct usage.

THINGS TO SUBSCRIBE TO

Dozens of periodicals—perhaps scores of periodicals—deal with language in one way or another. Let me recommend two of them: Verbatim, edited by Laurence Urdang, a quarterly published at $7.50 a year (Box 668, Essex, Conn. 06426), and Editor's Revenge, a monthly mimeographed sheet at $6 a year, published by J.T. Harding at Box 805, Morristown, N.J. 07960. Verbatim is the more scholarly of the two. Editor's Revenge is mostly fun in the city room. For writers who are deeply into word games, the quarterly Word Ways, put out by A. Ross Eckler, Spring Valley Road, Morristown, N.J. 07960, probably is useful. Its articles are mostly over my head, but for Scrabble nuts it may be the ideal gift for Christmas.

Just as no carpenter ever has quite enough tools, nor any general quite enough troops, a writer never can acquire all the reference works he would love to have. This abbreviated bibliography has left out the essays of Thomas Middleton, one of the most graceful and sensible critics in the field. I have overlooked Rudolf Flesch's salutary advice on the writing art; I omitted the Funk & Wagnall's *Handbook of Synonyms and Antonyms,* but if I start adding things to this list we will be here all night. Earlier I urged all would-be writers to "read insatiably," and high on the list of books a writer should read are books about writing and our treasury of words.

7 My Crotchets and Your Crotchets

Upon reflection, I am inclined to doubt that *crotchet* is truly the word I want for the glossarial notes that follow, but *foible* and *prejudice* are no better, and besides, *crotchet* is an interesting word. A *crotchet* is a surgical instrument; it is a quarter note; it is "a simple curved seta that is notched at the distal end and that is found in annelids." A *crotchet* is also a reaping hook, and a pair of *crotchets* make typographical brackets.

More to the point, Webster's III defines a *crotchet* as "an out of the ordinary attitude or habit, an opinion usually of little ultimate importance; whim, peculiarity." The OED defines *crotchet* as "whimsical fancy; a perverse conceit; a peculiar notion on some point (usually considered unimportant) held by an individual in opposition to common opinion." The OED tracks this meaning to the late sixteenth century and cites, by way of example, a reference in Burton's *Anatomy of Melancholy* to "that castle in the ayr, that crotchet, that whimsie."

A writer's heartfelt convictions on points of usage and syntax cannot fairly be termed whimsy. They may reflect simple ignorance or sheer obstinacy, but such convictions are passionately held. Read the strictures of Henry Fowler—or read Follett, Gowers, Nicholson, Bernstein, Copperud, Evans, Safire, Newman, the Morrises, or the American Heritage panel—and you will hear the adrenals pumping away. The "notions" of good and bad writing ought not to be dismissed as "of little ultimate importance." Every one of my one hundred crotchets is as dear to me as Audrey, the country wench, was dear to Touchstone. She was an ill-favored thing, sir, but his own. If I am tetchy about the placement of *only,* that's it. I'm crotchety.

Very well. Most of the points that follow have been explicated in most

151

of the standard reference works. Everyone who writes about writing has written about *flaunt* and *flout*, about *infer* and *imply*, about *less* and *fewer*. Little good purpose may be served by trotting these old horses once more around the track. Nevertheless, there has to be a first time for every experience, and it may be that some of these observations will be new to some budding writer, somewhere.

a

"A" and "An"

Early in 1983 I found myself entangled in a matter that provoked an astonishing mail. It had to do with the article adjectives *a* and *an*. These surely are not words well calculated to give offense, but it turned out that readers had strong views on the subject.

I wrote that far from finding a hard and fast rule on *a* and *an,* I could not find even a loose and sloppy rule. It seems all to depend, said I, on the ear and the eye. Thus, in the San Francisco Chronicle, a defendant admits guilt to "a indictment." Also from the Chronicle, a lawyer says something in "a interview." Still again from the Chronicle: "A Israeli colonel was quoted . . ."

Under a 48-point headline, The Harrisburg (Pa.) Patriot-News provides at the year's end "A Editorial Sampler" of opinions that had gone before. A columnist in the Philadelphia Daily News came up with "an hilarious story." The Philadelphia Inquirer proclaims in an eight-column streamer, "A Historic Challenge." The Portland Oregonian reports on "a apprentice telegrapher."

The general rule, of course, is well known: We should use *a* before all words beginning with consonants and *an* before all words beginning with vowels, but that general rule will throw you into *an unique situation* and *an one-cent* increase. Exceptions have to be made for the vowel sounds that the ear turns into consonants: *yew-nique,* and *won-cent.*

The ear is likely to deceive us in this business of aspirates. The rule in American English is that there is practically no such thing as a dropped "aitch." Some of my revisionist friends would rewrite *The Book of Common Prayer* so that we would confess our sins with *a humble* and contrite heart. To my ear, *an humble* is better. My ear doesn't hear the *h* in such words as *historic, hysterical,* and *hilarious;* I would use *an* with all of these. But my ear is an inconstant ear. I would write about *a hotel* and *a happening.* John Irving, it follows, wrote an hilarious novel about a hotel in New Hampshire.

My thought—it is by no means an original thought—is that the reading eye and the inner ear function in tandem in this regard. The eye reads, *a* L.A. Times editorial, but the ear hears *an* L.A. Times editorial. Was the fictional Lieutenant Kojak *a* NYPD detective or *an* NYPD detective? It depends on whether the eye tells the ear that the reference is to *El A* or to *Los Angeles,* or to *En Wye* or *New York.* Professor John Bremner states a rule that satisfies me: "It's a question of judgment." The venerable Fowler, in an uncharacteristically tolerant humor, says that the choice of *a* or *an* in certain situations "is the sort of thing about which we ought to be allowed to do as we please, so long as we are consistent."

A.M. in the Morning

One of these days perhaps all mankind will go to the twenty-four-hour clock. Then 3 o'clock in the afternoon will be "1500 hours" and 4 o'clock in the morning will be "oh-four hundred." Everyone will then be spared an irritating redundancy much beloved by broadcasters and occasionally by The Washington Post, which once reported that Jessica Savitch could be seen "at 8 P.M. tonight" and GSA boss Gerald Carmen "labored until 3 A.M. one morning." It's either 8 o'clock tonight or it's 8 P.M., but it can't properly be both.

Absolute Words

Our language contains perhaps a score of words that may be described as *absolute words.* These are words that properly admit of no comparison or intensification. When the ad writer urges us to buy Raid Roach & Flea Killer because "Raid kills bugs *dead,*" the ad writer is having us on. It would be unusual, not to say impossible, for someone not to die of a *fatal* wound. The abuse of *unique* has been sufficiently belabored; a thing cannot be more or less or rather or somewhat or very *unique.* A thing is unique, period.

Bernstein wisely cautions us against drawing up an arbitrarily definitive list of absolutes, "because if one goes hunting for such words he will find himself in a philosophical predicament and a literary straitjacket." Nevertheless, words that obviously are absolutes "should be inviolate." It is a matter, he reminds us, of preserving words that are not replaceable.

My own modest list of words that cannot be qualified by "very" or "rather" or "a little bit" includes *unique, imperative, universal, final, fatal, complete, virgin, pregnant, dead, equal, eternal, total, unanimous, essential,* and *indispensable.* Follett would have us add *discomfit,* which once meant to undo totally. In its present-day meaning of "to be embarrassed," *discomfit* no longer qualifies. A correspondent suggests, and I am inclined to agree, that *nude* is not subject to modification; a body can't be very nude or partly nude. The phrase we want is probably *partly clad,* but police reporters surely would howl if *partly nude* were denied them.

Argument continues over *perfect,* as in the assertion by the Quaker Oats people that their product is "nature's most perfect food." Notwithstanding Caesar's "most unkindest cut of all," or the Constitution's hope for a "more perfect union," I would be inclined to preserve *perfect* as one of Bernstein's inviolables. Christopher Morley, speaking through that remarkable canine Mr. Gissing, once reflected that "the just short of perfect—how perfect it is!" The terms of geometry qualify as absolutes. An object can't be *very square* or *a little bit round.* Perhaps it is *inevitable* that those who play with words will *forever* haggle over absolute words, for the list runs on. I suggest we come to a *stop,* and not, as the airline flight attendants tell us, a *complete stop* at the gate.

Abstract/Abstraction

That glob on the gallery wall that looks as if (a) someone had tipped over five buckets of paint, or (b) someone set out to make a design for linoleum, is not an *abstract.* It is an *abstraction.* It is a specimen of *abstract expressionism.* The noun *abstract* has to do with summaries of the main points of a document: an *abstract* of a will, an *abstract* of a deed. The adjective *abstract* has to do with things that are difficult to understand, e.g., the paintings of Jackson Pollock.

Access (v)

Webster's III, Random House, and American Heritage do not list *access* as a verb, but their horse-and-buggy lexicographers were caught in the dust of a computer age. Webster's New Collegiate (1979) matter-of-factly accepted *access* in the sense that now has been accepted universally, i.e., to gain access to the innards of a data processing system. None of my dictionaries has caught up with *to scroll*, but the New Collegiate is hep to *format, formatted, formatting*. Computerese is a language all its own, and we had better learn it. The day is at hand when millions of households will be accessing data banks. I venture no protest. These are useful verbs. They ought to be welcomed.

Ad Hoc

An *ad hoc* committee is a body created for a particular purpose; after its work is completed, the committee is expected to dissolve. Senator Harrison Schmitt of New Mexico made a verb of *ad hoc*. He said he was "tired of ad hocking it in education," and wanted a permanent body created.

Ad Nauseam

If you are determined to use this poor old thing, at least spell it right. It's not *ad nauseum*, it's *ad nauseam*. I'm sick of it myself.

Adages, Old

In the Rex Morgan comic strip, Dr. Morgan remarks that it has been three years since he has seen a particular patient. Nurse June replies, "To use an old cliché, time flies."

The president of the United States, at a "Day of Remembrance" ceremony, remarks upon the impact of photographs of victims of the Holocaust. He recalls "the old cliché that a picture is worth a thousand words."

Andrew Beyer, who brilliantly covers racing for The Washington Post, is in Louisville for the 1981 running of the Derby. "Ordinarily," he writes, "I consider the old handicapping adage that 'pace makes the race' to be a bunch of malarkey."

Newsweek magazine is covering an exhibition of photographs. "There's an old cliché that it's the handling, not the subject, that counts in art."

The Saturday Evening Post has a piece about Henry Catto and his wife. "Any foreigner clinging to old clichés about Texans is likely to be disappointed—or surprised, perhaps—that the Cattos are Texan."

From a bridge column by Charles Goren and Omar Sharif: " 'Third hand high' is an old adage of bridge players."

From The Washington Star, in an editorial on racial balance busing: "Some of its defenders . . . defend it on the basis of the old maxim, 'Let justice be done though the heavens fall.' "

Aaargh, aargh, and aargh again! Can't we have some new clichés, some new adages, some new maxims, some new saws, some new proverbs? These things are inherently *old.* And why resort to clichés anyhow?

Adapt/Adopt

No good reason suggests itself for the two words ever to be confused, but now and then they are confused. One *adapts* to a situation; the meaning is to accommodate or to adjust. One *adopts* a position, an amendment, or a child; the meaning is to embrace or to espouse.

Admonish

A very long time ago, when I was covering a United States District Court as a very young cub reporter, I wrote that "Judge Pollard admonished Allen to prepare a summary of the cases on which he would rely." I don't know where I got *admonished* or why I used the word, but attorney George Allen was justifiably annoyed. *To admonish* is close to *to reprove.* It carries a connotation of warning or disapproval. Had the court ordered Allen to stop badgering a witness, the word would have been properly used.

Adverse/Averse

These are trickers, because both adjectives carry a sense of opposition or hostility; both take the preposition *to;* and except in such constructions as *adverse* winds or *adverse* circumstances, both sound a little puffed-up. Of the two, *adverse* is the stronger; to be in adversity is to be in serious trouble—in suffering or destitution, flat broke, afflicted by calamity. By contrast, *averse* means to be disinclined: I am *averse* to hard exercise. To have an aversion to something is actively to dislike it. Generally speaking, things are *adverse,* people are *averse.* To say that Senator Helms was *adverse* to the Panama Treaty is clumsy; the senator was opposed to it. He was *averse* to voting in its favor. If ever you are tempted to use *animadversion,* resist the temptation. This is a five-dollar word for *calumny,* which is a four-dollar word for *aspersion.* There are better ways to speak of criticism that is not merely adverse, but also unfair.

Affect/Effect

Affect and *effect* continue to give trouble. The Sentinel, a Jewish newspaper, reports that daily study of Talmudic texts has had a "profound affect" on the lives of many American Jews. A spokesman for the Federal Trade Commission reportedly believes that changing policies at the FTC will have "relatively little affect" on consumers' pocketbooks. The Indianapolis Star, reporting on hearings for two groups of air traffic controllers, doubts that one group's hearings "will effect" the other. Wrong, all wrong.

To *affect* something is to influence it, to shape it, to bring about a change in it. To *effect* is to produce a result. Fowler offers as an example, "A single glass of brandy may *affect* his recovery," meaning to alter his prospects for recovery. "A single glass of brandy may *effect* his recovery" means that the brandy could make him well, a pleasant thought.

In a reckless moment, I once asserted airily that *effect* is both a noun and a verb, while *affect* is a verb only. Not so. Fifty psychiatrists wrote to say that *affect* is indeed a noun. It is "the conscious subjective aspect of an emotion considered apart from bodily changes." Okay by me.

Affidavit

Avoid "sworn affidavit." There is no such thing as an unsworn affidavit.

Affluent/Effluent

I doubt that the two are often confused, but I include them because of a news item I once saw about a pulp mill in Clifton Forge, Virginia. "The affluent created an almost intolerable stench." I thought it was a typo until I noticed, farther down in the story, that "to purify the affluent" would cost a bundle. Both words have the same root in *fluere,* to flow, but the *affluent* are the rich. The *effluent,* in this instance, was liquid waste. They say in Clifton Forge, "It smells like money."

Aggravate/Irritate

Aggravate comes out of the Latin *aggragave,* to make heavier, and ought to be used only in that sense: "The majority leader's problems were *aggravated* by a handful of liberal Republicans who became known as the Gang of Five." *Irritate* means to incite anger or impatience; it is closer to *annoy* or *rile.*

Alibi/Excuse

The Gresham's Law of Language, which teaches us that bad usages tend to drive out the good, has affected *alibi.* The word comes directly from the Latin for "elsewhere," and ought to be reserved for that meaning. A defendant who contends that he has an *alibi* is offering a specific defense: He was somewhere else when the crime was committed. Over the years *alibi* has come to mean almost any kind of justification offered in one's defense: "Wright said the President was full of alibis for the mounting deficits." The Texas congressman should have said that Mr. Reagan was full of *excuses,* but *alibis* is a zingier word. Besides, it fits better in a headline.

All Due Respect

This is one of those euphemistic phrases, drawn from parliamentary speech, that ought to be reserved for malicious occasions. The clear implication of *all due respect* is that no respect at all is due. The phrase hangs in the same elegant cloakroom on a hook next to *with deference to the learned opinion of my able and distinguished friend.* Such fulsome compliments are as necessary to parliamentary speech as oil is vital to an auto, but in ordinary writing and discourse *all due respect* should be reserved for the opinions of blithering idiots.

All-Important

It is a noisy world we live in. At any given moment, somewhere a horn is honking, somewhere a fender crumples. We seem to spend a great deal of our time quarreling with the godless Commies, and the godless Commies spend their time snarling back at us capitalist warmongers. A rock band plays music to chew gum by. The TV switch is always on. Sirens rip the black fabric of a city night.

As a consequence, a tendency develops to shout. It is wrongly supposed that this is the only fashion in which we may be heard. Out of the hypodermic needle squirts the verb *to hype,* and even the most respectable writers yield to the temptation to hype things up. Thus National Review in 1983 provided a few background facts "as the British prepare for the all-important election next month." The Washington Post, reporting on presidential primaries, has spoken of "all-important" New Hampshire.

Pfui. This kind of hyperbole may be tolerated in the sports pages, where even a high school tennis match is *all-important,* but we ought to avoid the exaggeration elsewhere. After all, what in the course of human events truly might be termed *all-important?* Two possibilities occur to me: The avoidance of nuclear war, and the Second Coming of Christ. I cannot think of others. Once I read a bridge column in which a spade finesse was *all-important.* Somehow this seemed unlikely.

If we intend to howl about calamities, we ought first to make certain that a calamity is at hand to howl about. The story is told of a long-suffering editor who summoned his junior editorial writers to a conference on New Year's Day. "Ladies and gentlemen," he said, "we are about to ration our reserves of alarm and indignation. During the twelve months that lie ahead, each of you may have six outrages, four disasters, and no more than two crises. If you exhaust your quota by July, thereafter you must retreat to the level of comment at which a given action is merely unfortunate, lamentable, regrettable, or disturbing."

I pass the advice along. Before we declare an event to be *all-important*—or *crucial* or *critical* or *vital*—let us recall the command that General Jackson was said to have voiced at the Battle of New Orleans. "Boys," he reportedly suggested to his gunners, "let us elevate them sights a little lower."

All-Time Record

It probably is captious to object to *new records,* despite the evident redundancy, but to be informed that Sebastian Coe set an *all-time record* for the mile is annoying. A record is a record. It is an "attested top performance." In whatever field, as the Guinness people tell us, a record is the fastest, slowest, highest, lowest, oldest, newest, longest, or shortest of its kind as of a given date. The *all-time* goes without saying; and if something goes without saying, why say it?

All and Not All

"Let me point out," said political adviser Lyn Nofziger, "that all of the people who supported Ronald Reagan in California were not opposed to him on this tax bill."

"It seems clear to me," said Justice Minton, dissenting in *Terry* v. *Adams,* "that everything done by a person who is an official is not done officially."

Chief Justice Burger, in *Chandler* v. *Florida:* "All of the dissenting justices in *Estes* did not read the Court as announcing a *per se* rule."

"All the evidence to date," said Princeton demographer James Trussell, "indicates that all places are not undercounted to the same extent."

A study of accidental injuries reported to the Consumer Product Safety Commission, said The Washington Post, "noted that all seventy-four hospitals did not report every month."

Says a TV commercial: "All Kitty Litters are not alike."

Most builders of kitchen cabinets, commented a Jacksonville columnist, "have yet to discover that all shelves need not be the same width."

From Response, a publication of the American Petroleum Institute: "All tracts are not drilled on the same schedule."

Ann Landers, about life in California: "Everyone in San Francisco is not gay."

Stanley Kauffmann in The New Republic: "But every painting of the Madonna is not a good painting."

And finally, a headline in the old Washington Star: "Everything Isn't What It Seems."

It is not surprising that in casual speech, where meaning can be conveyed by tone and gesture and inflection, *all* and *not all* should give little trouble. If our conversation concerns the Smith students who prevented Jeane Kirkpatrick from speaking on campus, we understand what is meant when a young woman says defensively, "Well, *all* of us didn't object." She means that *not all* of the students objected; some of them favored the Kirkpatrick address.

It *is* surprising that the solecism crops up so widely in print, and in such high-toned places as the Supreme Court Reports. Justice Minton

meant that "not everything that is done by an official is done officially."
Chief Justice Burger meant that "not all the dissenting Justices in *Estes*"
read the case the same way. As for Ann Landers, she knows better. In the
same column in which she imparted the eye-popping news that "everyone in San Francisco is not gay," she had it right in a preceding
paragraph: "Not everyone in California goes to the beach every day."

Before we launch into a sentence of negative construction beginning
with *all* or *every,* let us pause to reflect. "All of the members have not
voted" means that no one of them has voted; and the chances are that that
is not what we mean at all.

Alleged

Alleged is a useful word in its place, and its place ordinarily is in the
prudent counsel of a newspaper's lawyers. As Bernstein has remarked, if
the word did not exist in the sense of *the alleged thief,* the word would
have to be invented. No other word has been devised to describe a
suspect who has been charged with a crime, or indicted for a crime, but
not yet found guilty of the crime. But when we take cover behind the
barricade of *alleged,* we ought to be certain we know who is doing the
alleging—ordinarily an arresting officer or a grand jury. Before someone
becomes "an alleged thief," he is best described as a "suspect in the
theft of." Do not write of *the alleged suspect.* That conceivably might
protect you from a suit for libel, but not from a charge of redundancy.

Alternately/Alternatively

The thing to remember about *alternately* is that it means one *after* the
other. Numbers *alternately* are odd and even. The squares on a chess
board are *alternately* black and white. This has nothing to do with
alternatively, which conveys the sense of one *or* the other. We could go
to the movies; *alternatively* we could stay home and play Scrabble. An
alternator generates alternating current. An alternate is an adjective, a
verb, and a convention delegate.

Amend/Emend

Webster's says that to *amend* is to make emendations, which gets us
nowhere. The words are used in quite different senses. *Amend* carries the

connotation of formal and substantive change: The House *amended* the tax bill. To *emend* is to correct. An editor's role is to *emend* the text.

Among/Between

Contrary to the rule expounded in some antiseptic quarters, there is no rigid rule that *between* is used only for two things and *among* only for three or more. This is a sound general proposition, and of course *among* cannot be used for two. If only two teams are involved, a pennant race cannot be *among* the Cubs and the Cards; come the millennium, such a race would be *between* them. But a treaty properly would be described as *between* the United States, France, and the United Kingdom.

Anniversary

You wouldn't think *anniversary* would cause trouble, but in thoughtless moments it does. Thus a correspondent for the Associated Press once reported from Warsaw that on June 12, 1982, the Poles observed "the seven-month anniversary of the December 13 military crackdown." The AP's man couldn't even count correctly. The respected Wall Street Journal fell into the same error. It reported Poland's "six-month anniversary." No way. George Kelley of the Youngstown Vindicator has proposed *mensiversary* in the name of accuracy. A couple of lawyers, searching for a word to apply to monthly payments on notes, also have suggested *mensiversary*, but the coinage has yet to catch on.

Anxious/Eager

The distinction is worth preserving. To be *anxious* about something is to be worried or uneasy about it. To be *eager* is keenly to desire something. A student may be *anxious* about his grades but *eager* to see classes end.

Apparent/Evident

The two words cause problems, and Webster's is no help in solving them. As a general rule, use *apparent* when a matter is in doubt: He *apparently suffered a heart attack* suggests that we are not sure about it. He *evidently suffered* suggests that we have reasonably convincing evidence to support that conclusion. In a nose-to-nose race to the finish line, Rosebud *apparently* is the winner (appears to be the winner, seems to be the winner), but examination of the photographs discloses that Petunia *evidently* won by half an inch. John Bremner, as is so often the case, offers the best advice: Find some better words than *apparently* or *evidently* when the meaning is not clear. He suggests that we say *obviously* or *unquestionably* when we are sure, and *seemingly* or *probably* when we're not.

Appraise/Apprise

The two words can be scrambled only through ignorance or typographical error. When we read that the president has been *appraised* of opposition in the Senate, we should recognize something wrong. To *appraise* is to put a value on. A president could *appraise* the strength of his opponents. But to *apprise* is simply to inform.

Arbitrate/Mediate

An arbitrator and a mediator perform different functions. The former is a judge; he is expected to be neutral. Therefore do not write that the parties "have agreed upon a neutral arbitrator." A mediator's task is to bring the parties together, to conciliate, to reconcile differences toward the end that an arbiter's award may be avoided.

Author

William and Mary Morris asked their usage panel to vote on *He authored three books in a single year.* The vote was 9-1 against the verb. One panelist remarked that he could accept the sentence only with an addition: *and I readered all three.* Nothing on earth is wrong with *he wrote.* My own inclination would be to put *to author* on a high, dark shelf with *to host, to decision* (except in a boxing match), and *to impact.*

b

Bad/Badly

How do you feel? If you feel *badly,* something is wrong with your sense of touch; your fingers may be numb, or callused, or gloved—who knows? If you feel *bad,* you're ill, depressed, worried. The same distinction applies to other copulative verbs, such as *smell* and *taste.* If you smell *badly,* perhaps your nose is stopped up. If you smell *bad,* try a hot soapy shower.

Believe/Think

In casual speech and writing, the two words are interchangeable. The precise usage scarcely justifies prolonged fussing, but if you want to be fussy: *Believe,* as Bremner notes, has to do with the heart; *think* has to do with the intellect. Thus, I *believe* the president will veto the bill. (You have faith that the president will veto.) But, I *think* the bill is unconstitutional. (You have specific reasons in this regard.)

Bequeath/Devise

These are verbs of the lawyer's art, and ought to be used precisely. Real property such as a farm is *devised;* personal property such as jewelry is *bequeathed.*

Bill/Resolution

These are words of the legislative art, and they are not synonymous or interchangeable. A *bill* is a proposed law; if passed by both houses of Congress and signed by the president (or passed over his veto), the bill becomes a public law. It may be cited thereafter as such-and-such an act, e.g., the Voting Rights Act of 1965. With few exceptions, *resolutions* carry no such authority; ordinarily they express no more than the sense of a legislative body that a particular action should be taken, or that a particular sentiment should be expressed. The principal exception is the joint resolution resolving that such-and-such an article is proposed as an amendment to the Constitution. The saving grace of the Republic is that, while many bills are introduced, few are enacted.

Black/Colored/Negro

As recently as 1940, which wasn't so very long ago, the universal custom among Southern newspapers was to identify persons of color: "The accident was witnessed by Sam Johnson (c), of the 400 block West Leigh Street." Until well into the 1950s, city directories in the South followed the same practice. Warrants, marriage licenses, business licenses and other public papers all carried a routine notation of "colored." That was the accepted descriptive adjective of the time. All such designations have been swept away by the hurricane winds of *Brown* v. *Board of Education,* and the word *colored* survives, ironically, only in the name of the largest of the racially oriented organizations, the National Association for the Advancement of Colored People.

Colored gave way toward the end of the 1950s to *Negro,* which was lowercased in some newspaper style books but eventually capitalized in all of them. The designation survives in such organizations as the United Negro College Fund.

Ten years elapsed, and *Negro* suddenly was displaced by *black.* In Congress we have the Black Caucus. This is now the universally accepted term, and though the adjective is almost everywhere lowercased, the Afro-American press (which has survived all these changes with its own name intact) is pushing for an uppercased B in Black.

These changes in nomenclature have perplexed the Bureau of the Census. Until 1820 blacks were not counted by either race or sex; they were enumerated under Article I of the Constitution as "all other persons." In 1820, the Census began counting blacks by sex (901,000 males, 871,000 females), but in Southern states they were all lumped together as "slaves." After the census of 1860 the practice was abandoned, but not very happily abandoned. The census of 1890, for example, designated persons descended from forebears with three-fourths or more of "black blood," as *black, mulatto, quadroon,* and *octoroon.* In 1900, census tables classified only *blacks* and *mulattos,* but table headings and notes took to the use of *colored.*

This semantic shifting and grappling led to an international uproar with the census of 1930, in which Mexicans, Negroes, Indians, and Asiatics were enumerated as *colored.* Mexico formally objected, and the Mexicans were converted to whites in 1940. In the census of 1970, we find a racial classification according to "Negro or Black," but in 1980, recognizing popular acceptance of a changed nomenclature, the table headings were amended to read, "Black or Negro."

That is where the matter stands now. I recount all this only to echo the point that descriptive linguists constantly make, that language is shaped by the social forces of the time in which language is used. Today racial designations appear to be important only to the government, for purposes of enforcing civil rights; to the medical profession, which recognizes such diseases as sickle cell anemia as predominantly confined to one race or another; and to the politicians, who seek support from the burgeoning "black vote." Eventually all formal and official classifications by race will be abandoned—they will not be greatly missed—and people will be treated as the Supreme Court would have us treat schools: not black, not white, "but just schools," or just people.

Blatant/Flagrant

Parade magazine, reporting in 1982 on food adulteration, said that "one of the most *blatant* cases" occurred in 1969 in England, where a man was charged with selling phony grated Parmesan cheese. What he actually was selling was grated umbrella handles. The offense wasn't *blatant;* it was *flagrant.* The last thing the crook wanted was to be *blatant,* which carries a connotation of conduct that is conspicuous, or arrant, or noisy. *Flagrant* comes out of "burning," and has to do with offenses so obvious they cannot be ignored.

Blond/Blonde

You can't go wrong on *blond* and *blonde,* either as adjective or noun, if you reserve *blonde* for females and *blond* for males and other often inanimate objects.

Boat/Ship

Except for submarines, which were known in World War I as U-boats, a *boat* is any craft small enough to be carried aboard a *ship.* A yacht is neither a boat nor a ship; it is a yacht, and a damned expensive pleasure to maintain.

Bombshell

This is a worn-out and overworked word regularly employed by reporters and editorial writers who are too weary to think of a better word for "stunning event." On its face, *bombshell* is meaningless. Explosions result from explosives inside a bomb, not from the shell in which the bomb is encased. The word ought to be retired.

Boor/Bore

A *boor* is a vulgar, ill-mannered, insensitive person; he arouses disgust. A *bore* is a tiresome, tedious person; he induces yawns.

Boycott/Embargo

Governments do not put *boycotts* on trade with other nations, no matter what you may read in the papers. Governments impose *embargoes*. An *embargo* may be general, which halts all trade, or it may be selective as to certain goods or products, as an *embargo* on shipments of wheat, or an *embargo* on arms. By extension the term has slipped into government and journalism, where the widespread custom is for a document or text to be given to reporters in advance of its release. "The White House has embargoed the text until 6 A.M. June 24." *Boycotts,* so named for an Irish landlord who was ostracized because he refused to reduce rents, are concerted actions of persons refusing to do business or have dealings with someone in their bad graces.

Bring/Take

To *bring* is to convey someone or some thing *toward* the place from which the action is regarded. It is the opposite of to *take,* which connotes action away from the point of view. We bring food to the table, and we take the dirty dishes to the kitchen. A much neglected verb is to *fetch,* which may be used in either sense. Jack and Jill fetched the pail of water; an antique table fetches a high price; a retriever fetches game. I have no idea how *fetch,* which stems from "foot," was extended to *fetching,* which means "attractive," or "achieving a windward mark on a sailing vessel on the tack on which the term is used."

Bullet/Cartridge

To confuse *bullet* and *cartridge* is to drive the national gun lobby into apoplectic fits, no bad idea. A *bullet* is the lead pellet; a *cartridge* is the metal tube containing the bullet and the charge. On this general topic, we should be careful to distinguish the several handguns. A *pistol* is what men used to duel with; the chamber is part of the barrel. A *revolver* has a rotating chamber. An *automatic* relies upon the force of recoil to eject a spent cartridge shell and insert a new one.

Burglary/Robbery

The old distinctions between *burglary* and *robbery* have eroded in the twentieth century. At one time *burglary* had a specific meaning; it was the breaking and entering of a dwelling house in the nighttime. The one essential element that remains is the element of forceful entry; without a forceful entry, we have simple *theft* or *larceny*. *Robbery* at one time applied only to crimes against the person; *highway robbery, train robbery,* and *bank robbery* embraced the element of theft from individuals by violence or threat of violence. I suspect the distinctions faded in part because *burgle* is a funny verb and *burglarize* is no better. I doubt that anyone, in speech or in writing, ever cried to the cops, "My house has been burgled!" Even so, a holdup man isn't a burglar, he's a robber; and a second-story man isn't properly a robber, he's a burglar.

By and Large

Everyone knows what is meant by *by and large*. In the sense of "on the whole" or "in general," it is one of those yawing phrases that permit a writer or speaker to avoid specific facts or figures when he finds it prudent or convenient to do so. I include *by and large* only because it offers an interesting example of the way in which language picks up a word or phrase of precise and special meaning and adapts the word or phrase for broader use. In its original sense, *by and large* meant to sail a little off the wind, rather than close to the wind. This was the safer policy, especially for the sailor, always assuming he was in no hurry to reach his destination.

C

Can/May

Except in the most self-evident constructions, clearly involving physical ability, the distinctions between *can* and *may* are steadily fading. I would indulge a rare permissiveness: Let 'em fade. *My twelve-month-old granddaughter can walk; she just doesn't choose to.* In such a construction, *may* would make no sense. *The horse has recovered fully; he can run tomorrow.* The meaning clearly is that the horse is physically able to run. It is only in the sense of possibility that the distinctions are preserved, and in this context they cause little trouble. *It may rain tomorrow. We may go to town, but then again, we may not.* Incidentally, *may* implies a stronger possibility than *might.* Thus, *it may rain tomorrow* (50 percent chance); *it might rain tomorrow* (20 percent chance). In the context of granting permission, I would abandon the controversy altogether. "You may be excused" and "You can be excused" seem to me equally acceptable. There is no discernible difference between *The decline of Rome can be attributed,* and *The decline of Rome may be attributed.* Let it go.

Care Less (he could)

This is interesting only as an example of the reverse spin that sometimes affects phrases of the clearest meaning. Common sense tells us that *The senator could care less about the president's criticism* is not what is meant at all. What is meant is that *The senator could not care less.* That is, the senator cares not at all; therefore he couldn't care less. The mystifying *could care less* ought to be banished. I couldn't care less if I never ran into the phrase again.

Careen/Career/Carom

The three verbs have distinctive meanings that ought to be preserved, though the issue is not a large one. In its original meaning, *to career* meant to turn a boat on its side so that the keel could be got at for repairs. By extension, careen came to mean "to lurch from side to side," so that today if a drunken driver is *careening* down the highway, he is weaving back and forth. The verb *to career* has fallen out of favor, probably because the reader immediately thinks of *career* as a noun meaning lifework or profession, rather than as a verb meaning to travel at high speed. To *carom,* which comes out of billiards and crossword puzzles, means to bounce off something.

Causal

This is the most frequently misprinted word in the English language. It is not often misspelled, it is only misprinted, largely because typesetters as a breed are unable to believe that a writer means to say *causal.* The typesetter is certain that *casual* was intended, so that we read of the casual relationship between cigarettes and cancer. I have found one device that often is helpful. This is to write a sentence such as *A causal relationship has been established,* and immediately to insert the following bracketed instruction: [Typesetter: That word is not casual, dammit, that word is C-A-U-S-A-L.] This works unless the typesetter, preoccupied and half asleep, sets the bracketed phrase along with everything else, in which event you have the problem of getting it out again.

Cement

It is not a *cement sidewalk,* bless you, and we do not *pour cement.* It is a concrete sidewalk. *Cement* is merely one of the ingredients.

To Chair (a meeting)

I am aware, of course, that all the respectable dictionaries sanction *chair* in the sense of "to preside over a meeting," and I would agree that in diplomatic parlance, *The meeting will be chaired by a member of the Soviet bloc* is an almost unavoidable construction. The verb nevertheless grates on my ear with the squeaky sound of *to host* and *to headquarter.* While I'm on the subject, *chairwoman* and *chairperson* are ridiculous words. Chairman is an office, just as mayor, senator, representative, and treasurer are offices. The word chairman is a common noun; it embraces both sexes with equal affection.

Chord/Cord

Because we tend to think of *chord* in terms of music, and especially of striking *chords* on the strings of a guitar, we may be inclined to think the things in our throat are vocal chords. They're not. They're vocal *cords*. A cord of firewood is a stack four feet by four feet by eight feet.

Claim

We may *claim* a hat, presenting a claim check for that purpose. We may *claim* an inheritance. Those who made the run of '89 into Oklahoma Territory could *stake a claim* or *claim* a piece of land. We may file an insurance *claim*. But I beseech you, do not use claim in the sense of *to assert* or *to maintain*. This is a barbarism. The director of promotion for the National Basketball Association, who once "claimed that he tries to come up with something new every night," wasn't claiming. He was saying, or explaining, or asserting, or remarking, or boasting, but let us save *to claim* from the wordnappers who have abducted too many good words as it is.

Compared to/Compared with

I would not deceive you. I will never in my life comprehend the distinction between *compared to* and *compared with*. My ear hears nothing amiss in "This year's corn crop, compared *to* last year's," or in "This year's corn crop, compared *with* last year's." Let me recommend to you the disquisitions of Jacques Barzun, John Bremner, Henry Fowler, Wilson Follett, Theodore Bernstein, William Safire, and the Morrises, all of whom understand this matter perfectly and have confused me totally. The general rule is to use *compared to* when you wish to emphasize the similarity between the things compared, and to use *compared with* (as in "contrasted with") when you wish to examine dissimilarities. You are now on your own, and I wish you luck.

Complaisant/Complacent

The two words are not even close in their meaning. A *complaisant* person is an obliging person: *A complaisant House gave the president everything he asked for.* A *complacent* person is a self-satisfied person. *The president said complacently that he had expected the favorable outcome.*

Complement/Compliment

Once I went to a meeting of the heads of about fifty political action committees. They gave the press a handout describing a study they had commissioned: "The corporate effort will compliment an academic study." Knowing something of corporation presidents, and something of college professors, I found the prospect unlikely. *To complement,* in this sense, is mutually to fill out a project; to accompany, to make complete. *To compliment* is to praise. Now and then conservative industrialists *compliment* liberal academicians, but not often.

Component Parts

I had never thought about *component parts* until I received a letter from a professor emeritus at a small Southern college. A true Southerner, he began by buttering me up for five paragraphs of praise for my columns. These amenities out of the way, he inquired, "But why, sir, do you persist in writing of *component parts?* Parts are components and components are parts." Against so gentle a charge, I could plead only *nolo contendere.*

Compose/Comprise

The rule here is that the whole *comprises* the parts, and the parts *compose* the whole. *The Society of American Florists' membership comprises 900 grower members, 600 wholesale members, and about 6,200 retail members.* Thus *comprise* means to contain, or to be made up of. Turn the sentence around: *Nine hundred grower members, 600 wholesale members . . . compose the Society of American Florists.* The confusion arises because *compose* may comfortably be employed in either the active or the passive voice: The members *compose.* The Society is *composed of.* But it does not work the other way. The membership *comprises,* but it cannot be *comprised of.* If we can remember that *to comprise* is *to contain,* we may get it straight, for a membership cannot be contained of. My problem is that I cannot seem to remember this.

Consensus

Do not, under any circumstances, ever write of a *consensus of opinion.* That is what a *consensus* is—an expression of the opinions or sentiments or preferences of a group. To its shame, Webster's Collegiate cites John Hersey approvingly: "the consensus of their opinion, based on reports that had drifted back from the border . . ." Aaargh! Do not slavishly accept everything that appears in Webster's Collegiate, and do not sycophantically emulate the lapses of even so gifted a writer as John Hersey. Follow Roy Copperud, whose excellent survey of experts on language is entitled *American Usage: The Consensus.*

Contact

I have surrendered on this one. I may hesitate to use *to contact* in writing, especially formal writing, but in casual speech and informal writing, both as a verb and a noun, *contact* is a useful and inoffensive word. It replaces the idiomatic *get in touch with,* which itself presents a semantic contradiction; we may not touch our contact, we may call him on the telephone instead. Let us cease quibbling over *contact* and quibble over something else instead.

Continual/Continuous

The Jacksonville Times-Union, in an editorial about the construction of new schools, said that existing schools also "must be continuously inspected." Time magazine, reporting on the funneling of arms from Nicaragua to rebels in El Salvador, said the White House "had continuously vowed" to halt the traffic. Both usages were wrong.

The rule here is that *continuous* means constantly; *continual* means repeatedly. Thus, the Mississippi river flows continuously; barge operators ply it continually. At Arlington Cemetery, an eternal flame burns *continuously;* visitors *continually* go there. A useful mnemonic device may be found in the o-u-s ending on *continuous:* It is one uninterrupted sequence.

Convince/Persuade

In the spring of 1983, United Press International reported from Des Moines on a decision of the Iowa Supreme Court. The court "ruled Monday against a leukemia victim who is trying to convince a woman to donate bone marrow . . ." Life magazine told us about a jet-set debutante named Cornelia who travels with a lover named Roberto: "She recently convinced him to take her to Monte Carlo.'' The Washington Post informed us that ''If Venezuela can convince its banks to convert many of the short-term debts . . .'' Yeccch! In each instance, the proper verb was *persuade*. The leukemia victim, the swinging debutante, and the debt-ridden nation all were trying to persuade. *Persuade* properly takes an infinitive; convince never should. The distinctions are worth preserving. An argument that is persuasive may not be convincing. But once we are convinced of something, persuasion has done its job.

d

Days (long)

''The committee spent long days laboring over the resolution.'' They did? What's a *long day?* Twenty-six hours? Thirty-one hours? We constantly are reading of activities that consume long weeks, long months, and long years. ''Proust worked twelve long years. . . .'' ''She waited ten long months for his arrival.'' ''He ran five long miles. . . .'' The same objection applies to such formations as *full quarts*. A day is a day and a quart is a quart and a mile is a mile. Let them stay that way.

To Decision

A Marine Corps commandant issued an announcement toward the end of the 1970s: ''It has been decisioned that some form of unit rotations may be a desirable objective.'' Except in the context of prizefighting, *to decision* is a barbarism. Nothing on earth is wrong with plain old *to decide*.

Deserts/Desserts

These ought never to be confused, but occasionally they are confused— and such occasions make for unintended hilarity. If you were to write of a criminal or a playwright that the person *got his just desserts,* you would be saying that he got all the ice cream (or other rewards) that he had coming. The only meaning of *dessert* has to do with the fruit or pie or cake, or whatever, served at the end of a meal. It is always a noun; a hostess might *desert* you, meaning that she had left you for a time, but she could not properly *dessert* you any more than she could fish or meat or soup you.

Deserts, of course, are such barren places as the Sahara and the Gobi; and just as it generally is needless to speak of crossing the Atlantic *Ocean,* so it is a mild redundancy to speak of a caravan across the Sahara *Desert.*

Dialogue

At some point in recent semantic history, a curious notion took root that *dialogue* should be restricted to describe a conversation between two persons only. The word hasn't had that narrow meaning for several centuries. It means any kind of colloquy or discussion involving two *or more* persons. A phrase to avoid, as Bremner remarks, is *meaningful dialogue.* As a matter of fact, *meaningful* is a word to avoid in almost any construction.

Dilemma

I once wrote, apropos of the senator from Massachusetts, that "with Kennedy's withdrawal, the Democrats' dilemma becomes glaringly apparent." Whereupon I was roundly and soundly rebuked by members of the Society for the Protection of *Dilemma.* It came as a surprise to me to learn that *dilemma* does not mean just any old mess or disarray, as Webster's Collegiate implies; a dilemma is a situation involving two equally unsatisfactory alternatives. A *trilemma* involves three unhappy choices. So far as I am aware, *lemmas* do not go beyond *tri;* after that we have a multiplicity, a plethora, or simply a batch or bunch of poor choices. Avoid *to be caught on the horns of a dilemma.* While you're at it, avoid being caught *between Scylla and Charybdis* or *between a rock and a hard place.* Surely we can find fresher phrases if we try.

Discreet/Discrete

The Washington Post once reported on a quiet effort by Senator Mark Hatfield to persuade his colleagues in a certain direction: "Almost lost in the spectacle of the conservative rebellion was a more discrete effort by Hatfield to insist that the Senate approve at least some money for jobs creation." Wrong word! *Discrete* has to do with things that are individual, separate, distinct. What was intended was *discreet,* which implies an element of unpretentious modesty or prudence. To maintain a *discreet* silence is to keep one's mouth shut at a time when speech would serve no constructive purpose.

Disinterested/Uninterested

If we have to go into court, we want a *disinterested* judge and a *disinterested* jury—that is, we want our liberty or our property to be subject to persons who have no selfish interest in the matter. We would not want them to be *uninterested* in the case, once the trial began. To be *disinterested* is to stand neutral in a cause. To be *uninterested* is not to care.

Drapes/Draperies

A food and restaurant critic for The New York Times did a piece in 1983 about one of the nation's finest country inns, the Inn at Little Washington, Virginia. She loved the food and she loved the decor, about which she wrote: "The peach and cream drapes are patterned with stylized fruits."

At about the same time, the owner of Garfield the cat (if anyone ever owns a cat) was describing Garfield's flaws: "You claw the drapes, shed on the furniture, steal my food. . . ."

Drape isn't a noun. It's a verb. You can drape a suit; you can drape a corpse; you can drape a patient for surgery; an artist can drape a model. But those heavy things hanging in folds at the window are not drapes, they are *draperies*. *Curtains* are something else, usually distinguished by size (they are smaller than draperies), by material (they are less ornate), and by their maneuverability; curtains often can be tied back or rolled up or pulled to open or close them.

Dual/Duel

A *duel* sovereignty, I suppose, would be a sovereignty won at sword's point. In careful usage, *dual* should be reserved for two elements that are shared, or are alike in some way: *dual* personality, *dual* possession, *dual* carburetors. Dueling pistols had better be dual, or somebody is cheating.

e

Encounter

A gentleman in Carmel, Ind., once took me properly to task for writing that "In most of the books I have encountered on how to write . . ." No matter what I had innocently believed all my life, the verb *to encounter* does not mean simply "to run across." It means to meet as an adversary or enemy; to engage in conflict with; to run into a complication.

End Result

Do not say *end result;* say result. And while you're getting rid of a redundancy, get rid of a cliché also: Do not say *bottom line.*

Engine/Motor

Engine is the generic term. All *motors* by definition are *engines,* but not all *engines* are *motors.* Airplanes, ships, trains, and automobiles have *engines;* it would be unthinkable for the Indianapolis 500 to be launched with a cry of, "Gentlemen, start your motors!" As a general rule, a *motor* is a small *engine.* Thus a floor fan may run on an electric *motor;* a boat is powered by an outboard *motor.* If it's big, it's almost certainly an *engine;* if it's small, it probably is a *motor.*

Enthuse

This is a weak, feeble, fluttery word. I would abolish it. The Seattle Times in 1982 quoted a director of tourism: "'Within the next five weeks,' Taylor enthused, 'we'll have more requests for information about the state of Washington than we had in all of last year.'" Such verbs as *enthuse* mark the beginner's copy. Mr. Taylor's enthusiasm should be conveyed in the context of the remarks attributed to him.

Envy/Jealousy

The general rule is that *envy* applies to what is yours; *jealousy* applies to what is mine. Thus John *envies* Peter's trip to Tibet. William may be *jealous* about his wife, his reputation as a banker, or his low handicap on the golf course, though not necessarily in the order named.

-Ess Endings

In the name of tranquil domestic relations, if a man happens to be married to a sculptor, let him never speak of her as a *sculptress*. Do not speak of a *poetess* or an *authoress*. Mencken once resurrected a list of twenty-five occupations or professions, compiled by a contributor to *Godey's Lady's Book* in 1865, for which *-ess* endings were urged. Among these were doctress, instructress, janitress, paintress, portress, professoress, tailoress, teacheress. All these, happily, have been scrapped. The ending survives in many British formations (baroness, mayoress, patroness), but only a handful of *-ess* words remain in American usage: waitress, heiress, actress, hostess. The airlines gave up on "stewardess" some years ago; they are flight attendants now. By the turn of the century, all but *heiress* will be gone. Headline writers will cling forever to *heiress;* it is a word, like *concubine* or *paramour,* that makes a copy editor's life worthwhile.

Everyone Had 'His,' Dammit

There may be times when *everyone* takes a plural pronoun—"Everyone gave themselves up to merriment"—but such occasions are rare. In my book, everyone has *his* book, everyone blows *his* nose, and everybody goes *his* way. Only in a sideshow could everyone turn *their* heads. Honeywell's advertising agency does itself no credit by recalling in Business Week a time when "Everyone had their own software."

Objection is heard that if we insist upon singular pronouns, in deference to feminists we should at least say that everybody has *his or her* hat. The venerable Fowler had no patience with this formulation. "No one who can help it chooses it; it is correct, and is sometimes necessary, but it is so clumsy as to be ridiculous except where explicitness is urgent."

Expertise

This is a blowfish word. I would toss *expertise* back into the sea of language, and hook onto *knowledge, skill, talent,* or *know-how* in its place.

f

Facet/Factor

Even the most respectable dictionaries now sanction the use of *facet* in the sense of "any of the definable aspects of a subject or object under consideration." Thus, regrettably, a *facet* can be almost anything: a *multifaceted* agenda, a *multifaceted* tax bill, the various *facets* of academic life. My suggestion would be to put *facet* back in the cabinet with the good china, and to use *facet* precisely when the occasion arises. To the jeweler, a *facet* is the plane surface of a cut gem; to the biologist, a *facet* is a part of the eye of a fly, a crab, or some other arthropod; to the architect, a *facet* is a fillet between the flutes of a column. When we speak of the *facets* of the pesticide problem, we draft a sterling silver word for kitchenware employment.

The same considerations apply to *factor.* The word has a precise meaning in banking and commerce; it has a precise meaning in mathematics. When we borrow *factor* to mean "something that actively contributes to the production of a result," we are demoting a landscape gardener to a field hand. I would restore *factor* to commission merchants, money-lenders, and engineers, and abandon the *factors* in Bear Bryant's winning record.

One other point, while it's on my mind: Let us be rid of the redundant *money factor,* or *time factor,* and stop saying of a federal budget, "the *revenue factor* has to be considered." Let us write simply of money, time, or revenue, and not be pretentious. As substitutes for *facet* or *factor,* we might try *elements, areas, reasons, aspects, dimensions,* or *characteristics.*

Fact (the fact is) (true facts)

A life spent in newspapering has taught me to be careful about writing, *The fact is* . . . Beyond the most evident facts (the score was Cubs 10, Cardinals 4), experience should teach us that *facts* are among the hardest things on earth to come by. When we write that "Millard Fillmore was in fact a poor president," we are not writing *facts;* we are writing opinions. The key thing about a *fact* is its actuality; the thing or the event exists: Four-minute-mile runs are now a *fact.* It is thus redundant, and damned annoying also, to be asked to consider the *true facts.* If it is a fact, it is true. But note that this does not apply linguistically to *factual statements:* "The moon is made of green cheese" is a *factual statement,* but it is not a *fact.*

To be sure, facts may well be disputed facts. That is my point: It is often difficult to know where the truth lies. In a typical case involving charges of drunk driving, the defendant s version of the facts ("I had only two beers, your honor") is almost always different from the cop's version ("He was reeling drunk, your honor"). In such a case, the facts—the *actual events*—may be simply that the accused was arrested at such-and-such a time on a charge of such-and-such. Actuality is the key.

Faint/Feint

I wouldn't include *faint* and *feint* except that it affords an opportunity to cite a funny clipping from The Washington Post. In a review of Peter O'Toole's *My Favorite Year,* we find that O'Toole's young apprentice "feints when his mentor urges him to rappel off a skyscraper roof." The lad wasn't shadow boxing; he was keeling over. The reviewer may be forgiven for what may have been, after all, only a typesetter's error: She described the insobrietous O'Toole in the movie as "the old sloshbuckler." Good line!

Farther/Further

The venerable Fowler predicted more than fifty years ago that *further* eventually would displace *farther* altogether, but it hasn't worked out that way. As the Morrises' panel on usage demonstrated, *farther* is alive and well, though the panelists themselves seemed a bit wishy-washy. Eighty percent of the panel members insisted they make a distinction between farther and further, but most of them were in a class with Richard Rovere: He preserves the distinction "when I remember to."

My own equally loose and casual thought is that except where *physical* distance is plainly implied (and of course in the use of *further* as a verb) the words are interchangeable. I would employ one or the other depending upon the sound of the sentence. "A rifle will shoot *farther* than a shotgun." . . . "Before we develop this topic any *further,* let us proceed to . . ."

Feasible/Plausible/Practicable

There are nice distinctions here. A *feasible* arrangement is one that is capable of being carried out; the connotation is that something can be done. A *plausible* argument is an argument with some degree of validity; the connotation is that something can be believed: a *plausible* explanation. *Practicable* goes beyond *feasible;* the lingering shadow of possibility has been removed, and a practicable invention can be put to work.

Fever/Temperature

In a crossword puzzle distributed by the Tribune Syndicate, the clue for a five-letter word at 46 down was "temperature," and naturally the word turned out to be *fever.* Yeccch! Assuming a normal base level, a sick child might have a *temperature* of 102.6, which would give us four degrees of *fever.* To the solicitous question, "Do you have a temperature?" the proper response is, "My God, I hope so." Fowler sniffed at the distinction as "pedantry." Fowler was wrong.

Fewer/Less

The rule is clear, though occasionally it gives difficulty in particular applications: Use *fewer* for *numbers;* use *less* for *quantity.* "Jimmy Falls has *fewer* head of cattle this year; he is producing *less* beef." "We have allotted *less* space to the garden, so we will have *fewer* vegetables." Thus it grates upon the ear to read the boast of a manufacturer of margarine that his product contains "one-third less calories" than other margarines. Calories are countable. "The Cubs drew fifty thousand spectators on Thursday but less fans turned out on Friday." Wrong! Spectators are countable.

The uncertainties arise when it is not evident whether one is dealing with numbers or with quantity. I once was rebuked by a reader in Coral Gables after I wrote that a typical syndicated newspaper column "runs to eight hundred words or less." He thought I should have used *fewer,* because words are countable. My ear still tells me that *less* was better. Newsweek in 1982 reported of a six-thousand-mile auto race in Africa that "at the two-thirds mark this weekend, less than half of the 392 vehicles that had started the race were still operating." I might have used *fewer* because of the specific number that was cited, but if "half" is considered a quantity, *less* was correct. In September of 1982, we may have read in the papers that "White House strategists expect to lose less than twenty House Republican seats—just possibly less than ten." The strategists were wrong (the loss was twenty-six seats) and so was the reporter; here the essence of the item dealt with numbers, hence, *fewer*.

Fibula/Tibia

Dr. Johnson once was asked why he had defined "pastern" as the knee of a horse. "Ignorance, madam," he replied. "Sheer ignorance." Out of the same flaw, I once wrote of those well-known bones of the lower leg, the *tibia* and the *fibia*. I had recently jumped on the doctors for their know-it-all opposition to any treatments for cancer beyond surgery, radiation, and chemotherapy, and the doctors were sore at me. A hundred of them, more or less, retaliated with war whoops of scorn and derision, for there is no such word as *fibia*. The bone is the *fibula*. Several of my critics were kind enough to say that, for no accountable reason, the mistake often is made. Before we rush to print, let us check our copy! And let us make no bones about it.

Flaunt/Flout

It is discouraging, truly it is, that after all these years of reminders, reproaches, and reprimands, so many writers should so often confuse *flaunt* and *flout*. The old Washington Star once reported on no-smoking laws: "Since the laws have gone into effect, there have been widespread reports of smokers openly flaunting them." The Portland Oregonian, in forty-eight-point bold, gave us this headline in 1983: "Foreign tax havens flourish, flaunt law." Wrong! The authors *flouted* the words and *flaunted* their ignorance. To *flout* is to scorn, to mock, to abuse; to *flaunt* is to wave, to display ostentatiously.

Flotsam/Jetsam

There once was a nice little distinction here, but the distinction has floated away with decades of casual usage. I make no passionate plea for its recovery. *Jetsam* is something that is tossed overboard from a ship in distress, in an effort to lighten its load. In its narrowest meaning, known to people in the salvage business, *flotsam* is the floating wreckage of a ship that has sunk. By understandable extension, both terms now embrace any old floating debris.

Flags

I suppose the occasions are few for using the vocabulary of vexillology, but I happen to collect flags—I believe I own the only 3-by-6-foot flag of Sri Lanka in Rappahannock County, Virginia—and I cannot resist the temptation to show off. In precise usage, *half-mast* should be reserved for flags thus flown at sea, *half-staff* for the mourning symbol on land. For square or rectangular flags, such as the United States flag, the stripes form the *field,* the stars the *canton.* The *hoist* is the vertical dimension next to the staff. Hung horizontally in a hall, the hoist ordinarily will be to the left of the audience, but if you happen to be flying the flag of Saudi Arabia—a neat flag, by the way—the hoist is to the right. This is because the Arabic legend reads from right to left. The very next time you display Saudi Arabia, I expect you to keep this in mind.

Free Gift

Aaargh!

Fulsome

It is part of a writer's continuing education to discover that some words in his working vocabulary simply do not mean what he always had thought them to mean. Such discoveries at first arouse incredulity; they then cause embarrassment; finally they inspire a missionary zeal to inform the whole world.

At one time, in common with several million others, I supposed that *fulsome* was a friendly word. In my ignorance, I thought *fulsome praise* was the pleasantest praise a man could receive. Thus I once covered a retirement ceremony for a beloved high school principal, and reported in all innocence that speakers heaped precisely such praise upon the old fellow.

Too late, after the blunder had gone to press, Dr. Douglas Southall Freeman set me straight. "Fulsome," he said, "means 'disgusting.'" It means "insincere." If alliteration helps you to remember, *fulsome* is *phony.* Members of the United States Senate regularly engage in *fulsome* speech when they speak of a colleague as the able, distinguished, erudite, and dedicated senator, for whom they cherish unbounded affection and admiration. This is spatula speech. You pile on the icing and mound it. You wind up with a concoction of indigestible gooiness. That's being *fulsome.*

First Formed, e.g.

A clipping from The Columbus (Ohio) Dispatch informs us that "Walter Chrysler *first began* his automotive career with the Buick Motor Car Company, and after three years became president." Another clipping, not identified, tells us about the Berea College Chapel Choir: "*First formed* in 1949, the group has made two foreign tours." In these instances, the *first* is redundant. I see nothing amiss, however, in *first met,* as in, "I first met Lyndon Johnson in 1947," the implication being that some time elapsed before we met again.

g

Gay

If lovers of language could hold wakes over fatally wounded words, no sadder occasion could be imagined than a mourning for our lost *gay.* Make no mistake: it is gone, wordnapped, abducted. It no longer is possible to use *gay* in its grand old sense of merry, exuberant, high-spirited, or brightly colored. If contemporary lexicographers are on their toes, henceforth they will have to give "homosexual" as the first meaning, and not the fifth or sixth, of *gay.* We no longer can write of *gay* parties, or *gay* clothing, or a *gay* disposition without conveying a meaning that would never have been intended a generation ago. The adjective *adult* is barely clinging to respectable usage: *adult movies* and *adult entertainment* have achieved universal if euphemistic understanding, though *adult education* and *adult communities* appear to be holding their own. But weep for *gay.* It now belongs to the homosexual community solely.

Gerunds

A year or so ago a feature writer for The Washington Post interviewed actor Robin Williams. The second paragraph of his piece began this way: "It's impossible to sit with Williams for more than two hours without him suddenly taking a break. . . ."

Unless the reporter's intention was to emphasize the *him* (and in the context, this plainly was not the reporter's intention), the reporter was in trouble. He had stumbled over a *gerund.* In this construction, *taking* isn't a verb. It's a verbal noun, and the noun demands a possessive: ". . . without *his* suddenly taking a break."

Gerunds are great little parts of speech. Used properly, they can add zest and motion to our writing. Alas, they are often abused. The Associated Press once informed us of a woman who had won $50,000 in a lottery but failed to show up when the cash was awarded. "It was all contingent on you being there to claim the prize," a spokesman for the sponsors told her. He meant, *your* being there.

Here are other examples: "I hope you're not bothered by us singing in the upstairs apartment." Or, "It was me practicing on the trombone that finally got his goat." And, "They threw us out because of him playing the trumpet at 3 A.M." In popular speech we hear these solecisms all the time, but we ought to guard against their creeping into our writing. Better: *our* singing, *my* practicing, *his* playing.

Now, having clarified the matter, let me contribute a few words of confusion. In these gerundial constructions, the possessive isn't always required. Indeed, it isn't always possible. Professor Curme, in his masterwork on syntax, offers examples. "Some families may have moved away, but I do not know of any having done so." There is no way to make a possessive out of *any having done so.* "There is danger of a woman's head being turned." Surely it would be carrying things a bit far to write, "a woman's head's being turned." When modifying phrases come in, the rule goes out: "Did you ever hear of a man of good sense refusing such an offer?"

Professor Curme authorizes other exceptions that depend upon the thrust of a sentence. "She was proud of him doing it" is acceptable if the emphasis is on the doer rather than on the thing done. By the same token, if your purpose is to show contrast, the genitive need not be employed: "We seem to think little of a boy drinking too much, but we resent a girl drinking too much."

The confusion gets further compounded by the appearance of present participles that look like gerunds but aren't gerunds. Suppose a band of demonstrators is approaching. "We could see them coming up the road" is correct. Another example: "We could see him bowing to the audience." In the song from *Show Boat,* "Can't Help Loving That Man," the word *loving* is a gerund; but when Bess speaks of Porgy as a *loving* man, she's into a participle.

After I wrote a column on gerunds, I heard from Max C. Peterson of Hartford City, Ind., who might well be elected by acclamation as chairman of the Society for the Defense of the Inestimable Gerund. He loves the things.

"Primitive man must have leapt for joy," he wrote, "when he discovered that he could increase the richness of his vocabulary a thousandfold by adding a single syllable to his verbs and thus making them into nouns: *eating* is good, *killing* is great, *laughing* is fun. *Running* made him tired, *climbing* was difficult, and *seeing* was believing."

The use of the gerund reached its zenith, Mr. Peterson believes, when the Mock Turtle boasted to Alice of his *schooling* in *reeling* and *writhing* as well as *drawling.* Since then, my friend laments, it has been downhill all the way. Today gerunds yield to the Latinate *-ion* endings. "Thus, no one would think of someone's dying of *strangling;* it would have to be *strangulation.* The divorced father is given a right of *visitation,* not of *visiting.* In legal parlance, *recordation* has replaced *recording.* We are engaged not in *verifying* a document but in its *verification.*"

Another of my correspondents and mentors is Gar Fowler of Lake Forest, Ill., who once fascinated his brightest eighth-grade students by asking them to parse the sentence, "Swimming rapidly is difficult." The teenagers had been taught that adverbs may never modify a subject noun, but behold: What was obviously an adverb was here obviously modifying a subject.

"Despite the deficiencies of the textbook," Mr. Fowler wrote, "my kids learned to like that double-duty word, the gerund. They noticed that there was more vivid action in the subject than in the predicate."

Amen to all of this. In many constructions, of course, gerunds won't work, but *strangling* will always be more vivid than *strangulation,* and if creating a vivid image is the object of our writing, let us keep the dear old gerund in mind.

Get, Got, Gotten

I put it to you plainly: *Got* is an ugly word. It works happily in song: "I've Got Rhythm," "I've Got You Under My Skin." In formal speech or writing, *gotten* is almost always the preferred past participle. In the simple past (preterit), a felicitous substitute for *got* generally can be found, and surely we can avoid the redundant *have got,* as in, "I have got to go to the city." Nothing is wrong with, "I have to go to the city," or if the urgency must be emphasized, "I must go to the city." To my ear, "I've got worse since I got off my medicine" is an unpleasant sentence. It can be recast: "I've gotten worse since I went off (or stopped taking) my medicine."

The past participles of other verbs offer similar difficulties. *Proved,* for example, seems to me generally better than *proven:* "The hair spray has proved useful." But "a proven success" strikes me as better than "a proved success." By contrast, *weaved* seems to me generally better than *woven,* though I have problems with shifting from the active to the passive voice: "She weaved the rug," but, "The rug was woven by . . ." The verb *to dive* is another pesky one. Is the preterit *dived* or *dove?* I happen to prefer *dived,* but offer only this feeble rationalization for my choice: *Dived* can be pronounced in only one way, and it carries but one meaning. By contrast, *dove* can be pronounced to rhyme with either *love* or *stove,* and the word embraces not only the aquatic event but also plump gray birds that hang around all year eating my expensive bird feed. In context, perhaps there's not even an infinitesimal hesitation, but all the same, in my copy, swimmers *dived* in, not *dove* in. Apropos of the general subject, Webster's wrongly defines *to dive* as to plunge into water "headfirst." In many sanctioned dives involving somersaults or gainers, the diver enters feet first.

Gourmand/Gourmet

A *gourmet* is an epicure, a connoisseur of fine food and wine. A *gourmand* is not so high-toned. Anyone who is heartily interested in eating—anyone who delights in dining well—may be classified as a *gourmand.* A *glutton* is the hog who eats too much. I insert these observations chiefly to warn against advertisements for *gourmet restaurants* featuring *gourmet menus.* Such overblown beaneries are almost invariably dreadful.

Graduated

Precisely speaking, it is not the student who *graduates,* it is the school that does the *graduating.* The word comes out of the Latin *gradus,* meaning step or degree, and in the academic world the institution awards this step or degree. Thus, *He was graduated from Yale* is better than *He graduated from Yale*. Here I am being pedantic. Let it go.

h

Hail/Hale

Now and then we read of some poor wretch who has been *hailed* into court, where presumably he was greeted with applause and acclaim. We can *hail* a ship, or *hail* a winner, but when the bailiff hauls us before the judge, we are *haled*.

Heal/Heel

This sound-alike also gives trouble. Out of ignorance or simple mischance, a reporter now and then tells us that a rift between nations or politicians has been *heeled,* which is not what is meant at all. As a verb, we can *heel* a dog or *heel* a ship, but if we want to mend a rift we had better *heal* it.

Healthy/Healthful

The health food people lately have become touchy on this one. Some of the rest of us might get touchy about their converting a noun to an adjective, but never mind. The distinctions between *healthy* and *healthful* are scarcely visible to my eye, and the examples of usage cited by Webster's Collegiate are no help. Thus Webster's cites Saul Bellow on *healthful:* "He felt incapable of looking into the girl's pretty, *healthful* face." Webster's cites for *healthy* a "*healthy* complexion." The difference between a *healthful* face and a *healthy* complexion is not immediately apparent, but I believe I understand what the apostles of natural food are getting at. *Healthy* exercise (that is, vigorous exercise) will contribute to a *healthful* condition. If we eat *healthful* food we are likely to be *healthy.* Funny thing is, after you have written *healthy* and *healthful* this many times, both words look misspelled.

Hectic

Hectic has grown to be one of those jack-of-all-trade words, hired for any occasion of mild confusion. The word deserves a few days off. In its familiar sense, *hectic* has grown from a medical term having exactly to do with fluctuating fever to a descriptive adjective having generally to do with a time of excitement or confusion. I voice no complaint. Beyond *hectic* is *frenetic*, which is a condition somewhat wilder; *frenetic* comes out of the root for brain, and implies behavior that could be characterized as insane. *Frantic* carries an element of great anxiety; to be in a *frantic* hurry is to be keenly worried about being late or getting a task done.

Hold (a meeting)

Bill Schrader, editor of the Herald-Telephone in Bloomington, Ind., has a thing about *to hold a meeting,* and because I have so many crotchets of my own I am tolerant about the crotchets of others. He holds that *hold* as a substitute for *conduct* or *stage* or *convene* is wrong. I have to disagree. All my dictionaries define *hold* routinely in the sense of "to convoke or preside over a meeting." The OED traces the usage to 1735, when a historian wrote of King Edouard traveling with his retinue "to hold their own assembly." A reference from 1450 has to do with fiends who held a great council. If fiends could hold a fifteenth-century council, I see no reason why friends could not hold a twentieth-century get-together, but I voice no passionate convictions on the matter.

Home/House

Henry L. Keepers of Cincinnati has been crusading for several years on this one. "There is one word the misuse of which grates upon my nerves constantly. Newspapers are full of advertisements for the sale of *homes.* Now, any fool should know that you cannot buy or sell a *home.* What the advertisements refer to are *houses.* A *home* often includes a house, but it is made up mainly of intangibles. Happiness and sorrows and innumerable emotional qualities go into the making of a *home,* none of them salable." Enough said.

Hopefully

My beloved friend William Safire—the lousy quitter!—in 1979 capitulated to the social workers of language and adopted the orphaned *hopefully* as his own. Gazing upon a sentence such as *Hopefully it will not rain tomorrow,* he embraced the construction. This was not because he had ever been wet by a hopeful rain. It was because this Flying Dutchman of an adverb has fallen into "common usage." It is understood to mean, "it is to be hoped," or "one hopes." In this sense, *hopefully* gains entry as "time-tested and well-understood usage."

Well, in that sense, hopefully my brother will regain his old prescriptive and magisterial characteristics. In his reckless column in the Times on this matter, Safire began a series of paragraphs with *evidently, angrily, additionally, coolly,* and *doubtlessly* as introductory adverbs. His point was to equate them with a lead-in *hopefully.* No way. Nothing is wrong with recasting a sentence to say that "the word *evidently* has become a litmus test," or "traditionalists *angrily* hold that the word is an adverb." It makes as much sense to write that *Coolly, the language slob replies,* as it makes to say, *The language slob coolly replies.* The adverbs fit.

One of Safire's readers, Joanne L. Schweik of Fredonia, N.Y., sent him a hot letter. "It is to be hoped," she said, "that we will not ever be able to say: it is *evidented,* it is *angried,* it is *additioned,* it is *cooled,* or it is *doubtlessed.*"

Bill Safire, won't you please come ho-o-ome!

Host

I am beginning to waver on this one. Back in 1981 I wrote a column from Jacksonville, saying that the public schools "will host what they hope will become an annual event, an Academic Super Bowl." The verb evoked a howl of pain from Clyde M. Reed at The Parsons (Kan.) Sun. "Great balls of fire!" he cried. "What is the world coming to? How in tarnation can you expect the oncoming generation to respect English for what it should be when such grievous offense is committed in your name?"

I replied at the time that I was properly rebuked, reproached, chastised, and much chastened, and I promised never to sin in this regard again. Now, three years later, the devil winks and nudges. I'm not sure that anything of great value is lost by writing that "San Francisco will host the Democratic convention." It may be marginally better to add three or four words: "San Francisco will play host to . . ." or "San Francisco will serve as host for . . ."

Both Webster's and Random House dictionaries list *host* as a transitive verb. The OED traces the usage at least to 1485, when some statute dealt with those who "should host or take to sojourn within this realm of England any merchant stranger." Spenser used *host* as a transitive verb in *The Faerie Queen.* I waver, but I am pulled from the brink by Hal Borland's thought that if *to host* is valid, why not *to guest?* "The convention will guest San Francisco"? I would have guest not.

i

Impact

In a few specialized meanings, no objection can be taken to *impact* as a transitive verb: "The steam roller has *impacted* the subsoil." In the usage that has fastened like fatty tissue to the arteries of our language, the verb is a barbarism: Says the utility executive of his rising costs: "They have *impacted* us negatively." Says the writer on finance: "Mr. Reagan's budget sharply *impacted* the bond market." An article in the Journal of the American Health Care Association deals with "Using Management Trends to *Impact* on Cost Efficiency and Quality Assurance." The ear flinches and the hair curls.

Put to work as adjective or noun, *impact* suffers anew. A *federally impacted* area is a civilian community housing many families in the armed services. President Ford, engrossed with his WIN campaign, wanted business leaders to make *inflation impact* statements. The Office of Management and Budget demands *paperwork impact* summaries. Civil libertarians complain that the government's requirements on abortion have a *privacy impact.* Nothing can be done in the name of federal construction without an *environmental impact statement.*

In its precise meaning of *to compress,* nothing is wrong with the garbage impacter that *impacts* garbage. Fine. But as a transitive verb, this muscular fellow ought to be left to do his work in peace. As a noun, *impact* should be reserved for special occasions—the impact of an airliner on a mountain, the impact of a bullet on a brain.

Implement

The battle is over on *to implement;* in retrospect, it probably was not worth even a rear-guard action. A noun that started as a simple tool or utensil has been transformed by linguistic alchemy into a handy verb. In three syllables we achieve what might require "to give practical effect to," or "to take specific measures to assure the actual fulfillment of." The problem with the verb is that it gets worn out by overwork. John Bremner usefully suggests that we look for such alternative possibilities as *accomplish, achieve, carry out, discharge, execute, fulfill, keep, make, observe,* and *perform.*

Imply/Infer

These troublemakers have been arraigned time after time, but they ought never to cause problems. To *infer* is to deduce; to *imply* is to insinuate. We draw inferences, we leave implications. There are times, as Bernstein reminds us, when the words may be interchanged ambiguously: "Are you inferring that I have this headache because I drank too much?" Such instances seldom come along. Ordinarily the choice is easy: "In your letter you *implied* that I am a skinflint." "I *infer* from your letter that you find me parsimonious."

Infinitives (split)

Let us not get all wrought up about *split infinitives.* Let us adhere to a general proposition, that as a working rule of prose composition it is better to keep the parts of a verb together than to scatter them about your sentence. Regularly observed, the rule lends a quality of tightness and vitality to our sentences. Rigidly applied, this working rule can lead to cumbersome constructions.

Dear Abby once heard from a reader who wanted to encourage both adults and children "to expose anyone who attempts to sexually molest them." There is no way to improve that sentence by recasting: "who attempts sexually to molest them" or "who attempts to molest them sexually." No. In this instance we have to split the infinitive and get on with our work.

An offense to avoid is the banana split, in which two or even three adverbs are piled on: "The Senate plans to quickly and quietly approve the pending bill.'' A Virginia governor once pulled off a triple split: Mr. Truman, he said, was attempting ''to willfully, brazenly, and deliberately seek destruction of the Democratic party.''

The proper test to be applied to a specific sentence is a test of the ear: Does it sound better to say *mortally to wound* or *to mortally wound* or *to wound mortally?* On these questions, every writer must find his own answers. No rule book will help him.

Insightful

Let us put this one on the same high dark shelf with *meaningful* and other junk words. To write a piece of *insightful analysis* is to write what is known to editors as a thumbsucker.

Irregardless

There is no such word.

-Ize Endings

A suitable award is in order, perhaps in the nature of a cut glass flyswatter, to Randall Scott of the American Land Development Association. In an interview with The Washington Post, late in December 1982, he was asked about a proposal to eliminate tax deductions for mortgages on ''second homes.'' He opposed the idea.

Any such change, he asserted, ''would *disasterize* new housing production.'' Let us hear a flourish of trumpets for the worst *-ize* ending of the year.

As H.L. Mencken observed in *The American Language,* the practice of forming verbs by adding an *ize* to a noun, an adjective, or an adverb has been going on for centuries. *To apologize* was born before 1600 and *to criticize* appeared in Shakespeare's day. *To revolutionize* came along, understandably, before 1800. *To burglarize* appeared in the 1870s.

The process has given us many useful verbs: *immunize, hospitalize, memorize,* and so on, but for every *ize* word that has caught on, a score have wound up in the semantic dump. Mencken cited such abandoned abominations as *broadwayize, filmize, seasonize, rapturize, machinize, featurize,* and *flavorize.* Professional linguists collect these specimens with a horrid fascination, as if they were collecting interesting worms.

One that gives me the willies is *prioritize,* which we encounter almost daily in Washington, D.C.

A measure of tolerance is required. There are no handy substitutes for *socialize, tenderize, pressurize,* or *publicize.* We have had *scandalize* since 1566. I am of two minds about *finalize.* Theodore Bernstein termed *finalize* an "expendable novelty," but my guess is that the word is here to stay. It conveys a clear meaning. When we *finalize a contract,* we put the terms of the agreement in final form awaiting signatures. The closest verb to it is *complete,* but that is not quite the same thing. I don't believe I would use *finalize* in writing, and I'm not sure I would use it in speech, but it no longer grates upon my ear.

1

Late, the

We should be careful about when persons get to be *late* persons. "The bill was signed by the late president Johnson" creates a startling and indeed a macabre image. We see the Prince of the Pedernales rising from his grave, pen in bony hand, to perform his ministerial service. What we mean to say is that "the bill was signed by President Johnson." He wasn't *late* at the time.

Lay/Lie

At the time of Grace Kelly's death, The Salina (Kan.) Journal reported that "the body laid in state in the Ardent Chapel in the Grimaldi Palace." Well, no. But such errors are made so frequently that probably it is unfair to cite a single example from Salina. Many experienced writers fumble on *lay* and *lie.* The verbs are the two most troublesome verbs in the English language.

Start with *lay, laid, laying.* Apart from two or three exceptional usages, *lay* is always a transitive verb. Hens and comedians *lay* eggs, gamblers *lay* bets, masons *lay* bricks, governments *lay* taxes, and the best *laid* schemes o' mice an' men gang aft a-gley. The only exceptions that I know of come from Congress and from rowing. In the House and Senate, a motion may be made that a bill *lay* on the table. In rowing, crew members *lay* to their oars. But if you want a verb that takes an object, your verb is *lay.* We don't *lie* a table or *lie* blame; we *lay* them.

The trouble comes from the parts of the verb *to lie: lay, lain, lying*. Here we have a verb that is always intransitive; *to lie* never can take an object. We *lie* down, or we *lie* in wait. Ships *lie* at anchor. Enemies *lie* just over hills. A patient *lies* or is *lying* in bed; he *lay* there yesterday; he has *lain* there all month.

When in doubt, think of the humble brick: Do we *lay* it or *lie* it?

Lectern/Podium

A *lectern* is a slant-topped desk that may stand alone or may sit atop a larger table. A *podium* is something else entirely. The conductors of choirs and symphonies stand on *podiums* (or if you want to be finicky, on *podia*). *Podium* comes out of the root words for foot, *lectern* from the root words for read or reader. The *dais* and the *rostrum* are something else; in the concert hall or the lecture hall, the *dais* and the *rostrum* are the whole shebang on stage.

Lend/Loan

Except in a few contexts, I am ready to abandon the distinctions between *lend* and *loan*. Banks *lend* money; they also *loan* money. It is all the same thing. To be sure, if you were in need of help you wouldn't ask a neighbor to *loan* you a hand; it certainly would have sounded odd, if not indeed grisly, for Antony to have asked of his countrymen that they *loan* him their ears; we *lend* advice, not *loan* it. But such exceptions are well understood. When it comes to such inanimate objects as books or cups of sugar, we can *lend* them or *loan* them as we please. My own preference is to use *lend* as a verb and *loan* as a noun, but the past *lent* has an unfamiliar ring. I would smush the two together: *I lend, I loaned, I have been lending*.

Like/Such as

A couple of years ago, in a single issue of Time magazine, one could find these repulsive gobbets:

On trauma teams: They are active at places "*like* New York City's Bellevue Hospital Center and Chicago's Cook County Hospital."

On profits after adjustment for inflation: High-technology companies "*like* IBM and Intel" were the only ones to do better.

About a German pornographer: He may start mail order outlets "in sun-and-fun states *like* California and Florida."

On an art exhibition: The show's impact is muffled by the lack of key paintings by fundamental masters of realism "*like* Courbet or Honoré Daumier."

In the Press section, on the attempt to assassinate President Reagan: "Newspapers *like* the Chicago Sun-Times, Chicago Tribune, New York Post, and New York Daily News replated their late afternoon editions . . ."

But in that very same issue of Time, the editors and writers informed us in this fashion: "House budget makers propose to restore $7 billion in cuts that Reagan wants *in such programs as* Medicaid, food stamps and child nutrition." Here they got it right.

A couple of weeks later, Time spoke of "food mavens *like* Julia Child and Craig Claiborne," and here they got it wrong. In that same issue, a footnote spoke of "Sunbelt states *such as* Oklahoma and Texas." Here they got it right.

Newsweek has the same problem: An ex-convict spent eighteen of his first forty years "in places *like* San Quentin and Folsom." Wrong! Major trans-Atlantic carriers "*like* Air France, SAS and British Airways . . ." Wrong! From the San Francisco Chronicle: "Concerts by rock groups and artists *like* Arlo Guthrie and Bette Midler" . . . "Donations have come from Hollywood people *like* Tony Curtis, Steve Allen, Barbra Streisand and others." Wrong! From The Associated Press: "a divisional race with teams *like* Cincinnati and Houston. . . ." Wrong, wrong, wrong!

Newsweek can get it right: "National's old routes feed into Pan Am's international routes at major gateways *such as* New York, Miami and Los Angeles." "Kroetz's work has aroused intense controversy, including the throwing of stink bombs at one play that deals with *such subjects as* abortion and child murder." Dave Broder of The Washington Post gets it right: Bills have been introduced "*by such Senators as* McClure of Idaho and Hayakawa of California."

This particular crotchet is dear to my heart. I cherish it fiercely. It is not dear to the hearts of Wilson Follett and Theodore Bernstein. Follett sniffs that only "purists" object "to phrases of the type *a writer like Shakespeare, a leader like Lincoln.*" He finds no more than a "shade of difference" and "an extremely slight distinction" between *like* and *such as.* Theodore Bernstein was as indifferent: "Some nitpickers object to saying, 'German composers *like* Beethoven,' arguing that no composers were like Beethoven and that we should say *such as*. The argument is specious because *like* does not necessarily mean identical."

Pfui! Consider two parallel sentences: (1) *Writers like Follett and Bernstein dismiss the matter out of hand.* (2) *Such writers as Follett and Bernstein dismiss the matter out of hand.* To contend that the two sentences reflect only "an extremely slight distinction" is to exhibit an inability to read plain English. In the first sentence, we are not told that Follett and Bernstein dismiss; we are told only that other, unidentified writers who in some fashion are *like* Follett and Bernstein dismiss the matter out of hand.

Go back to some of the examples just quoted. Time intended to say that the German pornographer was considering outlets in California and Florida, not in states *like* them. The business profits after adjustment were the profits of *such companies as* IBM and Intel. The ex-con had been in prisons *such as* San Quentin and Folsom.

When we are talking of large, indefinite fields of similarity, *like* properly may be used: "In considering lives like Abraham Lincoln's, we are reminded that humble beginnings . . ." and so forth. When we are talking about specifically named persons who are included in a small field, we ought to use *such as:* Artists *such as* Arlo Guthrie and Bette Midler, food mavens *such as* Julia Child and Craig Claiborne, senators *such as* McClure and Hayakawa.

It takes a measure of temerity to disagree with such eminent authorities as Follett and Bernstein, but in this instance they were quite simply wrong.

Liable/Likely

The Washington Post's book columnist once told us that a writer named Roald Dahl "went further with his inflammatory anti-Zionist opinions than any other similarly well-known American author is *liable* to go." Wrong word. In precise usage, *liable* should be reserved for those contexts in which some adverse contingency is implied. Thus we are *liable* to be stung by a hornet if we get too close to a hornet's nest. In view of that prospect, we are *likely* to stay a good distance away. The book columnist wanted either *apt* or *likely.*

Literally

This is how a story began in The Washington Post: "Fannie Mae is her name and 'chicken' is the game being played in Washington about her future. At least that's the view of Wall Street analyst Elliott Schneider, as he literally explodes about the warfare in progress over the Federal National Mortgage Association."

Poor Schneider! His days of analysis are gone.

From The Associated Press: "The Jets' lanky wide receiver literally stole the ball from the defenders for the winning touchdown." He hadn't *literally* stolen anything; he had made a good catch.

From The Wall Street Journal: "An examination of the history of the Kaiparowits power project shows that environmentalists alone didn't kill the plant . . . Kaiparowits, it seems, literally strangled in red tape." It is an interesting way for a power plant to die, to be *literally* strangled in red tape.

Literally means actually. When we translate *literally,* we translate exactly, word for word. When we say that a public figure *literally* wears two hats, we must mean that, for whatever reason, he has two hats on his head. If we read that "McEnroe *literally* mopped up the court with his outclassed opponent," we must envision the poor opponent as tied to the business end of a mop. Now and then *literally* may be employed exactly, to good effect: "During his suspension, Allen's problem was that he literally had time on his hands." (The White House adviser had accepted two wristwatches from Japanese friends.) Ordinarily *literally* is a good word to leave out. It adds nothing, and indeed it usually destroys the metaphor it is intended to enhance.

Lion's Share

Webster's has it wrong, but it probably is too late in the day to restore the original point of Aesop's fable. Webster's says that the *lion's share* is "the largest portion," and offers by way of example, "the *lion's share* of the research money." If original meanings prevailed, the researcher would have won *all* the research money, for that is what the original lion claimed when he led his pride on a hunt: one-quarter for being king of the beasts, one-quarter for his superior courage, and one-quarter for his lioness and her cubs. "As for the fourth," he put it to his companions, "let who will dispute it with me."

The same kind of misunderstanding, incidentally, has taken the punch out of *Hobson's choice*. It now is taken to mean any difficult choice—a situation for which we already had an abundance of clichés. Hobson was an English innkeeper who kept a livery. His customers could have their choice of mounts; but like the first Henry Ford, who offered buyers any color as long as it was black, Hobson required his patrons to choose the horse nearest the stable door. In that way they had no real choice at all. Such was *Hobson's choice*.

Livid

Its meaning has not been improved by age. For at least a couple of centuries, *livid* meant only what the OED defined it to mean: "of a bluish leaden colour; discoloured as by a bruise; black and blue." It had nothing to do with being angry or enraged, and hence red in the face; if you were *livid*, you were ashen, pale, pallid. Only physicians and fuddy-duddies cling to the original meaning. When we learn that the president is *livid* at his budget director, we now infer that the president has a face like a Bloody Mary. So it goes.

Lot

When we speak of a *building lot*, or of one's *lot in life*, or of a particular parcel in a lottery or auction, *lot* is singular. In the more common usage, *She made a lot of food for the party; she made a lot of biscuits, too*, the noun takes its number from the prepositional phrase: A lot of food *was* left over; a lot of biscuits *were* eaten.

m

Madame/Madam

The thing to remember here is that the only *e-madame* is a French woman: *Madame de Villefort, Madame Defarge*. All other *madams*, including those who run houses of ill fame, are *madams* with no *e: Madam* Chairman, *Madam* President; *yes, madam*, and *no, madam*.

Meaningful

The Democratic National Platform of 1980, in a notably illiterate passage, contained this provision: "In order to encourage a lifetime of meaningful political participation for every Democrat, the National Education and Training Council shall attempt to reach every young citizen as they enter the electorate at eighteen years of age.'' Never mind the disagreement of *every* and *they.* My suggestion is that you look again to that high, dark shelf where you hid *insightful,* and that you put *meaningful* beside it.

Media

Media, which so often and so vexatiously is pronounced *mejia,* is the plural of *medium.* This means that media *are,* media *are,* media *are!* Why is it so difficult for people in the media to get this through their heads? It is beyond understanding. But time after time, in publications edited by professional journalists, we find: ''The media is entitled to'' . . . ''The Washington media is concentrating this week on'' . . . ''The national media increasingly is exercising its influence. . . .''

The same elementary rule applies, of course to *data,* which is the plural of *datum.* Like media, data *are,* data *are,* data *are!*

Writers seem to have little trouble with *alumni, alumnae, criteria,* and *strata.* They may even be trusted with the ending of *millennia,* even if they can't spell the middle of *millennia.* The plural of *curriculum* seems not to throw them. It is only when they get to *media* and *data* that they collapse. Media *are!* Data *are!* Media *are!* Data *are!* . . .

Militate/Mitigate

The New York Times, in a piece in 1982 on a ''Perfectionist on the Podium,'' told us about this finicky fellow: ''He also wonders whether the leisure-time orientation of Los Angeles itself mitigates against excellence.'' Dear, dear! Theodore Bernstein must have shuddered in his grave. The word the critic wanted was *militate,* which almost always means ''to have an adverse effect on.'' (It is rare to read of something that *militates in favor of;* when we are *militating,* we generally *militate against.*) The sound-alike troublemaker, *mitigate,* has nothing whatever to do with *militate.* When we *mitigate* something, we ease it. It means to alleviate, or to extenuate: *Mitigating* circumstances, in law, are the kind of circumstances that may justify a wife in braining a faithless husband— or vice versa.

Minion

Minion is an editorial writer's word. In any political campaign, our side has adherents, followers, supporters, boosters, aides, and team members. Your side has *minions*. It is written with a curl of the lip and a contemptuous spin on the ball. Your side has flunkies, hangers-on, sycophants, and gofers. Your side may also have myrmidons and fuglemen, but they have these only in Southern journalism, where pejorative writing has been raised to a high art. *Minions* are like *coffers*, e.g., *the money vanished into the Teamsters' coffers*. Only bad guys have coffers.

Moot

Among the fascinations of English, discussed a bit later on under the heading of contranyms, is the appeal of words that have opposite meanings. Among these is *moot*. I got onto this one through a gentleman in Miami Beach who was working a crossword puzzle. He got to 85-down, a four-letter word meaning "arguable," and he triumphantly lettered in m-o-o-t. "If I'm correct," he wrote, "it will be the first time I have ever seen or heard *moot* used correctly. Of the many places I have seen it used incorrectly, National Review shocked me the most. I would love to hear you and Mr. Buckley moot the meaning of *moot*."

Well! I dashed off a hoity-toity response, saying I had been covering appellate courts for the better part of forty years. "Moot," said I, "does not mean arguable or debatable. It means precisely the opposite. At the Supreme Court, where cases often are dismissed by reason of mootness, it means that nothing is left to argue about. The triggering statute has been repealed, or the litigants have settled out of court, or the petitioner has died. Finis. End of case."

Then I discovered that Webster's, among other dictionaries, says my correspondent was right: *moot* does mean arguable. I put the matter to Justice William H. Rehnquist. After a week's meditation he delivered a decision that provides a model of judicious indecision. The word *moot*, he said gravely, does indeed mean arguable, but only in an academic sense. In the real world, it means "no longer subject to argument." This explains why law schools have moot courts, where hypothetical points may be debated; and it also explains why appellate courts dismiss cases "by reason of mootness."

Momentarily

In precise usage, which all of us should strive for, *momentarily* does not mean *in* a moment. It means *for* a moment. Thus it is proper, though probably untrue, for a pilot to advise his passengers that "we will be delayed only momentarily." If a pilot wants to let his passengers know that the plane will be departing in a minute or two, he has a choice of *immediately, straightaway, shortly, at once,* or *right now.* The more accurate word would be *presently,* which means *before long, after a while, when we're good and ready.* While we're on the subject, *presently* also means *at the present time:* "Formerly in the House, Trible is *presently* in the Senate." Never speak of a *present incumbent.* Come to think of it, I don't believe you could have a *former incumbent* either.

Myself

Linguistically speaking, what can be said of *myself?* The pretentious reflexive causes persistent problems. For example: "Present at the board meeting were Virginia Beattie, Marie Pietri, and myself." Or, "I have prepared this document for the benefit of my wife, my children, my executor, and myself."

What should we do with such sentences? The self-conscious *myself* intrudes like the knock of a hotel chambermaid making her eight o'clock rounds. It is as if *myself* were a dissociated third person—a disembodied spirit—a mere name to be answered when the roll is called: "Beattie? Here. Pietri? Here. Myself? Myself? Myself has gone out for a pizza."

The sentence could be awkwardly recast: "Present were Beattie, Pietri and I," or we could switch to the declarative: "Beattie, Pietri and I were present at the board meeting," but minutes of a meeting are not usually so phrased.

The second of the two examples gives greater trouble: "I have prepared this document for the benefit of my wife, my children, my executor, and me." Aaargh! You simply cannot write that "I have prepared this document for the benefit of me." You could try: "I have prepared this document for my own benefit, and also for the benefit of my wife, my children, and my executor." Better, but longer; and in this version the thrust of the sentence is subtly shifted.

These are beetle-trap sentences: We fly into them and we can't back out. Such troublesome constructions come along infrequently, but the problem of *myself* seems to be getting more prevalent. It is no trick to change "My wife and myself" to "My wife and I . . ." But how do you escape from, "The assets of my husband and myself are in excess of . . ."? The first thing you know, you are into real trouble: "Thinking of my husband and me, our combined assets are . . ." Probably the most felicitous solution lies in, "My husband and I have combined assets of . . ."

The best rule of thumb, it seems to me, is to limit these *self* words to their natural functions as intensifiers: "Mother, I'd rather do it *myself!* " "If you *yourself* want to gamble, go ahead, but . . ." When the tone of a sentence demands an inverted construction, there's no course but to wince and surrender: "Present at the board meeting were Beattie, Pietri, and myself." I don't like that sentence, but it does convey the intended meaning. Suppose the lean and hungry Cassius had recast his famous observation, "The fault, dear Brutus, is not in our stars, but in us, that we are underlings."

Let it go. Fowler, that wise and pugnacious master of English usage, took a tolerant view of the matter. If a *myself* makes a sentence run more smoothly, he counsels, go ahead and use it. It's not exactly a felonious offense.

n

Nauseous

This is a tricker. Watch out for it. "I am nauseous" means *I am disgusting; I can make you throw up.* Some people are indeed *nauseous,* but ordinarily the required word is *nauseated.*

Negative Constructions

This entry might better be indexed under "nuance." *It is not improper to wear a dinner jacket before six o'clock. . . . They were not unwise in selecting Spode. . . . It is not unknown for Charles to sleep past noon.* . . Double negatives do not always constitute a positive. The implication in each of these examples is that a "but" clause should follow: It is not improper, *but* . . They were not unwise, *but* . . . It is not unknown, *but* it is unusual. If a positive statement is intended, let us be positive; let us write *he is a generous person,* and not *he is not an ungenerous person.*

Negatives can lead you astray. One of my readers in Norfolk, Va., for many years preserved a letter of recommendation that had been written for him when he applied for a naval commission: "David has no bad habits and associates with no elements of unquestionable character." But negatives also can be used with exquisite precision. Jody Powell, press secretary to President Carter, used to tell us that "the first duty of a press secretary is never unintentionally to mislead you."

Such constructions are akin to litotes—those understatements in which an affirmative is expressed by the negative of the contrary: "She is not a bad singer." This is not to say that "She is a good singer." Used with precision, litotes can convey subtleties not easily conveyed otherwise.

New Beginning

Some of my correspondents find *new beginning* an odious phrase. It doesn't strike me as grossly offensive, though *fresh start* usually would be better. If a composer can write a *beginning* of a concerto, or a politician can embark upon the *beginning* of a proposition, I see no reason why he could not scrap his original beginning in favor of a *new beginning*. The redundancy I object to is *first began:* "He first began to write poetry in 1925." Nothing is wrong with *first met, first tried, first tasted,* and the like, so long as we mean to say that some appreciable time elapsed between the first meeting, trying, or tasting, and the second: "Fred first met Ruth in 1941. They did not meet again until after the war." On this general subject, do not *ever* write of a *new innovation*.

Noisome

I have no way of knowing what you think *noisome* means. Some people have peculiar ideas about *noisome*. It does not mean "noisy" and it does not mean "annoying." It means smelly. A *noisome* thing stinks.

None Is/None Are

A few days before the congressional elections of 1982, columnist Richard Reeves was writing about the negative nature of the campaigns in California. "None of the candidates talk about themselves, their ideas or programs," he said.

How about it? Shall we have one more go at the old debate over *none is* or *none are?* A school of thought remains in action (I was once among its stuffy practitioners) that teaches a foolish doctrine—the doctrine that *none* is *always* singular. These pedagogues suppose that *none* must invariably be read as a contraction of *no one* or *not one*, and they are quite wrong in this.

This is the truth as I see it: *None* is usually singular but it sometimes is plural. It is as simple as that. If our intention is to emphasize *not a single one*, we should write: *Four eggs fell out of the nest, but by a miracle none was broken.* If our thought is somewhat broader, *none were* probably is better. Reeves had it right. More than a hundred candidates were running for high office in California. It is inconceivable that not a single one of them ever talked positively about his own ideas. Thus the plural, *none of the candidates talk*, rings true.

These are judgment calls. The issue doesn't turn on agreement in number; the issue involves the thought to be conveyed. Unless the meaning is clearly *not any*, my own inclination is to go with the singular every time. It looks better to my eye and it sounds better to my ear. Thus, "None of the crates were damaged [not any of the crates] when the truck went off the embankment, and none of the five occupants of the Cadillac [not a single one of them] was hurt." Some critics regard the singular verb as "intrusive" or "pretentious," to which I can reply only, to each his own crotchets.

Often a sentence will provide an internal clue to the better usage. Jody Powell, as a columnist, wrote a piece about racial prejudice in both the North and the South: "None of us are in any position to point fingers— except at ourselves." I would have written, "None of us is in any position to point a finger," but when Jody was pointing fingers in the plural, he had to have *none are*.

The problems created by *none* are first cousins to the difficulties that arise with *everyone, everybody,* and *anybody.* Here I remain stuffy. The image presented by, "Everyone bowed *their* heads in prayer" is not a felicitous image. I stumble over, "Everybody in the school brought *their* own lunch." When the question is asked, "Has anybody had *their* breakfast?" I wonder if everybody are eating from the same plate.

It is no use telling me that *everybody has their* is well understood, that the usage occurs constantly in conversation, that it crops up even in well-edited newspapers. I know all that. But I insist that *most people have their* is better. The late and truly lamented Washington Star once headlined a story about the accident in the nuclear plant in Pennsylvania: "Nobody's Holding Their Breath for Panel's Three Mile Island Report." Who can hold any breath but his own?

My thought is that when we say *every,* we mean each particular individual or thing. If "Everybody has *their* ticket to the play," nobody has his own ticket; we have one common ticket. Such a construction defies common sense.

Whether we agree or disagree on my stuffiness in this regard, perhaps we can agree that once a sentence has been launched in the singular, we have to stay on course. Jimmy Carter's first official act as president, you may recall, was to issue a proclamation granting amnesty to those who had evaded the draft between 1964 and 1973. This was his concluding sentence:

"Any individual offered conditional clemency or granted a pardon under Executive Order 11803 . . . shall receive the full measure of relief afforded by this program if they are otherwise qualified under the terms of this Executive Order."

Any individual who writes a sentence like that sentence should have their typewriter taken away. Otherwise he or she will most likely make their mistake again.

O

Officer

There was a time, and it wasn't so very long ago at that, when we had no hesitation in writing about persons in the police. A beginner in the department was a policeman, then a police sergeant. If he advanced further, he became a police lieutenant, captain, or major—and only at that point was he a police *officer.*

The movement toward gender-neutral terms has complicated matters. It becomes increasingly difficult to locate a policeman or a policewoman; egalitarianism has made police *officers* of everyone. In the armed services, *enlisted men* is now forbidden; sex is concealed behind the armor plate that shields all ranks of *armed services personnel.* The familiar *fireman* hangs on, holding his ground against *fireperson* and *firefighter,* and in the firehouse old distinctions remain: An *officer* in the fire department is just that.

One of Those Things

Back in September of 1981 I wrote a column that touched upon -*ize* endings. I said: "In Washington we encounter *to prioritize* all the time; it is one of those things that makes Washington often unbearable." As a consequence of this blunder, I took a good hiding from William H. Lane in Stuart, Fla.: "You kind of wonder about the competence of a nationally syndicated writer who uses an elementary grammatical barbarism in a column dedicated to improving the Writer's Art. In this instance, in the *ize* of this beholder you have joined the Philistines."

I was much chastened. I vowed to sin no more. The vow didn't take. In September of 1982, borrowing from Bill Shakespeare, I wrote a column about events in the Middle East: "With the expulsion of the PLO from Lebanon, Mr. Reagan may have caught one of those tides in the affairs of men which, taken at the flood, leads on to fortune." This time Mr. Lane didn't jump on me; perhaps he had abandoned me as hopeless. But Bill Buckley did. From National Review came an anguished note: "How *could* you?"

Some fight was left in me: "My ear hears *one* as the subject of the verb, in this case, 'one leads on to fortune.' Is it possible that you may be wrong?" From Buckley, by return mail: "It is not at all possible that I am wrong in this instance, *not at all.*"

In desperation I diagramed the offending sentence, and sure enough: *one* was not the subject of any verb; it was the object of *caught.* The word that governed the verb's number was *tides.*

Follett has some firm things to say about *one of those* and about professional writers who fumble their handling of the phrase. He cites eleven examples, e.g., *one of the few writers in the country who has made a living being funny,* and comments: "The contributors to this miscellany are all educated men; some are literary artists; not one of them would ordinarily put a singular verb with a plural subject. Yet, seduced by a certain pattern of words, they will automatically commit themselves to *writers who has made a living.* . . . Moreover, most of the specimens can be presumed to have passed under the eyes of experienced copy editors."

Follett concedes that "the error is easy to fall into." By a mental shortcut, the *one* in whom we are interested jumps over the class *(the few writers in the country)* and links itself to the defining words *(who has made a living being funny).* He adds stiffly: "The best of writers, when he falls into absent-mindedness, yields no better precedent than the worst." Alas, poor Follett! He died in 1963, and it is perhaps as well that he did not live to browse through the Harper Dictionary of Contemporary Usage. The editors put this question to their panel on usage: "Which is correct, *It is one of those things that happen* or *It is one of those things that happens"?*

I experienced a moment of consolation. Isaac Asimov answered, either one. Heywood Hale Broun voted for *happens.* Herman Wouk preferred *happen,* but thought the verb "depends on the sense." The final tally found 26 percent of the professionals voting that the singular and plural verbs are interchangeable; 22 percent, or better than one out of five, thought *happens* was correct.

In a sassy aside, Wouk remarked that the question about *one of those things* "is one of those things that bore you." Nonsense! As writers, we ought all of us to fuss incessantly about such things as *one of those things,* for fussing is one of those things that, cheerfully pursued, help us to master our trade.

One of the Only

Loretta Cairo of Shiremanstown, Pa., caught me in 1983 with the year's most surprising inquiry. She had received a flier from a real estate firm that boasted: "We are one of the only agencies with an in-house education director." She asked, "Can something be *one of the only?"*

It was a sockdolager. When you think about it (and I had never thought about it even once in sixty years), it is manifestly impossible to be *one of the only.* The idiom falls upon our ears as lightly as elevator music: We grasp the meaning and miss the elements. The firm may have been *almost the only* or *one of the very few,* but *only* speaks to an absolute condition.

After Ms. Cairo's letter came in, I brooded for several days over *one of the best.* Could Jacqueline's in Washington, D.C., be *one of the best restaurants* in the capital? By definition, *best* means "excelling all others." It is "the greatest degree of excellence." If there can be only one restaurant that is *the best,* what of the others? Are they to be demoted to merely *among the excellent* restaurants of Washington?

Upon reflection, I concluded that *best* need not be restricted to a single person or thing. It is idiomatic, but it is entirely acceptable to speak of the *ten best horses*, or the *ten best-dressed women*. I have banished *one of the only*, but *one of the best* may still hang around.

Only

On the matter of the misplaced *only*, I am as crotchety as an old bear with a thorn in his paw, and I nurse a lasting grudge against Fowler and Follett because of their indifference to a cause on which I feel so passionately. Both mentors believed in "freedom from confusion." Both sought precision in the placement of words. They had superb ears for the nuances of construction, but when it came to *only*, their ears turned to tin. Listen, if you please:

From Time magazine: "Under ecclesiastical law, miraculous cures can only happen through the intervention of a saint or in places of holy pilgrimage." The *only* belonged after *happen*.

From National Review: "The dispute over the Voting Rights Act isn't a dispute that can only be held in philosophical quarterlies." The *only* belonged after *held*.

From the Cathy comic strip: "I only date redheads." The lad meant that he dated *only redheads*, or that he dated *redheads only*.

From the headline over a Dr. Steincrohn column: "Black Widow Spider Bites Only Fatal One Percent of Time." No comment required.

From a report on Argentine invaders in the Falklands: "They can only be dislodged by a combination of shuttle and slow-boat diplomacy." The *only* belonged after *dislodged*.

From The Columbus (Ind.) Republic, in a report on a class reunion: "Only the whereabouts of seven classmates were unknown." The *only* belonged ahead of *seven classmates*.

From Miss Manners' column in The Washington Post: "One does not leave a tip of less than a quarter, even if one has only ordered coffee." She meant, *ordered only coffee*.

From a TV commercial for National Geographic: "You can only get the magazine by becoming a member . . ." Properly, *you can get the magazine only . . .*

From U.S. News & World Report: "The court holds that its restriction can only apply to counsel and the parties." *Apply only*.

From the Bulletin of the Republican Study Committee: "The fact that 'public interest' lawyers are only paid $25 to $30 per hour was deemed irrelevant." *Paid only*.

Is the nature of my complaint becoming clear? The careless mislocation of *only* can alter the entire meaning of a sentence. One of my Florida correspondents, Max Goldblatt of Margate, remarked that when he read that "French people only make love in bed," he wondered if they sleep on the floor, or perhaps standing up. The accurate location of *only* adds punch, precision, and clarity.

There are times, of course, when exceptions have to be made to the general rule that the modifying *only* should go next to the word it modifies. If an entire statement is being modified, you will want to use common sense: "If writers would only put words where they belong" is a better phrase than, "If writers would put words only where they belong." The *only* is nicely placed in, "The kids think they must only write one draft and hand it in." Such exceptions are few.

Oral/Verbal

When it comes to sex, the two words assuredly are not confused, and they ought not to be confused in writing either. The trouble is that while *oral* and *verbal* both apply to that which is spoken, only *verbal* applies to that which is written. My thought would be to set *verbal* aside for uses that have particularly to do with words: Bernstein's *verbal mastery,* Tom Stoppard's *verbal fireworks,* an editor's *verbal rules.* This would leave *oral* for such uses as *oral argument* and *oral agreement,* and it would avoid the confusion that results from the verbal agreement that more understandably would be identified as a *written agreement.*

Pair of Twins

Lewis Edward Lehrman, National Review once reported, was born in Harrisburg, Pa., in 1938, "one of a pair of twins." No, indeed. A *pair of twins* adds up to four. Lehrman was one of twins.

Parameters

A columnist for The Washington Post, assigned to do a piece for Bosses Day, wrote that bosses are much like normal folk: They fall within the usual parameters of intelligence from cretin to 104 or thereabouts."

An administrative law judge at the Federal Trade Commission discoursed in the Great Cereal Case on the meaning of unfair competition: "The Supreme Court has set some parameters as to what kinds of commercial conduct can constitute a Section 5 violation."

Intermedics, Inc., whose ad writers should know better, advertises the "nominal parameters" and the "operating parameters" of an implantable cardiac pulse generator.

The columnist meant "range," the judge meant "guidelines," and the company meant "specifications." Why did they use *parameters?* R.E. Shipley of Indianapolis once sounded off in a letter to me about the matter: "With no apparent rationale, nor even a hint of a reasonable extension of its use in mathematics, *parameter* has been manifestly bastardized, or worse yet, wordnapped into having meanings of consideration, factor, variable, influence, interaction, amount, measurement, quantity, quality, property, cause, effect, modification, alteration, computation, etc., etc. The word has come to be endowed with 'multiambiguous non-specificity.' *Parameter* has come to mean anything that does or could have some sort of relationship to something else, a truly sloppy, non-substantial, omni-definiens generic substitute for a multitude of valid words that have precise meanings."

What *is* a *parameter?* W.M. Woods of Oak Ridge, Tenn., whom I take to be a mathematician by profession, writes that "to understand what a *parameter* is, you have to understand what a variable is, for a variable is one of the many things a *parameter* is not." He offers an example in the operation of an automobile: The dependent variable, the speed of the car, depends on the independent variable, the position of the gas pedal.

"Now let's suppose that you—or the engineers who designed the car—change the lever arms of the linkage that connects the gas pedal to the butterfly valve of the carburetor. The speed of the car (dependent variable) will still depend on the pedal position (independent variable), *but in a somewhat different manner.* You have changed a parameter in the function that relates the speed of your car to the gas pedal position. . . .

"When the Fed changes the discount rate, it is changing a *parameter.* The Fed does not change the rediscount rate instantly, continuously. It changes this *parameter* of the economy, and then leaves it fixed for a time. From the borrower's point of view, when a large bank suddenly changes its prime rate of interest, it is changing a *parameter.* When you change the automatic gain control of your hi-fi or tape deck, you are changing a *parameter.* . . . "

My own thought on the subject of *parameter* is to ship this poor damaged noun back to the mathematicians, and to forswear its use hereafter. This will be asking a good deal of the Washington bureaucracy, but it would lower some high blood pressures in the world of science.

Peak/Peek

Some nodding Homer at The Wall Street Journal was snoozing when a story came across his desk about a new home computer from IBM: "Details about two models of the machine are being bandied about among dealers, industry observers and consulting organizations, some of which have had a peak at the machines." A *peak* at them? Yoicks!

People/Persons

The general rule in newspapering is to use *people* for large round numbers, and to use *persons* for small and precise numbers. Thus, "An estimated two hundred thousand *people* gathered in the Mall for the Fourth of July program." "The Air Florida crash took the lives of seventy-eight *persons.* " The Associated Press says that *people* should be preferred to *persons* "in all plural uses," and offers as examples: *Thousands of people attended the fair. There were seventeen people in the room.* I would agree on *thousands of people* at the fair, but my own preference would be for *seventeen persons* in a room. The AP's rule would require us to write of two *people* waiting at a bus stop. If one of them left, what would remain? One *people?*

Perceive

Some months ago, writing about the MX missile and the possibilities of nuclear war, I mentioned the Pentagon's contention that unless the MX is funded, "Soviet leaders will perceive the United States as a weak and timid nation." I said that "we can only surmise how the American character is perceived in the Kremlin," and I added that "perception is everything."

A professor of medieval history at Florida International University rebuked me soundly: "The use of *perceive* and *perception* to refer simply to the way somebody sees something is very widespread among the semi-educated who try to pass for better, and this includes most college graduates and even professors, but you should not be among them." To *perceive*, he instructed me, is "to become aware of something *as it really is,* and the current abuse of the word should be replaced by the use of words such as *regard, believe, view.* "

Let's think about it. Webster's III offers as one definition of *perception*, "mental image," as in "a *perception* of what is beautiful." The dictionary speaks further of "intuitive recognition." In a turgid amplification, Webster's III says *perception* is "a function of non-conscious expectations derived from past experience and serving as a basis for or as verified by further meaningful motivated action." I can't make much out of that spinach, but I think it confirms my thought that the Soviets' *perception* of American character is of great importance. What is their insight? What are their expectations?

To limit *perceive* to the observance of things *as they really are* is to bind the word too tightly. We can perceive that a pan is hot, or that a drink is cold, but beyond the obvious evidence provided by our senses, it often is difficult to see things *as they really are.* Images form in the eye; they also form in the mind.

Pinch Hitter

A *pinch hitter* is of course a substitute, but a substitute in a special sense. A manager summons a particular pinch hitter because of his supposed skills in a pinch: The manager needs someone who can bunt, or bat left-handed, or hit a long ball to the outfield. The word is too valuable to be debased by casual use: "Because Bishop Jones was ill, Father Brown was asked to pinch-hit for him as the luncheon speaker." Baseball provides a rich mine of analogy and metaphor, but the vocabulary of baseball ought to be used as we use other vocabularies, with tender loving care.

Plurals (pointless)

Is the *pointless plural* a recent phenomenon? Or is it that these irritants have been with us all along, and I have only recently become crotchety about them? These are *pointless plurals:*

"Four Plunge to Deaths" . . . "London's five-day fog caused the deaths of 12,000 people" . . . "Many Americans who get herpes suffer more from its social stigmas than from its physical symptoms" . . . "They demonstrated their handiworks" . . . "Mountain climbers find almost inexpressible satisfactions in overcoming difficult challenges" . . . "The EPA has done too little about illegal dumpings of toxic wastes" . . . "The flood caused $12 million in damages."

It seems to me that in each case a singular noun would be preferable— Four plunge to *death;* they demonstrate their *handiwork;* the flood caused $12 million in *damage.* When we are dealing with different things—many cheeses, many makes of automobiles—straightforward plurals plainly are required. When we specifically enumerate, again, the plural noun is better: the *assassinations* of Lincoln, Garfield, and Kennedy. But "Four Plunge to Death" is tighter and crisper than "Four Plunge to Deaths," and if you're writing headlines a saved *s* is often worth saving.

Pore/Pour

Few confusions in English composition produce more ludicrous consequences than the confusion of *pore* and *pour.* In Time magazine, we find terrorists who "poured over floor plans and street maps" in the ordeal of Patty Hearst. In The Washington Post, we find Bob Guccione of Penthouse magazine "pouring over 1,000 35-millimeter slides of a woman in various degrees of dress and arousal." A columnist writes of New York's Mayor Koch that "he had poured over the Bible to find a suitable passage." In these instances, we gain a messy vision of wet maps, ruined slides, and a soppy Bible. Let us *pore* over recipes, and *pour* over pancakes.

Possible/Probable

Nice distinctions ought to be preserved in writing of the uncertainties that encumber future events. *Possible* carries the greatest degree of uncertainty: Something is capable of happening—it just might happen— but the likelihood is slight. *Probable* is much stronger: If a thing is *probable,* it may very well come about.

Preplan

Is there any difference between an action that is *planned* and one that is *preplanned?* I can think of none. Let us also guard against *advance planning* unless there is some good reason for using the phrase.

Precession/Procession

I throw this one in because my best beloved copy editor, a usually meticulous and learned fellow, once flubbed the usage. Borrowing from Kipling, I had written of the vernal equinox that it *"preceded* according to precedent.'' He changed *preceded* to read *proceeded,* and this caused me indescribable pain and anguish. Spring in the Blue Ridge Mountains is indeed a *procession,* and a gorgeous one at that, but if it's an equinox we're talking about, the word is *precession.*

Prerecorded

In a news story dealing with fraud and deception at a radio station in Michigan, The Washington Post informed us that "The weather reports on the 11 P.M. nightly news were found to have been *prerecorded* five hours earlier.'' The writer gave us two redundancies at once. He meant to speak of the 11 o'clock nightly news, or the 11 P.M. news, and with that *pre-* prefix he gained nothing but egg on his face.

Prescribe/Proscribe

These are almost direct opposites, and ought not to be confused. To *prescribe* is to define a remedy, to ordain, to decree. To *proscribe* is to prohibit, to forbid, to ban. When the Food and Drug Administration *proscribed* Laetrile, it meant that no doctor lawfully could *prescribe* it.

Principal/Principle

Eliot Janeway, who has forgotten more about the financial world than most of us have ever learned, once free-lanced a piece to The Washington Post on international debt. He mailed in his copy; someone at the Post retyped it into a computer—but that someone wasn't paying close attention. For on Sunday we were startled to see Eliot Janeway saying,

"The fact is that much of the interest on these loans cannot be paid, and most of the principle will not be." A few paragraphs on, we were again amazed to hear him explaining that "Bank interest compounded on unrepayable principle will double the debt load in five years." The correct word, of course, was *principal.*

On the other hand, we once read in The Norfolk (Va.) Ledger-Star: "Pavilion Foods announced Monday that it has agreed in principal to acquire 100 percent of Pavilion Hotel Corporation." Unh-hunh. The agreement was in *principle.* The acquisition doubtless involved some *principal,* which is to say, some capital investment, but that is a different matter.

The problem at bottom is that *principal* is both an adjective (the principal parts of speech) and a noun (the principal of the school, the principal of a loan). *Principle* is a noun only. These little trickers have to be mastered head-on. I know of no mnemonic device to scoot around them.

Prone/Supine

These easily may be kept straight. If a person is lying on his back, which is to say, on his spine, he is *supine.* Face down, he is *prone.* If you are prone to forget which is which, think of spine.

q

Quality

The National Education Association informs us in a pamphlet that "Quality classroom instruction starts with quality teacher training." The Ford Motor Company says it "makes quality happen." The author of the NEA pamphlet should be summoned to the nearest blackboard, there to write fifty times: "Quality is not an adjective; quality is a noun." Ford's ad agency treats *quality* as a noun, but it treats it badly.

In the sense under discussion, *quality* is a measure by which we express degrees of excellence. That is all it is. Classroom instruction and Ford products come in various qualities—poor, fair, good, and first-rate. Would we write of a *speed car* or a *growth variety?* We would write of high speed and low speed, of fast growth and slow growth. It is a manifestation of the pervasive sloppiness of our time that we have fallen into a kind of vacuous praise: "Hey, that's a *quality* performance!" That's a poor quality construction.

Quantum Leap

Physicists once had exclusive rights to *quantum leap* (or *jump,* as you prefer), and I willingly would see the term returned to them. In physics, a *quantum jump* has to do with an abrupt transition of a particle from one discrete state of energy to another. Like the *parameter,* the *quantum jump* proved irresistible to bureaucrats and editorial writers. They dragged this nice and inoffensive expression into the arenas of politics and foreign affairs, and stretched it limb by limb. That eminent statesman, poet, philosopher, political zoologist, and former first baseman in the Soo League, Eugene J. McCarthy, once described the Leaping Quantum in a political bestiary we co-authored.

"This is the remarkable thing about the Quantum," said Professor McCarthy, "it only leaps. Or jumps. That is all a Quantum is known to do. He does nothing else. He has no time for anything else.

"This too should be noted: The Leaping Quantum comes from nowhere. He goes nowhere in particular, at least in the present, though frequently we hear of a Quantum Leap *into the future.* The Leaping Quantum was observed in the People's Republic of China when Mr. Nixon made his famous visit to Peking. Then it was said that China had made a Quantum Leap into the twentieth century. The Quantum Leap similarly was recorded in Spain following the death of Generalissimo Franco. Quantums recently have appeared in some numbers in Africa. They sometimes bound backward, as in India. Ordinarily, however, the motion is forward, upward, outward, and on to infinity."

Professor McCarthy added, in a helpful footnote, that "because of their incessant bounding around, Quantums make poor pets but they make excellent tight ends."

r

Raise/Rear

Other people's children sometimes are regarded as little animals, in which event we may properly say that they are being *raised.* That is what we do with animals: We *raise* them. We also *raise* crops. Occasionally we *raise* cain. But if we would cling to an old but vanishing distinction, we *rear* our sons and daughters.

Rebut/Refute

Rebut and *refute* have virtually identical meanings: to provide counter-proof, to demonstrate the falsity of, to contradict by formal argument. In ordinary use, they are among the words that John Bremner classifies as *loaded words.* They have the sound of smacking lips: "The president's statistics immediately were refuted by the speaker." "The majority leader did his best, but he was at once rebutted by . . ." This sort of thing is all very well on the editorial page, where we expect the semantic spitball, but in even-handed writing we should practice fair play: *were challenged by the speaker,* and *was at once answered by.*

Reiterate

Avoid redundancies! I have said it once. Avoid redundancies! I have now *iterated* that imperative. Avoid redundancies! Avoid redundancies! Avoid redundancies! That is a reiteration. I cannot recall ever having heard anyone use *iterate* in conversation, and I have met the stranger only once or twice in print. To *reiterate* carries a connotation of boring repetition. I would as soon forget both *iterate* and *reiterate.* They are uptown words for *repeat,* which is all we are trying to say.

Remains to Be Seen

Some years ago, when word processors and computers began to replace typewriters in our newsrooms, I ventured a proposal more in earnest than in jest. I inquired of one of the technicians if the machines could be so programmed that a sequence of four particular words would trigger a special effect. He said, "Sure." My thought was to rig things so that when the four words were entered in the proper order, a puff of smoke would erupt, red lights would blink on, the machine would explode in a jackpot jangle of cowbells, and a bucket of slop would fall upon the head of the offending operator.

The four words make up the dumbest, most portentous, most profoundly obvious statement in the English language. They constitute the ultimate banality, beyond which no greater stupidity lies. These are the four words: *remains to be seen.*

Time magazine blunders: "Whether Haig can recover authority over foreign policy remains to be seen." . . . "It remains to be seen how well this apparatus [the White House troika] would serve if events called for a 24-hour-a-day president."

Newsweek offends: "How and when the president may choose to make such a substitution remains to be seen." . . . "Investors bid up the price of Polaroid after the announcement, but it remained to be seen whether the bleeding had really been staunched." . . . "Whether Kennedy will challenge Carter openly remains to be seen." . . . "Just how much of the President's program would be enacted remained to be seen." . . . "Just how far age has moved in on Muhammad Ali is now what remains to be seen." . . . "Just how badly Ford and Reagan were hurt by the Democratic victory in New Hampshire remains to be seen." . . . "While 'Chariots' has raised hopes for a new wave of indigenous British filmmaking, it remains to be seen whether indigenous British cash will support it."

Barron's ponders a proposal by which the Securities and Exchange Commission would be authorized to "investigate" or to "study" a newspaper or magazine: "Whether Congress or the courts will agree remains to be seen."

The Wall Street Journal falls into sin: "It remains to be seen whether supply-side economics revitalizes American industry." . . . "Whether Friedman is also correct remains to be seen." . . . "How serious the Hunts' embarrassment is remains to be seen." Hogwash! Get the hogwash!

National Review, that polished journal of conservative thought, lost some of its sheen at the time of the Falklands war: "How the Argentine garrison will behave remains to be seen." Across the philosophical street, The New Republic gave us the word on Bible Belt moralism in politics: "Whether it is an asset or a liability remains to be seen." From the right or from the left, the construction cannot be defended.

Parade magazine looked at books about Jack Kennedy: "How much more of his private world will be revealed by the year's end remains to be seen." Parade also spoke judiciously on the consequences of the interracial marriage of Richard Pryor and Jennifer Lee: "Whether her career will suffer remains to be seen."

From Family Weekly: "Whether the inflatable seat belts can also be used as water wings remains to be seen."

The New York Times looked at Secretary Schweiker's proposals for

Medicare: "It remains to be seen when he can design a fee structure that also protects hospitals and patients." The Times wondered about collecting bad debts on student loans: "It remains to be seen whether the new law will be sufficient. . . ."

The Washington Post regularly imparts these words of wisdom. Could Mr. Nixon cut federal spending massively? "His success remains to be seen." How about Robert Strauss as Democratic chairman? "It remains to be seen how skillful he will be." And what about a deadlock in Congress on reform of the Criminal Code? Whether a compromise would work "remains to be seen." In Angola, said the Post, "whether Nascimento will now make a comeback remains to be seen." In Warsaw, "what still remains to be seen is how the Polish party intends to move from words to action." Eugene McCarthy was considering a campaign for the Senate in 1982, but "whether there's sufficient warmth to persuade him to announce remains to be seen." Teddy Kennedy's message is a message of hope, said the Post's top political writer, "but it remains to be seen whether he can make that hope real."

I have 150 such citations yet to go, but will now suspend. Is it not instantly evident, without even a blinking pause for examination of the truism, that *every* future event under moon or sun *remains to be seen?* I would beseech you to abandon this pompous phrase in everyday writing, and to reserve it exclusively for references to funeral parlors. There at least, remains truly may be seen.

Replica

On the matter of *replica,* let me quote Justice Cardozo on the writing of a dissenting opinion: "Deep conviction and warm feeling are saying their last say with knowledge that the cause is lost." I am resigned to the strong probability that *replica* never will be restored to the niche it once occupied so neatly. A replica, may it please the court, is a work of art (or any other object) that is *re-created by its original creator.*

A company called Fiberfab advertises a kit by which one may build a *replica* of the MG. Another company sells a true-to-scale twenty-one-inch *replica* of a Virginia pilot boat of 1805. The Smithsonian magazine asks if we wouldn't love to build and own an almost incredibly authentic *replica* of the *Titanic*—a *replica* that measures thirty inches in length. Moviemakers, we were told, had a fifty-five-foot *replica* of the ship.

At a cooking show, the French brought a three-and-a-half-foot *replica* of the Eiffel Tower made out of glazed uncooked pasta. An ad in The Wall Street Journal offers for $4.5 million a full-scale *replica* of H.M.S. *Bounty.* Newsweek reported that salons in Switzerland and Finland "are already snipping happily away at *replicas* of Princess Di's hair-do."

Now and then, *replica* appears in its old honest meaning. The Associated Press reported on Princess Di's figurative accession to Madame Tussaud's Wax Museum: "The dress is an exact *replica* of the one worn by Princess Diana for the wedding. It was made by the Emmanuels, *who produced the actual wedding dress.* "

On the face of it, it is patently impossible for anyone to produce a *replica* of the *Bounty* or the *Titanic,* or of a colonial musket, or of a Cellini salt bowl, or of the Eiffel Tower, for the creators of these things are long since dead. What we have, whether it be in plastic parts or glazed pasta, are *models, copies, reproductions, duplicates,* or *facsimiles,* but as we treasure the coins of language, these latter-day imitations are not *replicas.*

Replicate

For practical purposes, *replicate* and *duplicate* may be all the same thing, but every profession has its own vocabulary. In the laboratory, scientists do not *duplicate* the experiments of other scientists; they *replicate* them. They use the same methods and controls to see if they obtain the same results.

Rhetoric

Gresham's Law of Language is hard at work on dear old *rhetoric.* At one time the word had to do only with oratory, with skill in speaking. By extension, the art of writing became included in *rhetoric.* In those days the word had no pejorative connotation. Like *quality, rhetoric* came in degrees from poor to excellent. Now the dictionaries acknowledge the contemporary meaning of *rhetoric* as grandiloquent and bombastic speech or writing. The other party's candidate offers "merely rhetoric." Our party's candidate speaks in "ringing phrases." The devaluation of the old meaning is almost complete, and I see no prospect of ever returning *rhetoric* to the respectability it once enjoyed.

S

Scenario

There must have been a time when *scenario* was a nice fresh word, possessed of a specific meaning for stage and screen, but that time has passed. As a synonym for "hypothetical situation," *scenario* falls short. Except when we mean to suggest a *theatrical* sequence of events, I'd drop the word. "Let's suppose we have this scenario" doesn't say anything that couldn't be said by, "Let's suppose."

Sensual/Sensuous

The distinctions are important. When we speak of a *sensual* person, we are speaking of a person of voluptuous tastes, given to an exotic or erotic ife styie; the word carries a connotation of amorality if not of immorality; a sensual man or woman is likely to be a person both dangerous and exciting. A *sensuous* person would be a person of exceptional sensory gifts—someone who could read Braille, or identify a fine wine by a sniff of the cork, or detect the soupçon of tarragon in the vichyssoise. *Sensuous* pleasures are the pleasures of the senses; *sensual* pleasures are the pleasures of the flesh.

Set/Sit

The general rule is a simple rule: *Set* is transitive, *sit* is intransitive. We don't *sit* a table; we *set* a table. We *set* records and we *set* out the geraniums. The difficulties come with the exceptions. Thus, the sun doesn't *sit,* it *sets;* and we don't *set* a horse, we *sit* him. A pot of soup doesn't *set* on the stove; it *sits* there, just as a satellite *sits* atop a rocket. But drying concrete *sets.* English is not a consistent language.

Simply

Colman McCarthy of The Washington Post has had a lifelong crotchet about *simply;* it heads his expanding list of words that all of us can live without. "The word is all right in itself," he writes, "if a fact or feeling of simplicity is meant—as in, 'He simply painted the room,' meaning the room was painted with no frills or adornments. But simplicity is usually the last notion in the minds of *simply* users. 'I simply can't go.' 'It's simply a matter of money.' 'She simply refused.' In these usages, which some dictionaries have come to sanction, *simply* is used as a synonym for definitely, solely or emphatically. Why not use those words?'' My own feeling is that as a shortcut to *it comes down to,* nothing is wrong with *simply.* As an intensifier, *simply marvelous* strikes me as better than *very marvelous* or *emphatically marvelous.*

Sewage/Sewerage

Sewage is the waste that goes through the *sewerage.* There's nothing wrong with the adjectival *sewage lines,* but *sewerage lines* is redundant in the same way that *rice paddy* is redundant. *Sewerage* is lines.

Shade/Tint/Color/Hue

Artists tend to get irritated when the terms are confused. *Color* is the generic word. *Hue* has to do with the intensity of color. A *shade* is a color produced by a pigment that has some black in it. A *tint* is a variation of color produced by adding white. It is thus technically incorrect to speak of a *light shade* or a *dark tint. Shades* are always dark, *tints* are always light. Some years ago The Washington Star had a feature story on a waterfront fish peddler who had just painted his stall: ''He stood looking at his stand, which was slowly turning a brighter shade of white.'' No way. White has neither *shades* nor *tints.* White is just plain white. White is the absence of color, just as black is the absence of light.

(Sic)

At the highest Olympian slopes of academic writing, or in the composing of legal instruments, there may be a place for *(sic),* meaning *exactly so.* In less formal writing, this irritating insertion smacks of the smugness of the inserter. Unless the occasion requires literal exactitude—or unless you have something malicious in mind—it is common courtesy to clean up a misspelled word in a quotation. An intrusive (sic) says, What a better speller am I!

Single Most

From Newsweek magazine, on fluctuations in the value of the dollar abroad: "The *single most* important cause is high U.S. interest rates."

From a Texas newspaper, quoting a Democratic pollster: "Double-digit joblessness would be the *single most* understandable argument that Reaganomics simply had not delivered on its promise."

From a question put to Washingtonian magazine: "What is the *single most* valuable piece of real estate in the District?"

From the London Sunday Telegraph, praising the Southern accent of a blues singer: "It is her *greatest single* asset."

From the Arkansas Gazette: "The increased cost of gasoline is the *largest single* factor in the Postal Service's inflation problem."

From The Washington Post: "Together, the two financial institutions provide the *single largest* source of home mortgages here."

From Newsweek: "For thirty-four years, Henry Ford II was the *single most* powerful figure in the U.S. auto industry."

From UPI: "Dr. Camilio Calazans, perhaps the *most powerful single man* in the coffee world . . ." (As distinguished from the most powerful married man?)

The Detroit News speaks of *the single most important piece of evidence.* National Review looks at *Liebling's single most affecting piece of writing.* Newsweek comments upon *the best single episode in the novel.* Evans and Novak talk to *the single most influential group of Jewish leaders.*

I have the same animus toward *single* in these constructions that E.B. White had to *very* in almost every construction. There may be instances in which the intensifying *single* adds something useful that has not already been conveyed by the superlative, but I cannot recall such an instance. If we can do without a word, let us do without it.

Stalagmite/Stalactite

The mnemonic device here is that *stalactites* are stuck tight to the ceiling. *Stalagmites* form on the floor.

Subjunctive, Future

"I wish I would have had this soldering gun when I was learning to work with stained glass!" So burbles a mail-order catalog. I wish someone would abolish this bastard tense altogether. *I wish I'd had* suffices nicely.

Surrounded

From The Washington Post, in a review of a concert by a rock group: "The Rollers stood on a rectangular stage *surrounded on all sides* by screaming young women. . . ." Yeccch! The solecism is as flagrant, and alas, as frequent, as *surrounded on three sides*. An island is *surrounded* by water; a peninsula is *bounded* on three sides. Mistaken usages can be neither explained nor excused.

Tenets/Tenants

From The Christian Science Monitor, in a piece about a bill in Congress: "This 85 percent provision is also in the House bill and is based on one of the controversial tenants of the architects of these formula changes." Unless the architects were running an apartment house, the desired word was *tenets*.

That/Which

Even experienced writers have trouble with *that* and *which* in defining and non-defining clauses, but in most instances the trouble is easily avoided. This is the rule of thumb: If the clause is to be set off by commas, use *which*. Otherwise, use *that*.

The rule will not work in every construction, but as a general proposition the guideline holds fast. *The Cadillac, which is in the driveway* (non-defining), *needs a wash job. The Cadillac that is in the driveway* (defining) *needs a wash job.*

These sentences, all taken from editorials in Florida newspapers, should grate upon your ear: "These radical groups nourish a bitter resentment toward the United States which gave them Coca-Cola." . . . "Units of the ROTC which have seventeen or fewer juniors enrolled are put on probation." . . . "The thrust of their discussions will be directed at the elimination of barriers which restrict cooperation." . . . "The bill retains for public employees the appellate protections which they should have in a system which does not allow binding arbitration of strikes."

Each of these clauses was intended to be a defining clause, and each of them should have taken *that:* the United States *that* gave, units *that* have, barriers *that* restrict, appellate protections *that* they should have in a system *that* does not allow. In the fourth of these examples, only for the sake of euphony, I would not quibble over *appellate protections that they should have in a system which does not allow.* Here we could bend the rule. Otherwise, when we wish to define a particular thing, let us stick fast to *that.*

On a related matter, when we are dealing with human beings rather than with units, barriers, and protections, *who* is generally better than *that: The children who live in the ghetto.* Granted, there is abundant precedent for *that* as a personal relative pronoun: *He that is faithful in that which is least is faithful also in much.* A gentlewoman in Birmingham once inquired of me about the sentence, *I have a husband who/ that is interested in aviation.* I responded—I hope, properly—that unless she was married to a block of stone or to some other inanimate object, her husband is a *who,* not a *that.* Because I myself sometimes am mistaken for an inanimate object, I acknowledge the possibility of alternative pronouns, and let it go.

Thoroughbred

Mary K. Wicksten of Bryan, Texas, reminds me that there is no such thing as "thoroughbred Chihuahua puppies." Such puppies may be purebred, or they may be pedigreed, but *thoroughbred* ought properly to be reserved for specific application to specific horses. The Thoroughbred breed is a strictly defined breed descended from English mares and Arabian stallions. If your thought is to identify equine breeding, you would properly speak of a *registered* quarter horse or a *registered* Morgan, but to speak in the presence of horsy people of a thoroughbred Morgan would invite a whinny of reproach.

Times

It is a characteristic of the breed, I suppose, that writers who understand words seldom understand numbers. We have real trouble with *times.* We are all right in such constructions as *The '84 budget of $80 million is four times as large as the '81 budget,* provided the '81 budget was $20 million, but we are in deep water when we get to *times less* and *times more*. The problem lies in the fact that *times* carries an unavoidable connotation of multiplication, and in many constructions that is not what we mean at all. The Miami Herald, reporting on space exploration, said that scientists hope to discover why the tiny moon Iapetus is *six times darker* on one side than on the other. But darkness is not subject to calibration or to units of multiplication. The scientists hope to discover why one side of Iapetus is *six times brighter.* Brightness we can measure.

Louis S. Michael of Lake Worth, Fla., has explicated the matter nicely. Such words as *height, length,* and *thickness,* he reminds us, may be defined in terms of feet, yards, or millimeters. The measurement of *brightness* may be defined in photons; *age* may be described in units of time, and *wetness* in positive units of humidity. "To the best of my knowledge," Michael writes, "*no such units of measurement apply to the antonyms.*

"For example, let us envision a piece of plywood .25 inches *thick* and compare it with a section of veneer only .05 inches *thin.* If we elect to define the veneer as being *five times thinner* than the plywood, we must choose between: (a) "5 x .25 = 1.25 inches" (not the true thickness of the veneer), or (b) "5 x .25 = .05 inches" (a mathematical absurdity).

"Whether 'five times thinner' carries more impact or is more readily understood, it is still my contention that the expression is incorrect mathematically. I therefore object to 'times shorter,' 'times darker,' 'times weaker,' 'times lower,' 'times younger,' 'times drier,' and others that fit the pattern. For a specific example, we ought not to write that a new film is '100 times thinner than its predecessor.' Better: The new film is one one-hundredth as thick as the original, or as an alternative, the original film was 100 times thicker than the new."

We ought also to seek professional help, as Ann Landers is so fond of advising, when we get lost in percentages. "Rainfall decreased 300 percent in the Great Plains states this June against last June." How's that again? A 100 percent decrease would mean no rain at all this June.

Tortuous

Watch out for a nuance that hides in the shrubbery of *tortuous.* Ordinarily we employ the word innocently in the sense of *intricate, involved,* or *circuitous,* but the word has a pejorative spin. It carries a connotation of *tricky, devious, sly.* Thus, *tortuous reasons* may be understood to mean *sneaky* or *tricky reasons.*

Trademarks

I write my country columns from Rappahannock County, Virginia, under a dateline of Scrabble, Va. A couple of years ago a huffy letter came from the people who manufacture the word game Scrabble. They wanted me to knock it off. Scrabble, the lawyers said, was their own trademarked product. I wrote back that the mountain community known as Scrabble, Va., is a real, honest-to-God community. It is not like Camelot or Yoknapatawpha County; it appears not only on contemporary maps of the region but also on maps of the Civil War. Scrabble, in brief, had been in existence for a hundred years before anyone ever tried to make a triple-word score out of *quixote,* and kindly go straight to hell without passing go. That was the last I heard from those birds.

Yet the point the lawyers were trying to make is a point that professional writers should keep in mind. Trademarks are precious assets. A decent respect for both law and property requires that trademarked names be denoted by capitalization.

Some products that once were protected have become generic: *aspirin, dry ice, escalator, linoleum, shredded wheat, trampoline, yo-yo, thermos,* and *cellophane.* Many other familiar items still are under trademark. Watch out for *Band-Aid, Styrofoam, Kitty Litter, Kewpie doll, Frigidaire, Kotex, Kleenex, Formica, Coke, Sanka,* and *Xerox.* When in doubt, consult the dictionary. You will find that *Kodak,* which once was used indiscriminately to identify any hand-held camera, still is the capitalized trademark of cameras made by Eastman.

Transpire

It is hard to judge how the battle goes over *to transpire.* The verb does not mean—at least it ought not to mean—*to occur* or *to happen* or *to take place.* It means *to become known,* or in the vernacular, *to turn out that.* Bill Buckley gets it right: "The university in question has a considerable enrollment, and it transpires that it is an open admissions institution."

The following examples are all wrong: "Lewis warned the jurors that they were prohibited from publicly discussing what transpired in the jury room." . . . "Although Lego did not dispute the truth of the confession directly, he did tell his version of the events which had transpired at the police station." . . . "The Times Company declined to comment on what had transpired at the meeting." . . . "With less than six months having transpired in the 98th Congress, two major battles have developed over tax policy."

The verb is rooted in the Latin *trans* and the Latin *spirare*, to breathe through or to pass over. It is a familiar term in botany and in medicine. To use *transpire* as a substitute for *happen* is to engage in blowfish prose, by which an ordinary word is puffed up to a more pretentious word.

Try And

In the name of domestic tranquillity, let us not *try and* do something. Let us *try to* do it. When we write that negotiators in Geneva "have the assignment to try and write an arms control agreement," we write gibberish. We should try to remember this.

Tummy

If we are writing at the level of a two-year-old, maybe *tummy* is acceptable. At the levels of two-and-a-half and up, *tummy* ought to be banned.

Turbid/Turgid

These are not at all the same thing, and the words should not be confused. *Turbid* means muddy, opaque, unclear. Gobbledegook is *turbid* stuff. *Turgid* means swollen, pompous, overly resplendent. Sportscaster Howard Cosell in full flight is often *turgid*. He's often amusing too.

U-V-W

Up

Up is one of those little idiomatic barnacles that cling to the keel of a sentence. To be sure, *up* serves a useful purpose in *to throw up*, but it ought to be pruned from *rise up in wrath, saddle up the horse, sign up the contract*, and *finish up the task*. We need an *up* in *take up the challenge* but not in *grab up your suitcase.* When you look down on an *up* in your copy, see if the *up* can't be lifted.

Verdict

Only juries can render *verdicts.* Judges never can. Judges can find a defendant guilty, or hold a defendant guilty, or even rule that a defendant is guilty as charged. If the trial is a jury trial, what we get at the end is a *verdict:* The accused is either guilty or not guilty—though a newspaper's libel lawyers, fearful of a dropped *not,* often ask that we use *innocent* instead of *not guilty.* It is not at all the same thing, but libel lawyers are a careful bunch.

Watershed

This is another of those battered-child words, well born but much abused. Properly speaking, a *watershed* is not a single point or a sharp line; it is a whole region or area in which water drains in a particular direction. It probably is too late in the day to deter U.S. News from calling the Illinois primary a political *watershed,* or to persuade court reporters to find something else to call *Brown* v. *Board of Education* besides a *watershed* in Fourteenth Amendment law. If we are determined to use clichés, let us use clichés with some feeling for accuracy: *Brown* was a *landmark;* it created a *watershed* of cases that doomed discrimination by race.

8   The Games We Play

It seems unlikely that any sane and sensible person would want to fling himself deliberately into fits of frustration, but recently I heard from an old friend in Philadelphia, an eminently sane and sensible person, who has flung himself into precisely such fits. He is trying to *make* crossword puzzles.

My friend, of course, is a writer. He loves to play with words. I take it as an article of faith that virtually all writers share his pastime. Anagrams, cryptograms, double-acrostics, crossword puzzles, palindromes—all of them provide hours of innocent and sometimes maddening enjoyment. I know one venerable scribe, not yet over the hill, who plays Scrabble with his wife for the stakes that once enlivened Elizabethan boudoirs: He plays her for her virtue.

My Philadelphia friend had received as a birthday present a copy of *A Pleasure in Words*, by Eugene T. Maleska, for many happy years the puzzle editor of The New York Times. Thumbing back to front, which is how many word beagles browse through a promising coppice, he saw a chapter on how to construct crossword puzzles, and at once he was hooked. He ruled up a blank square of 15 by 15 little boxes; he inked in a symmetrical pattern containing a permissible forty-two black squares, and following Maleska's tips, he went to work.

"I didn't think it would be easy," he wrote, "but I never dreamed it would be so hard. It's no trick to find words with alternate consonants and vowels, which is one of Maleska's hints for beginners, but when Maleska stacks up such going-across words as *parapet, Alabama,* and *tetanus,* they make words going down. When I stack up such words as *aware, risen,* and *toned,* I don't get much of anything."

After five nights of hard labor, my friend finished his first puzzle. He enclosed a copy of the misbegotten thing for my inspection, but it was more than I could crack. After all, who ever heard of *gid, puisne,* and *orgeat?* In his puzzle a young man was an *ephebe.* He had rivers and mountains known only to God and the National Geographic. Maleska would have flunked him flat. But when I frittered away a frustrating hour, trying my own hand with a sackful of Scrabble tiles, I did even more poorly. Let us raise a glass to the professional puzzle makers who give us so much pleasure.

Writers need never apologize for the time they spend in word games. Even the easiest crossword puzzle may return an unexpected dividend in the discovery of a new word or the rediscovery of an old one. I never knew that *irk* was a noun until I was sitting in the Birmingham airport doing a puzzle in the News. Solving a cryptogram, wholly apart from a moment of triumph, teaches us something about letters and words. A Middleton Double-Acrostic requires leaps of linguistic imagination.

If this sort of thing amuses you—and it should amuse you—a wide literature is out there. I've mentioned *The Joy of Lex* by Gyles Brandreth, published by Morrow in 1980. Brandreth is a fiendishly witty English journalist, who evidently spends most of his waking hours in word play. Maleska's book is another treasure. In 1975 Willard R. Espy brought forth his *Almanac of Words at Play;* at the risk of indelicacy, I recall that it stayed in my bathroom through all of 1976. Joseph T. Shipley published *Playing with Words* in 1960 and followed with *Word Play* in 1972.

One of the most puzzling forms of word play is the rebus. Among Shipley's favorites is this one, from his 1960 book:

> Hill
> John
> Mass.

Until it was forbidden by act of Congress sixty-odd years ago, gamesters used to challenge the Post Office with rebuses such as that one. It's a classic. A letter so addressed, when you approach it with a wacko knack of triple vision, could go only to John Underhill, Andover, Mass.

Shipley has found rebuses as far back as the times of Emperor Darius and the Scythians. "Perhaps the neatest of all," he says, "is this French one":

> Ga

If you have the rebus eye, you will think it significant that the *G* is capitalized; it is a large letter. The *a* is lowercase; it is small. From that you will move to *G grand, a petit,* and then it will hit you: *J'ai grand appetit.* In brief, I'm really hungry.

Let me recommend another fun book: *Ologies & -Isms,* under the editorship of Laurence Urdang. It is in fact a work of serious scholarship, in which Urdang and his colleagues have rounded up three thousand words ending in *-ologies, -ities, -isms,* and *-ics.* The book is thematically arranged, so that if your need is to come up with the word that has to do with the science of making wine, the word is *oenology.* The fellow who contrives puzzles may be engaged in *enigmatography.* I myself happen to be into *vexillology.* You should look it up.

Josefa Heifetz Byrne had a great time in 1974 putting together *Mrs. Byrne's Dictionary of Unusual, Obscure, and Preposterous Words.* At random, from her bag of baubles, I give you *exosculate,* to kiss heartily; *mancinism,* left-handedness; and *scissile,* capable of being easily split. It is hard to know how we could get along without the words that follow scissile: *sclaff, scobiform, scolecophagous, scolion,* and *scollardical,* though it might be difficult to drag *scopelism* into a dinner conversation. It means, "the scattering of stones on a field to hinder farming."

Brandreth also collects exotic words in the same way that a philatelist collects exotic stamps: a *bronstrops* is a prostitute, *to quop* is to throb, *eldnyng* is jealousy, and a *wallydraigle* is a slovenly woman. Still another collection of stray cats comes from Russell Rocke in *The Grandiloquent Dictionary.*

A question on the run: What's unusual about *unquestionably?* It contains all five vowels and the letter *y.* I leave it to you to discover why *facetious, abstemious,* and *abstentious* are collector's items.

If there is a cheaper hobby in the world than the collection of homonyms and homophones, I have yet to find it. Homonyms are words that are spelled and pronounced alike, but have quite different meanings. There is *quail* the noun and *quail* the verb. You can *post* a horse, *post* a letter, and *post* a notice; indeed, you could *post* the notice on a *post.* Homophones are words that are pronounced alike but spelled differently: *to, too,* and *two; so, sew,* and *sow; air, ere,* and *heir; bole, boll,* and *bowl; read, reed,* and *rede; rain, rein,* and *reign; for, four,* and *fore; seas, sees,* and *seize; rode, road,* and *rowed,* and so on.

Kathryn Passarelli of Fort Lauderdale, playing the game, recalls the passenger who arrived at a railway station in 1:58 for a 2:02 train. The passenger had to wait from two to two to two-two. Her friend had to wait from two to two to two-two, too. Judy Ceniceros of Portland has collected six hundred of these things, "but not with any sense that I have exhausted the possibilities." Her collection includes about sixty three-way homophones and even a few prize four-ways: *or, oar, ore, o'er; right, write, rite, wright; rase, raise, rays, raze; you, yew, U,* and *ewe.*

Let me quote a little more from Judy Ceniceros, because her letter reflects a cast of mind that word lovers should cultivate:

> There are other categories of words that are fun to play with, such as pairs of anagram-synonyms (words that contain their own synonym), such as *replicate, repeat; retrogression, regression; appropriate, apt.* I have found about 50 of these without trying. An even more sophisticated example of an "elegant anagram" that I ran across somewhere is *Alec Guinness, genuine class.*
>
> Yet another category, known as homographs or heteronyms, is made up of words that are spelled the same but pronounced differently. Often the switch comes in the change of parts of speech, such as from noun to verb, as in *desert* and *wind.* Sometimes it's from noun to adjective, as in *invalid.* Two nouns: *primer, sewer.* Other combinations: *wound, tear, read.*

In that last classification, my correspondent might have included a couple of noun-verbs out of football. At RFK Stadium in Washington, D.C., where the Redskins play, the fans are in love with their de-fense. When the de-fense performs well, the announcer says they de-fensed that play beautifully. The Redskins also of-fense pretty well, though in the 1984 Super Bowl they offensed offensively.

In the glossary of "My Crotchets and Your Crotchets," I touched upon some of the Troublesome Twos that cause great embarrassment. At the risk of repetition, let me urge that all of us get straight on: *appraise* and *apprise, capital* and *capitol, principle* and *principal, pore* and *pour, complement* and *compliment, peal* and *peel, affect* and *effect, karat* and *carat, pear* and *pair, peak* and *peek, sole* and *soul, waste* and *waist, heal* and *heel,* and *exercise* and *exorcise.* Let us not emulate the gentleman in Florida who advertised for a female companion; he was a fastidious fellow, and wanted a lady who had been formerly educated.

These sound-alikes can throw the inattentive writer. J.T. Harding of New Jersey, whose copy pencil is a samurai sword, regularly cites examples of unhorsemanship. How is one to criticize the actor who plays a small roll? What of the orchestra that performed East Asian music with a great flare? There was a reporter who was sent out to get a picture but couldn't find won. Another reporter had voters going to the poles, though not in Warsaw. I am especially enchanted by the student who described some itinerant Hapsburg as a Pretender to the Thrown. Another student—I guess it was another student—advertised for an "English tudor for a brief review." A classified ad in a North Carolina paper offered a boat wench for sale at $150. Harding also notes: Pontius Pilot, back-peddling, and bails of marijuana dropped from a low-flying plain.

At one point in my column, I got off on the subject of contranyms. It turned out that hundreds of word hounds hunt them all the time. A contranym is a word that embraces contradictory meanings. *Moot,* for example, can mean both arguable and no longer arguable. To *cleave* is to whack in two and also to bind together. When a door is *bolted,* it is locked in place; when a horse has *bolted,* he has taken off.

I learned that contranym collecting has been going on for years. An article in Word Ways, a quarterly published by A. Ross Eckler, recalls the researches of Jack Herring in 1962. Among his contranyms were *fast* and *scan.* When we say a sailboat is *fast,* what do we mean? When we *scan,* are we looking intently or looking casually?

The piece in Word Ways cited a dozen others. Applied to fabrics, *wear* means both to put on (wear it), and to decay (wear out). *Distraction* is both amusement and confusion. In everyday use, a *commencement* is a beginning; in academia, a *commencement* is an ending. On the golf course, a *handicap* is an advantage; elsewhere it's a disadvantage. And thinking of golf and how you're feeling today: What do we mean by *below par* and *above par?* When we *wind up* a watch, we start it; when we *wind up* a speech, we stop it. The word *sanguine* means both cheerful and murderous. In the nation's capital, congressional committees deal in *oversight;* they are both accused of it and charged with it. To *sanction* something is to approve it; to impose *sanctions* is to punish.

Isn't English wonderful? It is wonderfully confusing—and among the confusions is the *amphiboly.* I had never run across an amphiboly until I stumbled over the word in an essay in Modern Age. To quote Webster's III, an amphiboly is an "ambiguity in languge; a phrase or sentence susceptible of more than one interpretation by virtue of an ambiguous grammatical construction."

Example: *Nothing is too good for my mother-in-law.* There's also the advertisement that tells us, presumably unintentionally, that *nothing is more effective than Esoterica.* My friend in Fort Lauderdale, Mrs. Passarelli, was impressed by the ad. "Naturally, I use nothing." Equally off-putting was an article in Gourmet magazine on Mexican cuisine. It was subheaded, "Little Known in Its Entirety—Equal to None."

My own pet amphiboly became a popular song toward the end of the 1970s: "If I told you you had a beautiful body, would you hold it against me?" For a neat doubletake: "Nobody goes downtown because it's too crowded." Imperative sentences have a way of leaping the fences of literal meaning: *Send no money . . . Mention this to no one . . . Take one capsule three times daily . . . Store kerosene in an approved container clearly labeled in a cool dark place . . . No liquid containers permitted.* In Indianapolis, a newspaper item reported that a suspect had been arrested "for entering a bedroom of the opposite sex." And of course there is the Marlboro man, who rides off on a horse with a cigarette in his mouth.

Amphibolies can slip up on you all unawares. I plead guilty. Once I was trying to say something complimentary about two writers whose work I greatly admire, Calvin Trillin and E.B. White. I said that, "Trillin is the best thing that has happened to magazine writing since E.B. White retired." A plaintive letter came from Dick Wolfsie of WISH-TV in Indianapolis. How *could* I have written that sentence? The feeble answer is, It just came out wrong.

Lane Jennings, writing in The Futurist a few years ago, put a profoundly simple thought in a profoundly simple sentence: *Change is the natural state of any living language.* On the conservative side of the semantic fence, many of us tend to make Great Harrumphing Noises about coinages that come along. We cry *yeccch!* and *aarghh!* and we roll our eyes at the degeneration of our mother tongue. This is mostly buncombe. We howl, with some justification, at *disasterize* and *prioritize,* and we scoff at coinages stamped from semantic lead. But any person who loves words is bound to love new words—and of new words there are thousands.

In 1973 Harper & Row produced the first *Barnhart Dictionary of New English.* It contained five thousand new words (or new usages of old words) that were not then contained in standard dictionaries. The editors had planned to wait ten years before a second edition. The language couldn't wait. In 1980, three years ahead of schedule, out came the

Second Barnhart—and it contained *another* five thousand words or usages that had arrived in the meanwhile.

In a note on coinages, the editors remarked upon the difficulty that lexicographers encounter in tracing the inventors of new words. Somewhere in the mazes of a great corporation or a large advertising agency are the individuals who thought up *Instamatic* and *Granola;* they remain unidentified. Other coinages have owners: *basilect,* a combining of *basic* and *dialect,* was contrived by linguist William A. Stewart to define a variety of speech that has the least prestige among speakers of a language. Norman Mailer invented *factoid* to mean a published statement taken to be a fact just because of its appearance in print. Tom Wolfe coined the *me decade* to capture the self-centeredness of the 1970s. Not surprisingly, perhaps half of the Barnhart's latest collection comes from science; here the coinages fly by at supersonic speeds, and many of them leave no more than a fleeting boom behind.

New coins of speech are minted everwhere. These are among the "A" entries in the Second Barnhart: *AC/DC* (a bisexual person), *acid rain, anchor* (to anchor a TV program), *antinuke, après-sun* and *après-swim, Archie Bunker,* and *armpit* (a grimy, undesirable place, as "Muncie is the armpit of Indiana"). Among the "B's" are *bag lady, ball-park figure, basket case, beautility* (invented by Ada Louise Huxtable of The New York Times as a combining form of *beauty* and *utility*), *big enchilada, blissout, blue flu,* and *Brand X.*

A reader inquired about *blissout:* Would it survive? I give *blissout* a half-life of maybe five years before it zaps out. It appears to be closely related to *make out,* which I understand to mean what we did in high schools in the thirties when we *pitched woo* or *necked.* The indefinitely adverbial *out* also appears in *bug out* and *freak out,* though it must remain a matter of conjecture where the *out* is that we have blissed, bugged, or freaked to.

In putting together their "B" entries, the Barnhart editors overlooked a coinage from William Safire that I happen to like: *blowsoft.* Everyone is familiar with the *blowhard.* In legislative halls, in business, in every trade or profession, we also find the *blowsoft*—the fellow who just stands there and quietly insists, and insists, and insists, and will not go away.

Neither did the Barnhart editors pick up *appallment.* Colman McCarthy of The Washington Post once used *appallment* in a column. Michael Gartner, editor of The Des Moines Register & Tribune, sent him a reproachful note; Gartner was filled with *appallment.* McCarthy wrote back, saying don't blame me; blame Robert Penn Warren, he invented it. Sure enough, Warren owned up. "If you're writing and a word is needed," Warren said, "you create it. This is a word that ought to exist. I've invented several other words. *Appallment* is my latest." I would like to think about *appallment* for a while. *Shockment? Dismayment? Disgustment?* I don't believe *appallment* will fly, even if Robert Penn Warren did invent it.

New verbs drift to the surface of contemporary speech. Out of labor-management contracts comes *to grieve.* Doyle Alexander, then pitching for the Yankees, was fined $12,500 for breaking a finger when he banged his hand in frustration against a dugout wall. "A player can grieve a fine of that size," The Associated Press reported. He grieved; and he won.

As a verb, *helicopter* has been around since 1926, and now appears regularly in the press. Webster's Ninth Collegiate dates *to chopper* from 1955. The Seattle Times has created a related verb: "President Reagan will Air Force One his way into the area Tuesday to address the American Legion convention."

I once proposed to nominate a series of Verbs of the Week. Readers sent in hundreds of possibilities. Some of the citations were old. To *helm,* meaning to steer, has been around since 1603. To *novelize* dates from 1828, to *scapegoat,* from 1943, to *plateau* from 1939, and to *thermalize,* from 1948. Others had not been discovered by the time Webster's Ninth New Collegiate was put together: *personnel, agenda, conference, deluxe, detariff, fraud, mother-hen, nonchalant,* and *information.*

From the world of politics comes the abbreviated *to primary:* Wisconsin voters will *primary* next week. When we accept the idea that American voters will *general* in November, I will buy *to primary* in the spring.

Other verbs float by: A reporter on The Portland Oregonian has a mash on *to conquest:* The Cadillac Cimarron "never was intended to conquest buyers" of certain other cars. At a computer training center in Washington, D.C., an instructor held a seminar in *futuring,* a construction I would just as soon past. But I have embraced *to total,* in the sense of to wreck an automobile totally. In the context, it's a good vivid verb, and ought to find its place. I am less certain about a related back-formation: "There is a *disabled* blocking the right lane of the expressway." Maybe so. The usage saves the airtime millisecond that might otherwise be needlessly expended on *disabled car* or *disabled vehicle,* and the meaning is as clear as the extended meanings of *giftable* and *unmentionable.*

My powers of prophecy are poor. I have no idea how many of the Barnhart ten thousand will still be in popular or technical use in the next generation. To browse through Mencken's *The American Language* is to be impressed by the number of desert flowers that have blossomed briefly in our speech and then disappeared altogether. The newspapers had a good time in 1982 and 1983 with the slang of the Valley girls in California. Whole vocabularies were compiled of Valleyspeak. Now the Valley girls have grown up and the glossaries have grown old.

All this is good. My impression is that the English language never has been healthier. It is, to be sure, a disorderly language. Most of our "rules" for spelling and pronunciation are so riddled with exceptions that they are no rules at all. I have a granddaughter named Charlotte; I have a friend named Charles. Why is it *Sharl* in the one case and *Charl* in the other? And what about *character, chameleon*, and *chaos?* Foreigners must despair at mastering English pronunciation. We punctuate as we damn well please. We turn nouns into adjectives and adjectives into nouns. Mr. Reagan's advisers reminded him before his forensic bout in 1980 with Mr. Carter that "televised political debates focus on image attributes more than issue positions." What is an *image attribute?* What is an *issue position?* We borrow words of specialized meaning—*parameter* is an example—and we never get around to returning them. It is a continuing process of fermentation, and the descriptive linguists are as happy as master brewers. They cannot keep up with the bubbles and froth.

Those of us who play the prescriptive role ought not to despair. Lexicographer Lawrence F. Scanlon, writing in The Hartford Courant a few years ago, scoffed at prescriptivism as "pointless." He recalled the labors of Jonathan Swift and Samuel Johnson to purify the English of their day: "Not only did they not have much effect on the course of the language, many of the things they were concerned about seem positively silly in retrospect." Fair enough—but many of the things Swift and Johnson were concerned about remain valid concerns in our own time. They were concerned with precise meanings that would convey thought precisely; they were concerned with rules of grammar and syntax that would support a solid structure of communication. They did not hesitate to prescribe standards of good, better, and best usage, and we may be grateful for their labors and for the labors of prescriptivists who have come after them.

We will never run out of English words, and we will never run out of writers who treat words with loving care. For such writers, a loving audience always will be out there somewhere. Depending upon our skill in fitting words together, we will win their applause, or we will earn their disdain.

Index

List of Words
and Phrases